Television Producers
Jeremy Tunstall

What News?
The market, politics and the local press
Bob Franklin and David Murphy

In Garageland
Rock, youth and modernity
Johan Fornäs, Ulf Lindberg and Ove Sernhede

The Crisis of Public Communication
Jay G. Blumler and Michael Gurevitch

Glasgow Media Group Reader, Volume 1
News content, language and visuals
Edited by John Eldridge

Glasgow Media Group Reader, Volume 2
Industry, economy, war and politics
Edited by Greg Philo

The Global Jukebox
The international music industry
Robert Burnett

Inside Prime Time
Todd Gitlin

Talk on Television
Audience participation and public debate
Sonia Livingstone and Peter Lunt

Media Effects and Beyond
Culture, socialization and lifestyles
Edited by Karl Erik Rosengren

We Keep America on Top of the World
Television journalism and the public sphere
Daniel C. Hallin

A Journalism Reader
Edited by Michael Bromley and Tom O'Malley

Tabloid Television
Popular journalism and the 'other news'
John Langer

International Radio Journalism
History, theory and practice
Tim Crook

Media, Ritual and Identity
Edited by Tamar Liebes and James Curran

De-Westernizing Media Studies
Edited by James Curran and Myung-Jin Park

British Cinema in the Fifties
Christine Geraghty

Ill Effects
The media violence debate, second edition
Edited by Martin Barker and Julian Petley

Media and Power
James Curran

Journalism after September 11
Edited by Barbie Zelizer and Stuart Allan

Media Perspectives for the 21st Century

Media Perspectives for the 21st Century brings together key international scholars to explore concepts, topics and issues concerning the communication environment in contemporary democratic societies. It combines qualitative and quantitative approaches to provide an interdisciplinary and truly global perspective that reflects the trends, theories and issues in current media and communication research.

The collection raises significant questions about the study of the media by challenging approaches to major media and societal issues, and analyses in more depth the range of concerns that shape both the present and the future media landscape and the issues these can create for communication. It also investigates the main effects of technological developments on the domain of the news media and journalism.

Divided into two main sections, Part I provides accounts of the role of media in society, and deals with agendas that affect the field of communications studies. Part II goes on to examine the world of new media and offers analysis on the developments of the 21st century. Chapters deal with various dimensions of media from a number of different perspectives and socio-political contexts, covering a wide range of topics including social networking, political communication, public journalism, global infotainment and consumer culture.

Media Perspectives for the 21st Century will be highly useful to undergraduate and postgraduate students, as well as researchers and academics, in the fields of media and communication studies, mass communication, journalism and new media.

Stylianos Papathanassopoulos is Professor in Media Organisation and Policy and Head of the Faculty of Communication and Media Studies at the National and Kapodistrian University of Athens, Greece. He has written extensively on media developments in Europe. His other publications include *The European Media* (with Ralph Negrine, 2011), *Television in the 21st Century* (2005), *Media and Politics* (2004) and *European Television in the Digital Age* (2002).

Communication and Society
Series Editor: James Curran

This series encompasses the broad field of media and cultural studies. Its main concerns are the media and the public sphere: whether the media empower or fail to empower popular forces in society; media organizations and public policy; the political and social consequences of media campaigns; and the role of media entertainment, ranging from potboilers and the human interest story to rock music and TV sport.

Media Perspectives for the 21st Century

Edited by
Stylianos Papathanassopoulos

Routledge
Taylor & Francis Group

LONDON AND NEW YORK

First published 2011
by Routledge
2 Park Square, Milton Park, Abingdon, Oxon OX14 4RN

Simultaneously published in the USA and Canada
by Routledge
270 Madison Ave, New York, NY 10016

*Routledge is an imprint of the Taylor & Francis Group,
an informa business*

Editorial selection and material © 2011 Stylianos Papathanassopoulos

Individual chapters © 2011 the contributors
The right of Stylianos Papathanassopoulos to be identified as
the author of the editorial material, and of the authors for their
individual chapters, has been asserted, in accordance with sections
77 and 78 of the Copyright, Designs and Patents Act 1988.

Typeset in Baskerville by Bookcraft Ltd, Stroud, Gloucestershire

Printed and bound in Great Britain by CPI Antony Rowe,
Chippenham, Wiltshire

British Library Cataloguing in Publication Data
A catalogue record for this book is available from the British Library

Library of Congress Cataloging in Publication Data
Media perspectives for the 21st century : concepts, topics and
issues / edited by Stylianos Papathanassopoulos.
   p. cm.
   Includes bibliographical references and index.
   1. Mass media. 2. Mass media--Social aspects.
   3. Digital media--Social aspects. I. Papathanassopoulos,
   S. II. Title: Media perspectives for the twenty-first century.
   P90.M3679 2010   302.23--dc22
   2010027112

ISBN13: 978-0-415-57498-3 (hbk)
ISBN13: 978-0-415-57499-0 (pbk)
ISBN13: 978-0-203-83407-7 (ebk)

Contents

List of tables and figures

Tables

Figures

List of contributors

Markus Beiler, Dipl.-Media Scientist, is holder of the Chair of Journalism II of the Institute of Communication and Media Science of the University of Leipzig, Germany. His research includes online communication, search engines, Internet governance and international media systems.

Gustavo Cardoso is an associate researcher at CIES-ISCTE-IUL and Professor of Technology and Society at ISCTE – Lisbon University Institute. He also works with the Department of Communications and Performance Studies of the University of Milan and with the Portuguese Catholic University. His international cooperation in European research networks brought him to work with IN3 (Internet Interdisciplinary Institute) in Barcelona, WIP (World Internet Project) at USC Annenberg, COST A20 'The Impact of the Internet in Mass Media' and COST 298 'Broadband Society'. Between 1996 and 2006 he was adviser on information society and telecommunications policies to the Presidency of the Portuguese Republic and in 2008 was chosen by the World Economic Forum as a Young Global Leader. He is co-editor, with Manuel Castells, of the book *Network Society: from Knowledge to Policy* and Associate Editor of the peer-reviewed journals *IJOC* at USC Annenberg and *IC&S* at Routledge. He is a member of the evaluation panels of the European Research Council (ERC) and of the ESF (European Science Foundation)

Nicolas Demertzis is Professor at the Faculty of Communication and Media Studies of the National and Kapodistrian University of Athens and Dean of the School of Communication and Applied Arts at the Cyprus University of Technology. He has taken part in numerous conferences and has published extensively in Greek and English journals and volumes. His current academic and research interests include political sociology, political communication, and the sociology of emotions.

Mark Deuze holds a joint appointment at Indiana University's Department of Telecommunications in Bloomington, United States, and as Professor of Journalism and New Media at Leiden University, the Netherlands.

Publications of his work on media life and media work include five books – including *Media Work* (Polity Press, 2007), and articles in journals such as the *International Journal of Cultural Studies*, *New Media & Society*, and the *Journal of Media Sociology*. Weblog: deuze.blogspot.com, Twitter: twitter.com/markdeuze.

Eszter Hargittai is Associate Professor of Communication Studies at Northwestern University where she heads the Web Use Project. She is also Fellow of the Berkman Center for Internet & Society at Harvard University. Her research focuses on the social and policy implications of information technologies with a particular interest in how these may contribute to or alleviate social inequalities.

Shanto Iyengar is Professor of Political Science at Stanford University. Iyengar's teaching and research address the role of the news media and mass communication in contemporary politics. He is the author of several books including *Media Politics: A Citizen's Guide* (W. W. Norton, 2007), *Going Negative: How Political Advertisements Shrink and Polarize the Electorate* (Free Press, 1995), *Explorations in Political Psychology* (Duke University Press, 1993), and *News That Matters: Television and American Opinion* (University of Chicago Press, 1987). Iyengar currently serves as the editor of *Political Communication*. He is also a regular contributor to Washingtonpost.com. His scholarly awards include the Murray Edelman Career Achievement Award for research in political communication, the Philip Converse Award for the best book in the field of public opinion (for *News That Matters*), the Goldsmith Book Prize (for *Going Negative*), and the Distinguished Alumni Achievement Award from the University of Iowa.

Marcel Machill is a Full Professor of Journalism and International Media Systems at the University of Leipzig in Germany. He is a graduate of the John F. Kennedy School of Government at Harvard University. In his research he deals with international media policy, search engines and with the regulatory frameworks for journalism in the digital age. Professor Machill is also a graduate of the French journalism school 'Centre de Formation des Journalistes' in Paris and has worked at several media in Europe and the U.S.

Matthew P. McAllister is Professor of Communications in the Department of Film/Video and Media Studies at Penn State. He is the co-editor (with Joseph Turow) of *The Advertising and Consumer Culture Reader* (Routledge, 2009).

Andrew Mendelson (PhD, University of Missouri) is currently Associate Professor and Chair of the Department of Journalism at Temple University. His research interests include visual communication, photography, and, society and psychological processing of mediated messages.

Tristan Mattelart is Professor of International Communication at the Department of Culture and Communication of the University of Paris 8, France. His works include *Le cheval de Troie audiovisuel: Le rideau de fer à l'épreuve des radios et télévisions transfrontières*, *La mondialisation des médias contre la censure: Tiers monde et audiovisuel sans frontières* and *Médias, migrations et cultures transnationales*.

Ralph Negrine is Professor of Political Communication in the Journalism Studies Department, University of Sheffield. His most recent book is *The Transformation of Political Communication* (London: Palgrave) and he is now working on a study of aspects of the media in Europe.

Zizi Papacharissi (PhD University of Texas at Austin 2000) is Professor and Head of the Communication Department at the University of Illinois-Chicago. Her work focuses on the social and political consequences of online media. Her book, *A Private Sphere: Democracy in a Digital Age* (Polity Press, 2010), discusses how online media redefine our understanding of public and private in late-modern democracies. She is also presently completing an edited volume on online social networks, titled *A Networked Self: Identity, Community, and Culture on Social Network Sites* (Routledge, 2010). She is author of three books, and over 30 journal articles, book chapters or reviews.

Stylianos Papathanassopoulos is Professor in Media Organization and Policy and currently Head of the Faculty of Communication and Media Studies at the National and Kapodistrian University of Athens. He is currently a Board member of the Hellenic Audiovisual Institute. He has written extensively on media developments in Europe and especially on television issues in various journals including the *European Journal of Communication*, *Media Culture and Society*, *Political Communication*, *The Communication Review* and *Journalism Studies*. He also edits the Greek communication journal *Zitimata Epikoinonias* (Communication Issues) and is member of the editorial board of *Global Media and Communication*. Among his most recent books: *Television in the 21st century* (Athens: Kastaniotis, 2005); *Media and Politics* (Athens: Kastaniotis, 2004); *European Television in the Digital Age; Issues, Dynamics and Realties* (Cambridge: Polity Press, 2002), and with Ralph Negrine *The European Media Landscape* (Polity, 2010).

Jessica Roberts has a master's degree in journalism from the Annenberg School at the University of Southern California. A PhD student at the University of Maryland's Philip Merrill College of Journalism, she is researching citizen journalism, civic behaviour and ethics.

Linda Steiner is Professor and Director of Doctoral Studies and Research at the University of Maryland's College of Journalism. Several books and journal articles address how social/political movements use media and gender issues in journalism; research interests include media ethics and public journalism.

Daya Kishan Thussu is Professor of International Communication and Co-Director of the India Media Centre at the University of Westminster in London. His research interests include political economy of global communication; global news flow; media and mediated culture in India and among South Asian diaspora. He is the Founder and Managing Editor of the Sage journal *Global Media and Communication*. Among his main publications are: *Electronic Empires – Global Media and Local Resistance* (1998); *International Communication – Continuity and Change*, second edition (2006); *News as Entertainment: The Rise of Global Infotainment* (2007) and *Internationalizing Media Studies* (2009).

Frank Webster is Professor of Sociology and Head of Department, City University, London and Visiting Professor, Department of Journalism and Mass Communication, Tampere University. He has written extensively on information developments and information society issues for many years. His latest book, with Kevin Gillan and Jenny Pickerill, is *Anti-War Activism: New Media and Protest in the Information Age* (2008). He is working on a book provisionally titled *Democratization and Information*.

List of abbreviations

ABC	American Broadcasting Company
API	Application Programme Interface
APTN	Associated Press Television Network
APTV	Associated Press Television
BBC	British Broadcasting Corporation
CD	Compact Disc
CJ	Citizen Journalism
CNN	Cable News Network
DAB	Digital Audio Broadcasting
DTT	Digital Terrestrial Television
DVB	Digital Video Broadcasting
DVD	Digital Video Disc
DVR	Digital Video Recorders
EBU	European Broadcasting Union
EC	European Commission
ECJ	European Court of Justice
EPG	Electronic Programme Guide
EU	European Union
FM	Frequency Modulation
GATS	General Agreement on Trade in Services
GATT	General Agreement on Tariffs and Trade
GDP	Gross Domestic Product
HDTV	High Definition Television
ICTs	Information and Communication Technologies
IDTV	Integrated Digital Television
IFPI	International Federation of the Phonographic Industry
IMC	Integrated Marketing Communications
IP	Internet Protocol
IPTV	Internet Protocol Television
ISDN	Integrated services digital network
MPEG	Motion Picture Experts Group
MSNBC	Microsoft–NBC (combination)
NBC	National Broadcasting Company
NHK	Nippon Ho-so Kyo-kai (Japan Broadcasting Corporation)

NPR	National Public Radio
ONS	Office of National Statistics
P2P	Peer to Peer
PBS	Public Broadcasting Service
PJNet	Public Journalism Network
RFID	Radio Frequency Identification
RTP	Rádio e Televisão de Portugal
SMS	Short Message Service
SNSs	Social Network Sites
TSD	Truman Show Delusion
TVWoP	Televisionwithoutpity.com
U&G	Uses and Gratifications
UGC	User-generated content
VHS	Video Home System
WAN	World Association of Newspapers
WAP	Wireless Application Protocol
WIP	World Internet Project
WMD	Weapon of Mass Destruction
WTO	World Trade Organization

Introduction: Media perspectives for the 21st century

Stylianos Papathanassopoulos

We live in an era of continuous change to our communications environment. The communications landscape has never been static but the scale of contemporary change has been almost global due to the extensive use of new technologies and the implementation of market-led, neo-liberal policies.

Communication and media studies need to change when the media change. This also helps explain the fact that communication studies are often in 'crisis' and under constant scrutiny. Even if communication and media studies are able to respond to what is happening in the communications sector and with media audiences, there is no one-to-one correspondence between the external conditions and the content of communication and media studies. Studies are dependent on what actually happens in the communications environment, yet communication (and in effect social) phenomena are always open to interpretation and rival theorization.

A look back over the last three decades reveals an explosion in the development of communication technology. In contrast to the past, the new developments are shaping a communications landscape that differs greatly from what we were familiar with (Wang and Servaes, 2000: 1). We have seen a movement away from the dominance of print mass media to the prevalence of audiovisual media and, most recently, a transformation of the media towards the development of integrated and digitized communication technologies which are creating a more complex multimedia environment. This development has blurred the traditional frontiers between reading and writing and between communications based on audiovisual images and communications based on text. In effect, the continuous developments of the new media (Internet, online communication and mobile technology) have differed from the old media in a number of ways, such as in the production, distribution and reception of media content. The problem is that old media like newspapers and magazines do not have an audience problem – newspaper websites are a vital and growing source of news – but they do have a consumer problem. Similarly, although nowadays some refer to audiences as users or consumers (Pavlik, 1998), media studies cannot take the concept of 'audience' as a redundant academic device (Ruddock, 2008).

The traditional concept of a one-way mass communication process has been challenged by new relations between media and their users. Though traditional mass media still exist in powerful forms, there are an increasing number of possibilities for interactive services and individual-ized consumption. Yet, at the same time, these new technologically-driven possibilities arrive in changing economic and political contexts, some of which create the potential for greater power over cultural production and distribution by large, global organizations (Bondebjerg and Golding, 2004: 9–10). Some commentators have argued that even with technolog-ical and social change the basic dimensions of theory concerning media and society will not actually change (see McQuail, 2005, and Warnick, 2007) but many believe that the widespread adoption of transforma-tive technologies and the new relationships amongst content producers, distributors and audiences force us to alter our old way of thinking. As Paul Taylor (2009: 7) points out, digital technologies signify 'a profound paradigm shift in which all former Media Studies (MS 1.0) bets are off' and the 'new media technologies offer some significant challenges to the previous conceptualisations of' conventional media studies (see also Deuze and Cardozo in this volume). William Merrin (2009: 17) goes further by arguing that media studies:

> was a product and reflection of the broadcast era of media, being formed in and analysing a specific historical period of media produc-tion, distribution and consumption. The rise of digital media, the transformation of 'old' media into a digital form and ongoing devel-opments in digital technology take us into a post-broadcast era, defined by new alignments of productive and distributive power and media consumption and use.

As Deuze argues in this volume, a future media studies can perhaps benefit from a new ontological turn – after and next to the cultural, the linguistic and the spatial turn. In effect, we need new concepts to inter-pret recent and new developments. For example, the traditional concept of 'audience' appears weak in the age of user-generated content. In other words, basic concepts and models appear no longer to suit media studies. Although it is difficult to eradicate old media studies, one has to acknowledge that the spread of the new interactive media has generated an enormous pool of academic research and general public discourse, with assessments concerning the social implications of emerging commu-nications and media technologies (McAllister and Turow, 2002; Jankowski *et al.* 1999).

Nevertheless, when we refer to the current state of communication and media studies, most of the time we refer to the complex relationships between the state, the media and individuals either as a society or as indi-viduals and we try to reassess these whilst using a new prism (see also McQuail, 2009: 387).

Regardless of their fragmentation, the field of communication and media studies has always been a fertile ground for debate, disputes and discussions. More so, when the landscape of communications has itself been undergoing enormous change. As relationships, processes and flows are all scrutinized by commentators, new insights and new interpretations come to the fore. One of the main aims of this book is to bring together diverse scholars in theory and research and to provide them with a forum in which they can explore contemporary issues and themes.

In the recent past, discussions about the future of communication and media studies contained two main and interrelated issues. The first was whether there would be something called communication science in the twenty-first century. The second concerned the relations between the different approaches within the field which derive from different sciences and disciplines.

On the first, many media scholars have given a positive answer. The convergence and the digitalization of the media, and before them the deregulation and privatization of the communications sector, have given rise to new concerns, problems and insights. The new media technologies have even stimulated reappraisals of the interpretative power of older theories such as the 'limited effects' of the media (see Iyengar's chapter in this volume; Ruggiero, 2000). Furthermore, so long as they are open communication systems and with divergent interpretations of what the future holds in the field, communication and media studies will be in high demand. However, a necessary condition for a fertile field of communication and media studies is an open, democratic, liberal society.

Communication and media studies perhaps inevitably privilege the social sciences, especially sociology, in part because the media (traditional and new) constitute a recognized social institution with its own rules, logic and priorities (McQuail, 2005). But the scope of their activities is defined by social change since the media are first and foremost part of the social systems in which they exist (Altheide and Snow, 1979; Wright, 1986; Thompson, 1995; Viswanath and Demers, 1999; McQuail, 2005; Hjarvard, 2008). By and large, this is an issue that characterizes all social sciences, and communications and media studies are no exception.

To an extent, the old divisions that have traditionally populated the field, such as the dichotomy between the dominant and alternative paradigm, or administrative as against critical research, have become obsolete. Communication phenomena, issues and concerns contain economic, political, social and cultural aspects, and they cannot be approached simply through a single perspective, much less a single discipline. Communication and media studies is an interdisciplinary, if not a multi-disciplinary, field. Communications studies draws elements from established disciplines like history, political science, sociology, psychology, anthropology, linguistics and literature. It also overlaps with newer disciplines and interdisciplines like cultural studies, popular cultural studies, film studies, journalism, speech communication, information studies, ethnomusicology (Chattopadhyay, 2008; Valdivia, 2006), and feminist studies. Although 'communication and media studies' is a relatively new (inter-)discipline, roughly dating back to the 1920s as a set of studies and the 1950s as a 'formal discipline' (Valdivia, 2006: 1), there have been few sustained efforts made to develop a single communication theory (Shoemaker, 1993). As Denis McQuail (2005: 16) has argued:

> It is unlikely that we can find any single definition that can adequately cover the diversity of the relevant phenomena and perspectives. It is also unlikely that any 'science of communication' can be independent and self-sufficient, given the origins of the study in many disciplines and the wide-ranging nature of the issues that arise, including matters of economics, law, politics and ethics as well as culture. The study of communications has to be interdisciplinary and must adopt varied approaches and methods.

In any case, the existence of a single exclusive media theory is unlikely to be accepted as such, at least in the near future. As Everett Rogers has pointed out, the field of communication studies is not integrated, but is 'divided into two sub-disciplines – mass communication and interpersonal communication – for reasons that are largely historical and somewhat accidental' (1999: 618). Besides, as Crowley and Mitchell (1994: 3–4) note, the tendencies for holistic theories have been eliminated. It is also true that there has been a rise of several specialized theoretical approaches which have rendered new important information about communication phenomena. In effect, during the last decades communication and media studies have been developed all over the world as subfields in humanities and social sciences (McQuail, 2008), reflecting the interdisciplinary and multidisciplinary character of the field.

On the other hand, this has always been the case in communication and media studies, and most perspectives always have tried to analyse the complex communication phenomena and realities. By and large, communication research has focused on three sets of issues: the nature of human communication, the effects of mass communication and the connections between the media systems and the society in which they are embedded (Lang and Lang, 1993).

In general, there are various views and perspectives on the media, their role and their influences in society. In practice, these views are as old as the media themselves. Apart from the 'dominant vs. critical/alternative' dichotomy, there are, as we have seen, other approaches which, from their own perspective, continually review and reappraise the role of the media in society.

Two dedicated volumes published by the *Journal of Communication* in 1983 and 1993 with the title 'Ferment in the Field' (Levy and Gurevitch, 1993), as well as the publication of two books in 1989 by the ICA with the title *Rethinking Communication* (Dervin *et al.*, 1989a, 1989b) revisited the question of the discipline's status since there was a considerable diversity in perspectives, either in terms of theory or methodology, with regards to the analysis of the communication phenomena. In effect, having experienced a remarkable growth within social sciences and humanities, political economy and cultural studies have tended to dominate the discussion of how researchers can best approach and interpret communication phenomena (Garnham, 1997; Cottle, 2003). As Craig (2008) notes:

> Some were optimistic that the field was emerging toward disciplinary status; others seemed equally certain that no such thing was happening. Some saw the continuing fragmentation of the field as a problem; others celebrated fragmentation as an invaluable source of adaptive strength. Some called urgently for efforts to define the intellectual focus of the discipline; others just as urgently insisted that any such effort to define a theoretical core would be not only useless but counter-productive. Still others were unclear about the possibility or desirability of becoming a discipline but nevertheless proposed various conceptual definitions of the communication field. None of these views clearly dominated the field by the mid-2000s.

Such segmentation and specialization is not necessarily disadvantageous to the field of study. On the contrary, the very nature of mass communication demands an interdisciplinary, if not a multidisciplinary and interdisciplinary perspective, and the tendency towards segmentation and specialization could be regarded as very vital for its future development. Besides, as Donald Swanson had pointed out, a basic constituent of the quality of the research and of education is to have a high element of differentiation (Swanson, 1993). In effect, in our hyper-modern societies which are characterized by complexity, communication phenomena cannot be analysed by a single, solid discipline as in the nineteenth century (Levy and Gurevitch, 1993). It should be noted that this interdisciplinarity is not limited to the initiatives of media scholars. When researchers in other fields recognized the dynamics of communication in almost all aspects of daily life, they started using the ideas, models and perspectives of media scholars and researchers.

Moreover, media scholars in the past two decades have sought to reconcile oppositional perspectives. Since the mid-1980s, one has seen efforts to revise the main theoretical approaches in the field of communication theory and research as well as a tendency towards a convergence among divergent 'camps'. As James Curran and David Morley (2006: 1) note:

> Now we see scholars on both sides of that debate more readily granting intellectual recognition to the claims of the other. The business in hand is then how better to articulate the insights by these different perspectives, rather than how to adjudicate their relative importance in the theology of the field.

A true convergence, however, has not taken place in the field yet, regardless of these efforts, and we still analyse new media with the 'old analytical tools'. Few researchers or scholars would argue that the 'old' tools have offered an integrated analysis of the complex phenomenon that is communication. Additionally, the theoretical pluralism which derives from the multidisciplinary character of the field leads to cooperation amongst researchers rather than to their isolation. This book, for example, is the outcome of this *osmosis*. We realized during the preparation of this volume that the different perspectives contained here can contribute to a better understanding of the communication phenomenon. In other words, although there have been diverse and oppositional perspectives, together they constitute the body of our current communication theory. Practice supports this argument since the conditions of complexity and uncertainty require a true multidisciplinary approach with each discipline's contributions epistemologically integrated into the study as a whole.

The case of Euro-American media research

Although studies of communication were born in the 1930s and 1940s, they were relatively underdeveloped in Europe as a field of study. In fact, there has been an American (or Anglo-American) influence in the field of communication in terms of both theory and research (Downing, 1996). In practice, North American scholars have strongly influenced communication (or mass communication) theory since the Second World War. According to McQuail (2008), this was due to the fact that 'the large task of postwar reconstruction and regeneration in Europe overshadowed issues relating to the media'. The bulk of published papers in such mainstream journals as the *Journal of Communication,* published by the US-based International Communication Association, are related to US concerns and research. However, as in the case of European scholars of television consumption, it has been possible to develop, as above noted, a theoretical model 'alternative' to mainstream American media theory, mainly as contributions to critical analysis and cultural media studies. European scholars have also developed their own approaches to research through such journals as the *European Journal of Communication* and *Media, Culture and Society*, which (especially the former) frequently present a picture of European media research and theory. In effect, the uniqueness of European media studies was beginning to emerge by the end of the 1970s. With a few exceptions, for example some studies in Germany, the Netherlands and Belgium, much of the European media research concerned historical accounts rather than media analysis. In fact, European media research is tied closely to the work of British scholars, since the theory and research of mass communication from the 1960s until the mid-1980s was in practice the predominant preoccupation of British media studies, with some exceptions from Scandinavia, Germany and France (Averbeck, 2008). However, one should also recognize the influence of semiotics in European media studies so cementing the importance of the French influence. James Curran (2002) has also drawn attention to the influence of Italian scholars in European media studies since they offered a complex and multifaceted interpretation of society, i.e. hegemony, in which power relations are in play in different situations and at different levels. These power relations cannot be reduced to a binary and all-encompassing opposition of class interests, nor can they be traced to the mode of production or social formations. French and German perspectives have also been adopted with some adjustments and variation by some media researchers and, undoubtedly, some of the most interesting studies that appeared in recent years fit under this category. On the other hand, a number of European researchers considered that the role of media is reduced to a succession of reader–text encounters (Curran, 2002), while some others argued that such a perspective does not differ importantly from the American liberal tradition in media studies and social sciences (Fiske, 1994; McQuail, 2008).

According to Nordenstreng, the evolution of the field since the 1950s can be seen as passing through a number of successive stages which coincide with the history of leftish thinking, as he calls 'six ferments one for each decade' (Nordenstreng, 2004: 6). In the first formative stage (1950s) the field 'emerged and established itself in the media industry throughout Europe and North America' (p. 6). In the 'second ferment' (the decade of the 1960s) the socio-political revolt affected all social sciences and consequently in communication research and particularly in the 'dominant paradigm'. In the third ferment (1970s) the leftish thinking was established as 'the main challenger of hegemonic powers in media as well as academia' (p. 6), while in the fourth ferment (1980s) these views were challenged. In effect, developments in European communication and media studies gradually offered new perspectives in film studies, popular music, fashion, advertising and sports analysis (Moores, 1993) and new terms have entered the media vocabulary such as 'genre', 'typology', 'discourse', 'realism', 'hegemony', 'polysemy', etc., but as new terms and perspectives started to be widely used, some gradually lost their analytical rigour.

To come back to Nordenstreng's framework, in the fifth stage (1990s) the field was 'influenced by neoliberal and populist-conservative politics on the one hand, and new information and communication technologies … on the other' (p. 7). Finally, the last, sixth, ferment (2000s) has been influenced by the globalization deluge and its contradictions. In effect, media researchers have produced studies covering a whole range of areas. These range from studies regarding the effects of the media. Violence and politics were, as usual, the most researched areas. Researchers were also interested in the wider role of the media in the structures and the performance of the political system, the effect of the media in social integration, and the construction of identity and social change. In other words, researchers shifted their focus to the political and social role of the media and the role of the public service. This tendency, however, has also been the outcome of increased contribution and intervention of media scholars and researchers, especially from northern Europe.

As Nordenstreng points out:

> It is possible to see it [the sixth ferment] as the writing on the wall for true leftist ideas – as the final stage when the Left is being totally co-opted by the System, not least through the active role of the leftists in applying ICT not only as technical instruments but above all as conceptual tools in the construction of a new network theory of society à la Manuel Castells. On the other hand, there are also good grounds for an optimistic reading of the trends, whereby the Left is not only sustained but even invigorated by the logic of the socioeconomic development itself, including the new social movements and radicalisation tendencies within the middle class. Moreover, the Bush administration has helped to politicise cultural studies not only in the USA but also worldwide, thus narrowing the gulf to the political (Nordenstreng, 2004: 8).

By and large, during the last decades the multiplication and diversification of media outlets, either old or new, has given an impetus to communications and media research and studies. However, our knowledge of how the media work at a European level, how the media are received and used in the different national communities and on a comparative, transnational level is still elementary, regardless of its proliferation in the recent decades (Nordenstreng, 2004).

Nevertheless, the study of mass media generated many new lines of research in Europe from both social sciences and the humanities. Media studies in Europe is therefore a truly interdisciplinary and multifaceted field. Though the American influence is still apparent, it has, at times, merged with the European tradition so providing a Euro-American dimension to media studies. In the last two decades there has emerged, as Jeremy Tunstall (2008) has pointed out, a Euro-American media culture and this has fed into, and drawn on, different traditions and perspectives. For example, while European media studies have focused on ideological and institutional analysis, the US approach from the beginning has favoured behavioural levels (McQuail, 2008).

Broadly speaking, the production of studies in the media field has mushroomed in the last two decades. There has been an explosion in the number of outputs in the field – in book form, in journals, in audiovisual format – and though most of these focus on Euro-American media circumstances and conditions, there has been a notable increase in the volume of work coming out of South East Asia, India and Africa. This situation has subsequently led to an increase in the number of research areas, topics and cases.

As regards to the focus of the work that is now being carried out, much of it is accounted for by the following main agenda items, at least in respect of work in North America and Western Europe: news research, agenda setting and framing; journalistic roles, professionalism and media ethics; television production (fiction, genres); media audiences and popular culture (audience and reception research); media production (content analysis and text research); children, young people and the media; media and everyday life; public sphere and cultural identity; the future of public service broadcasting and the emerging public media; nationalism and identity, 'Europeanization', and globalization; democracy, political culture and media framing; political communication (campaigning, advertising and debates); the role of new media in all aspects of communication; media policy, media law and media concentration; information society and Internet studies, new information order and development; modernity and media representations. However, there are many variations and subthemes regarding not only the approaches taken but also the ways in which these topics are explored. As this volume seeks to show, developments in technology and polity may signal the appearance of a new phase in the study of the phenomena of communication.

Thematic development of media perspectives

The aim of this book is to address general issues and topics that can be studied through concrete analysis of the history, structure, contents and effects of the media. The chapters in this book deal with various dimensions of media, culture and economy from a number of distinct dimensions and socio-political contexts. At the same time, the chapters attempt to discuss and to interpret the marked changes in the communication domain through a number of topics and issues discussed by the contributors of the book. Most importantly, the chapters in this volume attempt to set a research agenda for the first quarter of the twenty-first century by exploring directions and analysing cases which, though not necessarily new, deserve to come under renewed scrutiny.

The chapters attempt to reflect the developments in the field by combining both qualitative and quantitative approaches, and 'soft' and 'hard' analyses. By default, the perspective of this book is interdisciplinary since its contributors present different traditions, geographical locations and dimensions of the field. Its distinctiveness stems ultimately from the fact that most of us were fortunate in this enterprise to have the opportunity to gather as a group and to debate and discuss the issues facing mediated societies today. Our experiences during a workshop that gathered in Athens in 2008 have in fact strengthened our belief that:

- interdisciplinarity is a prevailing instrument for charting, mapping and realizing the potentials as well as the limits of emerging media situations and the new media;
- debates on the way the media evolve contribute to our understanding of the contemporary communications field;

- media analysis definitely requires a social science perspective, which at the same time takes into consideration the structure as well as the logic of media.

This introduction has also sought to show how communication and media studies benefits from ideas and concepts chosen from the traditional perspectives of the field, from fresh analyses, as well as from the cooperative endeavours involving several perspectives and approaches. For instance, the rapid convergence and digitalization of the communications sectors have already had strong impacts on media markets, political communication, communication policy, media content, social structures and imbalances and cultural forms. We are told that we live in the era of choice, but do the changes which have taken place in terms of structures and content actually undermine some of the major characteristics of media production, distribution and reception?

This book thus reflects trends in current communication research. It comments upon and at the same time appraises them. As the essays in this volume deal with topics and cases in the communication field, they also provide an account of trends in media analysis and regard the media as a force that is related to social, economic, political and technological transformations in the field.

In sum, this book discusses and explores topics such as:

- the main issues of communication in the twenty-first century;
- 'new' relationships between the media and society;
- the new environment of political communication;
- the main effects of technological developments on the domain of the news media and journalism;
- the ways in which technological forces are altering our social relationships and the role of the media in public life.

The book uses either case studies or topics and discusses some aspects of these questions. By and large, it explores the new communication environment by combining the existing body of knowledge with core questions about some major media and societal issues.

The book is divided into two parts. The first part provides accounts of the role of the media in society. The second part offers analyses of new media developments and tries to explore the role of the new media in the social production of meaning. Needless to say, there are a number of crisscrossing themes in the essays and between the parts of the book. Finally, by bringing together American and European authors, the book seeks to raise significant questions about the study of the media from within different traditions. In doing so, it touches on the range of concerns that shape the present, and the future, media landscape and the issues these can create for communication, be it political or civic.

Media in the contemporary age

In Chapter 1, Frank Webster examines the argument that information is a necessary foundation of democracy and offers a systematic critique of the 'social democratic consensus' that, to ensure reliable and robust information, state support and/or intervention in the market is necessary. Webster critically reviews arguments for and against in a context of new media, globalization, postmodernity and new thinking about the state's role. He argues that the dominance of 'public sphere' thinking may now need to be critically reviewed.

But in the digital era, there is increased 'mediated visibility' (Thompson, 1995). This has transformed the relations between visibility and power and has forced political rulers to appear before citizens in ways and on a scale that previously never existed. Skilful politicians exploit this to their advantage with the help of their PR consultants and communications advisors so as to create and sustain a basis of support by managing their visibility in the mediated arena of modern politics. This new situation has led to the transformation of political communication and Ralph Negrine and Stylianos Papathanassopoulos' Chapter 2 sets out to explore this.

In Chapter 3, Shanto Iyengar argues that the developments in technology have also changed the ways in which we consume news. Citizens/viewers now have access to thousands of online sources ranging from well-established news organizations to relatively unknown bloggers whose reports and views are widely circulated through email, viral videos and other forms of content sharing. Given the prospect of imminent information overload, a basic question for communication researchers concerns consumers' coping strategies; that is, just how do they sort through this vast array of news sources? The question is particularly challenging because the use of newer forms of information is correlated with not only demographic attributes (e.g. age), but also with levels of political motivation and political preference. It is well established, for instance, that younger media users disproportionately avoid conventional news channels and choose instead to congregate in online interactive environments where they are not merely consumers, but co-producers of messages. Similarly, the people who seek out news on the Internet are much more involved in political life than their counterparts who perhaps spend more of their time online on other activities.

Daya Thussu, in Chapter 4, focuses on the growing worldwide commercialism of broadcast journalism resulting from privatization, deregulation, digitization and the opening up of new markets that have resulted in a shift from public-conscious to ratings-conscious television news services. The proliferation of all-news channels, broadcasting to a heterogeneous global audience and dependence on corporate advertising have encouraged a tendency among broadcasters to move away from a socially relevant news agenda – privileging information and education over the entertainment value of news – to a more market-led, 'soft', version of news, with its emphasis on consumer journalism, sports and entertainment. Thussu discusses these changes in a global setting and explores the key implications. As he argues, the main aim of the increasingly globalized corporate media is to ensure diversion of audiences from the real scandals caused by neo-liberalism.

Nicolas Demertzis explores the topic of emotions in the media and the mediatization of traumas by combining media theory and the newly emerging subfield of the sociology of emotions. In Chapter 5, he notes that unlike the field of sociology, the topic of emotions could be found at the heart of media and communication studies from the early days of the development of the field. On this premise, his chapter is concerned, on the one hand, with a brief assessment of the status of emotions in communication and media studies and, on the other hand, with the intersection of media studies, cultural studies, media ethics, and the sociology of emotions, namely, mediatized traumas and the moral dilemmas they convey to the members of the audience.

In Chapter 6, Tristan Mattelart combines media studies and history in order to focus on media and transnational cultures. He points out that since the end of the 1980s, the literature on diaspora and migrations has become, in the Anglo-Saxon academic field, one of the main places where cultural transformation in times of globalization are considered. The concept of diaspora has in particular been used metaphorically to describe contemporary cultures and identities as being in a constant state of flux, as being constantly redefined under the pressures of transnational cultural flows. In this analytical framework, works on media and migration flows have emerged in many ways as a kind of testing ground to study the advent of 'hybrid' identities and cultures, fruits of the increasing intercultural encounters. National borders and the associated national forms of belonging are, in these works, presented as losing significance whereas transnational ones are presented as increasingly important. By exploring some of the key texts that have given birth to these ideas, this chapter shows how this body of literature on media and migration flows has emerged and underlines some of the major ruptures that they have encountered in ways of thinking about media internationalization.

Communication in the digital era

The second part of the book examines cases in the new media world. In Chapter 7, Gustavo Cardoso argues that one can identify a number of changes in the context of communication in our societies and that those changes can be interpreted in the light of the emergence of a new communication model, which is not based on the idea of 'mass' but one of 'networked' communication. Cardoso enumerates the main characteristics of this new communication model and also highlights, among other things, what are considered to be the main manifestations of change of context or, if we prefer, of present futures, in the context of communication, its technologies, appropriations and uses.

Mark Deuze attempts to analyse the ways we live in the new mediatized world. His chapter addresses the most fundamental aspects and themes of everyday life – such as work, family, love and play – as these are understood in the context of a life lived in media. As media research has shown us, people spend more of their time using media devices than in the past, and this behaviour has become a foundational feature of everyday life. Media devices, what people do with them, and how all of this fits in with the organization of our everyday life, disrupt and unsettle well-established views of the role media play in society. Instead of continuing to wrestle with a distinction between media and society, Deuze proposes that contemporary media studies should take as its point of departure a view of life not lived *with* media, but *in* media. The media life perspective starts from the realization that the whole of the world and our lived experience in it can be seen as framed by, mitigated through, and made immediate by (immersive, integrated, ubiquitous and pervasive) media.

This is also a prerequisite for the advertising industry to reach consumers. Thus Matthew McAllister, in Chapter 9, explores the concept of commodity fetishism in new media context, by focusing on how brands are both celebrated and production contexts co-opted in digital forms. Consumerist characteristics of digital media are briefly reviewed, including the ease of mixing textual forms, digital image manipulation, and the proximity of purchasing with persuasive messages, ease of feedback/mass customization, mobility, and democratizing consumerist production. In applying commodity fetishism to new media, the chapter first discusses the 'cyber-celebration' of brands via promotional websites. To this end, it focuses on the archival function and collective memory contributions of commercial websites, integrated marketing activities – which highlight convergence of marketing and commoditization – and niche, database and customer relationship marketing that are structured around feedback and surveillance of consumer habits and preferences. McAllister then argues that digital consumer discourse, rather than ignoring or completely masking capitalist production, instead appropriates production discourse as a form of 'production fetishism', articulated via the proliferation of web distributed 'insider information' and through the framing of the consumer as labour. This latter construction is manifested in impromptu 'focus groups' found in commercial website discussion boards, the consumer as distributor through viral marketing, and finally in user-generated commercials. McAllister concludes with reflections about what such developments mean for identity, community and the role of product brands, along with possibilities for cultural resistance and agency.

When researchers began to explore the dynamics of the Internet back in the early 1980s and wanted to create an open network for freely exchanging information, they could never quite imagine how the

Internet would affect journalism. Marcell Machill and Markus Beiler in Chapter 10, and Linda Steiner and Jessica Roberts in Chapter 11 deal with the future of journalism. Marcell Machill and Markus Beiler summarize and comment on a research project that has focused on the use of the Internet by journalists in Germany. Their study focuses on the use of search engines by journalists, among a variety of other methods, electronic and interpersonal, traditional and new, for news gathering, checking and reporting. Among their findings is that for most journalists, email and phone presented primary methods of research and that Google and other search engines function as gatekeepers, presenting primary points of entry for journalists looking up information online, since the Internet is employed as a complement or alternative to other methods of fact-finding, rather than a substitute.

A similar trend is evident in the US. A survey conducted by Cision (2010) and Don Bates found that an overwhelming majority of reporters and editors nowadays depend on social media sources when researching their stories. Among the journalists surveyed, 89 per cent said they turn to blogs for story research, 65 per cent to social media sites such as Facebook and LinkedIn, and 52 per cent to microblogging services such as Twitter. The survey also found that 61 per cent use Wikipedia, the popular online encyclopedia. By and large, the survey made clear that reporters and editors are aware of the need to verify information they get from social media. Eighty-four percent said social media sources were 'slightly less' or 'much less' reliable than traditional media, with 49 per cent saying social media suffers from 'lack of fact checking, verification and reporting standards'.

Linda Steiner and Jessica Roberts analyse and respond to criticisms of public journalism generated over the last decade by scholars and practising journalists, including how it is sometimes distinguished from and sometimes conflated with citizen journalism. They argue, in Chapter 11, that public journalism continues to offer a model whereby professional news organizations can take citizens' interests seriously and partner with citizens. Nevertheless, they argue that democracy still suffers, but as a critique of conventional journalism, a reform movement in journalism, and a set of journalistic practices, public journalism lost its momentum. The death of public journalism resulted not from its own flaws or failures but from two linked processes that significantly challenge journalism: the continuing development of technologies enabling citizen journalism, and economic crises that significantly undermine conventional professional journalism. After analysing criticisms of public journalism, Steiner and Roberts address the extent to which citizen journalism solves the problems of civic culture identified by the advocates of public journalism. At least some forms of citizen journalism abandon the information model at the heart of both conventional and public journalism. Whether citizen journalism's emphasis on engagement solves problems of democracy is yet to be determined.

As new technologies emerge, the where, when, and how of media use and consumption continue to change. In recent years, social networking sites have become not only popular but also a new global communication platform. Social network sites (SNSs) such as Facebook, MySpace, LinkedIn, Twitter and CyWorld provide individuals with the opportunity to present themselves and to connect with existing and new social networks. In Europe, the population of social networkers is forecast to rise from 41.7 million in 2008 to 107.4 million by 2012 (Reding, 2008). To what extent does this rapid development of the sector present wider social utility? In their chapter in this volume, Zizi Papacharissi and Andrew Mendelson note that social network sites might be, for some, just a way of expanding their personal connections and entertainment. They point out that conducting research in a converged media environment requires researchers to develop theories and analytical tools that examine uses, effects, activity, involvement and content across media. They propose a theoretical model that combines elements of the uses and gratifications and the social networks approaches with a consideration of technological affordances, so as to explain the emerging patterns of media use, activity and sociability. They also note that the uses and gratifications and social networks approaches acknowledge the social character of online media and the social capital generated by their use, since individuals are able to fulfil traditional mediated and interpersonal needs simultaneously, while at the same time expanding their social connections.

In the final chapter of this volume, Eszter Hargittai challenges the popular account that digital media are predominantly used by young people who are universally savvy with information and communication technologies. Hargittai, in Chapter 13, presents evidence that implies considerable disparities in Internet skills and uses among young adults. It shows that although the majority of youth are now online in many countries, and thus access differences (the so-called 'digital divide') are no longer the main barrier to benefiting from digital media, know-how and actual uses exhibit considerable differences across the population. Far from being randomly distributed, online skills and uses vary by socio-economic status suggesting that rather than meeting its potential to level the playing field, the Internet may be contributing to increasing social inequality.

All the essays in this volume have sought to provide an initial map of some of the current media issues and, to an extent, some of the contested themes in the field. Such a project, by default, has its limitations. There are many other topics and cases in the field which are not covered and the rapid rise of communications and information technologies, among other things, have quickened the pace of globalization. The issues covered here, though, are important because they constantly reappear on our agendas. In this new age of networking and political and economic crisis, how we see them and how we understand them is, therefore, critical.

References

Altheide, D.L. and Snow, R. P. (1979) *Media Logic*, Beverly Hills, CA: Sage.

Averbeck, S. (2008) 'Comparative History of Communication Studies: France and Germany', *The Open Communication Journal*, 1 (2): 1–13.

Bondebjerg, I. (2001) 'European Media, Cultural Integration and Globalization; Reflections on the ESF-programme Changing Media – Changing Europe', *Nordicom*, 22 (1): 53–64.

Bondebjerg, I. and Golding, P. (2004) 'Introduction', pp. 9–18, in Bondebjerg, I. and Golding, P. (eds) *European Culture and the Media*, Bristol: Intellect.

Chattopadhyay, S. (2008) 'A Review of Angharad N. Valdivia, Ed. *A Companion to Media Studies*', *Mass Communication and Society*, 11 (3): 357–363.

Cision (2010) 'National Survey Finds Majority of Journalists Now Depend on Social Media for Story Research'. Available: http://us.cision.com/news_room/press_releases/2010/2010-1-20_gwu_survey.asp>.

Comscore.com (2008) 'Social Networking Explodes Worldwide as Sites Increase their Focus on Cultural Relevance'. Available: <www.comscore.com/press/release.asp?press=2396>.

Cottle, S. (2003) 'Media Organization and Production: Mapping the Field', pp. 3–25, in Cottle, Simon (ed.) *Media Organization and Production*, London: Sage.

Craig, R.T. (2008) 'Communication as a Field and Discipline', in Donsbach, W. (ed.) *The International Encyclopedia of Communication*, Blackwell Publishing. Blackwell ReferenceOnline.Available:<www.communicationencyclopedia.com/subscriber/tocnode?id=g9781405131995_chunk_g97814051319958_ss75-1>

Crowley, D. and Mitchell, D. (1994) 'Introduction', pp. 1–25, in Crowley, D. and Mitchell, D. (eds) *Communication Theory Today*, Cambridge: Polity Press.

Curran, J. (2002) *Media and Power*, London: Routledge.

Curran, J. and Morley, D. (2006) *Media and Cultural Theory*, London: Routledge.

Dervin, B., Grossberg, L., O'Keefe, D. and Wartella, E. (eds) (1989a) *Rethinking Communication; Vol. 1*, Newbury Park: Sage.

Dervin, B, Grossberg, L, O'Keefe, D. and Wartella, E (eds) (1989b) *Rethinking Communication; Vol 2*, Newbury Park: Sage.

Downing, J.D.H. (1996) 'Internationalizing media theory', *Peace Review*, 8 (1): 113–117.

Fiske, J. (1994) *Media Matters: Everyday Culture and Political Change*, Minnesota: University of Minnesota Press.

Garnham, N. (1997) 'Political Economy and the Practice of Cultural Studies', pp. 56–73, in Ferguson, M. and Golding, P. (eds) *Cultural Studies in Question*, London: Sage.

Hall, S. (1982) 'The Rediscovery of "Ideology": The Return of the Repressed in Media Studies', pp. 56–90, in Bennett, T., Curran, J., Gurevitch, M. and Woollacott, J. (eds) *Culture, Society, and the Media*, New York, NY: Methuen.

Hjarvard, Stig (2008) 'The Mediatization of Society; A Theory of the Media as Agents of Social and Cultural Change', *Nordicom Review*, 29 (2): 105–134.

Jensen, K.B. and Rosengren, K.E. (1990) 'Five Traditions in Search of the Audience', *European Journal of Communication*, 5 (2&3): 207–238.

Lang, K. and Lang, G. E. (1993) 'Perspectives on communication', *Journal of Communication*, 43 (3): 92–99.

Levy, M.R., and Gurevitch, M. (eds) (1993) 'The future of the field: Between fragmentation and cohesion' [special issues]. *Journal of Communication*, 43 (3/4).

Luhmann, N. (2000) *The Reality of the Mass Media*, Cambridge: Polity.

McAllister, P.M. and Turow, J. (2002) 'New Media and the Commercial Sphere: two intersecting trends, five categories of concern', *Journal of Broadcasting and Electronic Media*, 46 (4): 505–10.

McQuail, D. (2005) *McQuail's Mass Communication Theory*, London: Sage.

McQuail, D. (2008) 'Communication as an Academic Field: Western Europe', in Donsbach, W. (ed.) *The International Encyclopedia of Communication*, Blackwell Publishing. Blackwell Reference Online. Available: <www.communicationencyclopedia.com/subscriber/tocnode?id=g9781405131995_chunk_g97814051319958_ss67-1> .

McQuail, D. (2009) 'Editorial: EJC Symposium Special Issue', *European Journal of Communication*, 24 (2): 387–389.

Merrin, W. (2009) 'Media Studies 2.0: upgrading and open-sourcing the discipline', *Interactions*, 1 (1): 17–34.

Moores, S. (1993) *Interpreting Audiences: Ethnography of Media Consumption*, London: Sage.

Nordenstreng, K. (2004) 'Ferment in the Field: Notes on the Evolution of Communication Studies and its Disciplinary Nature', *Javnost/The Public*, 11 (3): 5–18.

Pavlik, J.V. (1998) *New Media Technology: Cultural and Commercial Perspectives*, 2nd edn, Boston: Allyn and Bacon.

Rantanen, T. (2004) *The Media and Globalization*, London: Sage.

Reding, V. (2008) 'Social Networking in Europe: success and challenges', Safer Internet Forum, Luxembourg, 26 September (SPEECH/08/465).

Reese, S.D. and Ballinger, J. (2001) 'The Roots of a Sociology of News: Remembering Mr. Gates and Social Control in the Newsroom', *Journalism and Mass Communication Quarterly*, 78 (4): 641–658.

Rogers, E. (1999) 'Anatomy of the two subdisciplines of Communication Study', *Human Communication Research*, 25 (4): 618–631.

Ruddock, A. (2008) 'Media Studies 2.0? Binge Drinking and Why Audiences Still Matter', *Sociology Compass*, 2 (1): 1–15.

Ruggiero, T.E. (2000) 'Uses and Gratifications Theory in the 21st Century', *Mass Communication and Society*, 3 (1): 3–37.

Servaes, J. (1989) 'Après le déluge', pp. 214–218, in Dervin, B., Grossberg, L., O'Keefe, D. and Wartella, E. (eds) *Rethinking Communication; Vol. 2*, Newbury Park: Sage.

Shoemaker, P.J. (1993) 'Communication in crisis: theory, curricula and power', *Journal of Communication*, 43 (4): 146–153.

Swanson, D.L. (1993) 'Fragmentation, the field and the future', *Journal of Communication*, 43 (4): 163–172.

Taylor, P.A. (2009) 'Editorial introduction – Optimism, pessimism and the myth of technological neutrality', *Interactions*, 1 (1): 7–16.

Thompson, J.B. (1995) *The Media and Modernity: A Social Theory of the Media*, Cambridge: Polity Press.

Tunstall, J. (2008) *The Media were American*, New York: Oxford University Press.

Valdivia, A.N. (2006) (ed.) *A Companion to Media Studies*, Malden, MA: Blackwell.

Viswanath, K. and Demers, D. (1999) 'Mass Media from a macrosocial perspective', pp. 3–30, in Demers, D. and Viswanath, K. (eds) *Mass Media, Social Control and Social Change: A Macrosocial Perspective*, Ames, IA: Iowa State University Press.

Wang, G. and Servaes, J. (2000) 'Introduction', pp. 1–18, in Wang, G., Servaes, J. and Goonasekera, A. (eds) *The New Communications Landscape: Demystifying Media Globalization*, London: Routledge.

Warnick, B. (2007) *Rhetoric Online: Persuasion and Politics on the World Wide Web*, New York: Peter Lang.

Wright, C.R. (1986) 'Mass Communication Rediscovered: its past and future in American sociology', pp. 22–33, in Ball-Rokeach, S. and Cantor, M.l. (eds) *Media, Audience and Social Structure*, Beverly Hills: Sage.

Part I
Media in the contemporary age

1 Information and democracy: the weakening of social democracy

Frank Webster

The social democratic perspective has long been dominant in discussions of information and democracy. Its analysis highlights capitalism's shortcomings in providing information to the public: it suggests that what the market best provides is diversion, gossip and trivia, being inept when it comes to supplying reliable news, disinterested debate and the in-depth scrutiny that an informed citizenry most needs. In response, the social democratic approach recommends state intervention in order to ensure that informational needs can be adequately fulfilled (this penchant for intervention is why it may be conceived as social democratic). Such a policy unavoidably introduces unease since many advocates are sensitive to the growth of 'spin' within the polity itself, the expansion of which they have encouraged as a counter to market inadequacies.

Democratic deficit

A starting point of this approach is the shortcomings of actually existing democracies. There is widespread concern about a 'democratic deficit' in the mature democracies. In such countries, democracy appears fully established: citizens have long had the vote, there are well-established procedures for conducting elections and there are multiple channels for political debate. Yet not all is well: voter turnout is low even at national elections, membership of political parties has plummeted, and it is often difficult to persuade candidates to run for local offices.

Critics observe other deficits. These include high levels of ignorance amongst the public (Jacoby, 2008), survey evidence showing high proportions of the public incapable of naming members of the government (and often more able to identify celebrities) or being uninformed about foreign policy. Chris Hedges (2008) conjures 'America the Illiterate' to conceive a *majority* that is 'informed by simplistic, childish narratives and clichés'. Recent analyses of presidential speeches have evidenced a decline in complexity of language use (from vocabulary through to reasoned argumentation) and a marked shift towards use of emotive and easily understandable phrases (Lim, 2008).

Critics generally go beyond observing public ignorance to identify as the major culprit a commercial media system dedicated to profit maximization. This leads to content that is escapist, shallow and hucksterist because the media producers must achieve highest possible audience figures while creating least possible controversy (there is a surfeit of *faux* controversy in the tabloid press about celebrities and the personality traits of politicians, most of it inconsequential). Certainly, audience size does not translate directly into profitability since it is audience demographics that most appeal to a commercial media. Hence, if a demographic attracts advertisers because it is well educated and affluent, then the product will be able to reflect something of this, perhaps offering content that addresses its lifestyle or even social concerns. However, the determinant remains profit maximization, with media reliant on and prioritizing the ratings or the sponsor. Either way the consequences for content are major, with a general narrowing of the range of coverage, a deluge of trivia, and a disposition towards conservatism (Miliband, 1969, chapters 7–8).

For many critics, public ignorance is exacerbated by an inadequate media system that supplies abundant information, but of an inappropriate kind, being obsessed with personality, glamour and the ephemeral. Infotainment is what media offer, 'junk information' comparable to foodstuff that is pervasive yet bad for one's health. A likely consequence is that vulnerable audiences, befuddled by a diet of garbage information, will be incapable of sifting nutritious from junk information, thereby pressured into reliance on image, appearance and personality traits – accoutrements of the celebrity culture that finds accord with commercialized media – in coming to decisions about issues of great moment (Popkin, 1994).

While it is commonplace for critics to suggest that the market is incapable of supplying reliable information to the citizenry, it is also usual for them to argue that political and business élites manipulate information. The charge then is not merely that markets operate in ways such that adequate information is not made available, but that business leaders and politicians more generally intervene to manipulate information in ways that favour themselves. In evidence, critics point to the spread of PR, spin doctoring, media management and suchlike as contributors to the spread of interested information.

It follows from this that neither the market system nor politicians can be trusted to supply the information required of democracy. But a problem then for the social democrats is that their advocacy – let the state intervene to ensure resilient and reliable information availability – must be suspected since we have so much evidence to show that politicians endeavour to shape information to suit themselves.

An informed electorate

It follows from concern about the democratic deficit, and the conviction that inadequate media play a key role in fermenting this condition, that critics wish for reform. The premise is that any meaningful democracy must have an informed electorate. If the public is ignorant, then to such critics democracy is weak. If people are unaware of the great issues of the day, then government cannot respond to the general will of the people. If citizens lack reliable information, then they may also be manipulated by those in the know. This is the underlying logic of the position that moves readily from identification of flaws to recommendation of state intervention to ensure that the public may be appropriately informed.

The importance of statistics

Let us point to something that vividly illustrates the importance of reliable information being available for the conduct of meaningful democracy. Accurate national statistics are an essential foundation of any democratic society – and for the most part, they must be paid for out of general taxation as a public good since market mechanisms are unlikely to deliver what is required.

It is worth emphasizing this since the importance of statistics is underestimated in everyday life. Yet without reliable data on, say, population trends, mortality rates, migration patterns and consumer expenditure, meaningful participation in democratic affairs is hard to envision. Access to such information is a requisite of debate since otherwise one must rely on personal experience only. It is essential that an infrastructure is in place that ensures the gathering and dissemination of such statistical data. These statistics are gathered from diverse sources, but the major responsibility rests with government.

Such statistics come to citizens chiefly via the media that use them as a matter of routine. This is probably the reason why many people underestimate the import of statistical services; they receive them at second hand, pre-digested in a politician's speech or inflected in a newspaper report. However, it is vital to appreciate that democracy relies enormously on the resource of accurate statistical data.

How else might a society know itself were not diligent and impartial statisticians gathering information, traceable often to particular households yet also aggregated into data sets, which allows us to understand the changing shape of the nation? Imagine how disabling it would be were politicians not able to discuss, say, changes in standards of living or regional development, without recourse to authoritative data. A rudimentary knowledge of social statistics reveals imperfections, but to concede that there is need for improvement on the data of, let us say, criminal activity or illegal immigration is a far cry from arguing that statistical information is unimportant. On the contrary, it is a prerequisite of democratic debate and discussion. While statistics might be unglamorous and they can be contentious, and while their generation involves expense and high-level technical skills, it is important that we recognize that democracies are impoverished without their being available.

Distrust of the market

The social democratic approach hinges on the perceived inability of the market to deliver robust and reliable information. There are several reasons why this should be so, but an important one is that it may not be in the interests of commercial organizations to make available what they know to the wider public. As profit-making outfits, their concern is to maximize returns to their investors – and this may encourage private organizations to keep information to themselves. If information is proprietary, then it is likely that it will be limited by copyright to protect the interest of the owners. Indeed, changes in technology have meant that producers of information have been at once challenged when established mechanisms of ensuring a return on their product are threatened (one thinks of the ease of swapping files of music and movies on the Internet), and at the same time galvanized to use new media as opportunities to seek greater returns on their 'intellectual property' (e.g. on digitalized stocks of newspapers).

Further, there are pressures to provide information based on willingness to pay and its profitability to the producers. Together this means cheapest costs in terms of investment and maximum sales of information. A result is programming that has mass, lowest common denominator, appeal, such as soap opera television, sports and movies. In a market system, this pushes to the margins information of particular value to the democratic system (either by alternative information being prohibitively expensive or by the provision of news and current affairs in diminished amounts and at the outreaches of the schedule). Add to this the ongoing spread of information management, from politicians as well as the business community, and then social democrats have powerful reasons to distrust the information made available in democracies.

The public sphere

It is at this point that the concept – and its institutional expressions – of public sphere becomes significant. This idea was developed by Jürgen Habermas in the early 1960s, and it is surely one of the most striking instances of the practical influence of a philosophical notion. The public sphere has been extensively discussed elsewhere, so I do not need here to go into detail (Webster, 2006). It is an arena, independent of government (even if in receipt of state funds) while also being autonomous of economic interests, which is dedicated to open-ended discussion and debate, the proceedings of which are open to entry and accessible to scrutiny by the citizenry. Habermas (1989) offered a historical account, but here it will be enough to make a few observations about its recent pertinence.

My view is that many of those who favour state subsidy of informational activities articulate their defence in terms of a 'public service' ideal that owes much to Habermas' notion of the public sphere. The argument is that large private corporations have developed market practices in ways that thwart effective democratic engagement. Against this, other institutions have emerged that rely on state subsidy for their continuation. At the heart of their defence is the view that they support the supply of reliable information so that discussion and debate may be conducted at the optimal level. This is crucial, attest supporters, so that democracy may thrive and discussion and decision-making may take place that is informed by reliable information and the deliberations of democracy made available to the widest possible public.

Those who support public service institutions such as the British Broadcasting Corporation (BBC) and the Office of National Statistics (ONS) routinely argue that they offer what the market cannot deliver as regards information. The range, depth and reliability of, for example, news and current affairs programmes on the BBC are superior to what one might expect from Rupert Murdoch's News Corporation (and, runs an important argument, the public service ethos of the BBC has exercised a positive influence on commercial rivals at home). Similarly, it is thought inconceivable that commercial organizations could deliver what the ONS offers in terms of statistical portraits of how we live today.

Moreover, it is essential for them to have autonomy not just from market pressures to provide this public service, but also to be at arm's length from government so that they may resist efforts at information management that are widespread in politics today. In 2008, a motive to insulate the UK Statistics Authority from political interference – though it is entirely reliant on public funding – was to separate it from a government department and provide it with the independence that comes with being answerable only to Parliament as a whole.

In Britain especially, the idea of public service has a great deal of congruence with public sphere conceptions. To be sure, the meaning of public service has shifted over the years. But at its heart is found a reluctance to admit market practices since they can jeopardize the mission of the organization, a commitment to impartiality and disinterestedness in terms of information that is generated and made available, a necessary autonomy from politics albeit that income comes predominantly from the public purse, and a self-perception that those who find employment in such organizations are motivated by a vocational calling to serve the commonweal.

This is inevitably an idealized version of public service institutions. On the ground things are a good deal messier and it is not unusual to come across careerists, political interference, and a falling from professional standards. Nonetheless, it is also easy enough to find in national statistical services, public television, museums and art galleries, and even in the education system, adherence to these sorts of belief. It may appear grandiose to formulate things in this way, but such public service institutions can find legitimacy in the claim that they provide an informational infrastructure without which democracy would be less healthy than it is.

The demise of public service institutions?

There is widespread agreement that public service institutions have been under siege over the last generation or so and with this there has been an accompanying assault on their distinctive contributions to information and democracy. There is a range of reasons for this, including the following.

- The widespread dislike of taxation increases pressure for reductions in public expenditure. Public service institutions are dependent on state funds, hence on tax revenues, and they are thereby in the front line when policies of reduced public expenditure are proposed.
- This combines with suspicion of non-commercial organizations in a market society. The retreat of collectivism since the early 1980s and the advances of market practices pose challenges to organizations that can appear as quasi-socialist institutions insofar as their income comes from the state.
- A related attack on public service advances the view that they are aloof from the 'real world' in that they were cushioned from market disciplines, thereby assured of continuity however poorly they perform.
- Consonant with this immunity from the market is the accusation that public service institutions are self-serving and élitist. They have a vested interest in increasing their revenue (hence increasing public taxation) since this has led to their own expansion and aggrandizement and they are also élitist in that they are not answerable to customers since they are aloof from market disciplines. To some this has meant that employees of public service institutions are not giving customers what they want, but instead are presumptuous in offering what they as employees feel their 'clients' are in need of. Such a 'nanny' attitude is said to be widespread in public service institutions such as libraries and the BBC.
- Indeed, many of the pressures upon public service institutions have come not from audiences, but from politicians who set the budgets. Critics of public service criticize this political interference while bemoaning the lack of answerability of public service institutions to their users. Their proposed resolution has been to free such organizations from political control while insisting on a closer relationship with customers as a counterbalance to élitist tendencies.
- Reductions in state resources to public service organizations have stimulated them to turn to the market to make up the shortfalls, thereby contributing to their longer-term demise. The more that public service organizations have turned to sponsorship, or to charging for their services, or to mounting exhibitions chiefly because they would be popular with audiences, the more they have risked jeopardizing their founding principles.
- Further, profit-seeking companies have found the pro-market ethos conducive to their own entry into the activities of public service groups.

Thus Sky Television, Waterstone's Books or even Amazon can claim to provide all that public service institutions offer (and frequently more), hence making the BBC and public libraries redundant.

- Finally, ongoing technological innovation has posed enormous challenges – as well as presenting opportunities – to many established organizations, including those conceived in terms of public service. The development of cable and satellite television, and especially the Internet, has led to a profusion of alternative communication platforms. One of the major consequences has been the fragmentation, and hence diminution, of significant audience shares. No longer being able to command the mass audiences of yesterday has inevitably led to questioning of, most notably, television and radio services paid out of public funds and delivered to the entire nation. There was a time that the BBC could command audiences for major television events in excess of 25 million; today that is inconceivable, a major hit getting less than 10 million viewers. The days of mass broadcasting to an undifferentiated audience can never be returned to in an era of YouTube, Sky and iTunes. This presents serious challenges to public service institutions whose justification for being has been supply of national service to all citizens.

These factors are elements of the advance of neo-liberalism across the world since the 1980s, with which has emerged a globalized world market system, rapid technological innovation, and the penetration of commercial principles and practices into hitherto relatively untouched areas of life. Combined they have exercised an enormous influence on the information-contributing characteristics of public service institutions. There has been a discernible turning away from provision of information on non-market terms from organizations once impervious (and frequently hostile) to the imperatives of the market.

Beyond the public sphere?

The notion of the public sphere – and its cousin public service – has long appeared sacrosanct. Critics conceded that the public sphere was flawed: it was a largely a male preserve, the practice did not live up to the ideal, it was nowhere fully achieved and it tended to overlook working class experiences. Rarely, however, did one encounter critics who thought that the entire notion could be jettisoned, since the consensus was that state intervention was essential to overcome deficiencies of the market system when it came to matters of information.

However, more recently it has become possible to identify criticisms that suggest the notion of the public sphere might be becoming irrelevant to meeting the informational needs of democracy, and that the time is approaching when it ceases to make a useful contribution to our thinking about this issue. One of the criticisms observes that *globalization* is leading towards the establishment of *multiple public spheres*. John Keane (1991) sees developing, from ongoing trends, a mosaic of networks that he distinguishes at *meso*, *micro* and *macro* levels, which do away with a need for state support. Thus at the macro level he discerns the emergence of what has been called a transnational public sphere, instanced in satellite television services that transcend national borders and the emergence of international news agencies such as Al-Jazeera (cf. Castells, 2008). At the meso level Keane identifies national broadcasting as a continuing important information source, but one which is intercut both by macro organizations and micro-level information agencies such as local radio and the blogosphere.

Keane retains the term *public sphere*, though in adopting the plural noun public spheres the concept loses a good deal of its traction since what is abandoned is the notion of a privileged location in which audiences may find and exchange information that is unsullied by market interests. In its place it is suggested that we now have a multiplicity of sites – better described perhaps as public spaces – where audiences may receive and give information, irrespective of its provenance. What we have then is acknowledgement that there are various places from which we may gather and disseminate information, but this is a far cry from the concept of a public sphere which calls for state support on the grounds that the market is inadequate when it comes to meeting the informational needs of a democracy. At the root of Keane's argument is a vision of a pluralized information domain brought about by globalizing trends combined with technology that does not require intervention since market limitations are overcome by virtue of the 'complexities' new forms of information entail.

Another argument has it that *postmodernity* makes obsolete public service broadcasting. TV executive Michael Jackson (2001) asserts that public service television is now a 'redundant piece of voodoo ... drained of all purpose and meaning' (p. 4). His reasoning is that public service broadcasting worked on the presupposition that audiences were ignorant and thereby required to be informed (and educated and entertained) by an élite of cultural custodians in organizations such as the BBC. His charge is that such an approach, in which the 'mass' received from on high information those at the top deemed was necessary, is now out of time. To Jackson this is because the days of a common culture – if it ever existed – which would have been transmitted to everyone by national broadcasters, are gone.

There are several reasons for this, but what Jackson seizes upon is postmodernity with its 'versatile culture' wherein 'mass' television programmes such as soaps and quizzes are treated 'much more ironically' (p. 4) by audiences who are reluctant to uncomplainingly approve of them, while 'minority' programming is 'more profuse, and in much less of a ghetto' than hitherto. Postmodern culture means that minorities are the new majority, that diversity and fluidity mean that public service broadcasting can no longer dole out what it decides audiences need. Such a deficit model of the public, believes Jackson, is upended in an era when audiences are more unpredictable, open to innovation, and highly differentiated in their responses. Accordingly, Jackson concludes that the days of a 'directed culture and command economics' (p. 11) are over, and with them any pressing need for state intervention to secure the presence of organizations capable of ensuring that high quality information is made available to the public. Jackson stops short of arguing that postmodern culture can be left to the market, but since the chief target of his opprobrium is the paternalistic presumptuousness of a public service broadcasting system largely funded by the public purse, endorsement of the market is his logical conclusion.

Other commentators pay particular attention to the potential of *new media technologies* to displace the public sphere. Those seeking change today can readily create a website, set up electronic subscriber lists and electronic newsletters, and thereby can begin to participate in campaigns without reliance on the formerly necessary expensive printing and distribution of written materials and the exhausting and time-consuming rounds of public meetings. The remarkable victory of Barack Obama also testified to the import of new media, the President elect acknowledging in his victory speech the key role of the Internet in raising unprecedented amounts of campaign funds from thousands of small contributions of 20 to 100 dollars. There has been much comment on Obama's marshalling of YouTube, text messaging and the Internet in a campaign that took him from rank outsider to decisive winner in the two years up to November 2008. Such innovative use of new media led a senior advisor to the Republican Party to observe that the 2008 election marked 'the year the paradigm [for US campaigns] truly became bottom up instead of top down' while, even more memorably, the Republican chief strategist noted that 'the great impact that this election will have … is that it killed public financing for all time' (Nagourney, 2008).

New media also have the effect that campaigners are less dependent on traditional political parties. Nowadays activists have the tools to enter the symbolic sphere at a rate that is no longer prohibitive. The Internet means that their voice may be heard without benefit of support by organized forces such as trade unions, business sponsors or established political parties. As such, grass rooters are empowered since they may be heard courtesy of new media and without approval of organized interests. By the same token, there is less need for public sphere institutions to be succoured because new technologies allow even relatively poor activists the means to achieve a public voice (McNair, 2006).

Fragmentation and cocooning

If a combination of globalization, new media and postmodern sensibility is announcing the demise of public service organizations, we also observe another related feature of the current context. This is that while there is now a profusion of information available round the clock and vastly increased opportunities to produce as well as receive information, an accompaniment has been the fragmentation of audiences. A primary force has been the increase in programming offered, from all-day service provision to many more channels coming from established as well as from new providers from within and beyond national borders. In such a situation it is inevitable that audiences will fragment, so that while people may watch more than ever, they now watch more selectively.

Fragmentation of audiences is not limited to television and radio. It is also a feature of, and is indeed exacerbated by, the emergence of the Internet. Here is programming that can challenge established television and radio directly by offerings such as YouTube and podcasts and also go further to present information resources of vastly greater range than any established system. Fragmentation necessarily accompanies its development.

Abundance of information can lead to fragmentation *plus* difficulties of coping with information excess. For instance, Cass Sunstein (2006) contends that to cope with information abundance filtering processes are established which can result in audiences inhabiting 'information cocoons' that allow in only safe and self-confirmatory information. While it might be imagined that the advent of the web, blogging and email would expand the horizons of audiences, profusion of information may as readily lead to fragmented groups paying heed only to that which suits their prejudices and predispositions. Such 'cocooning' may make personal life easier, but it contributes little to the opening of minds and expansion of informational horizons. By the same token, the consequences for democratic debate cannot be presumed to be advantageous just because there is a greater amount and even diversity of information available nowadays.

Furthermore, there is evidence that filtering to cope with information overload tends to exclude that which is disturbing, contentious and challenging. What we then can see is a form of 'cyberpolarization' whereby filtering stimulates information cocoons that relegate and even reject nuanced positions (Sunstein 2009). That is, websites are established to which audiences may be drawn because they concur with their point of view, but these sites link overwhelmingly to like-minded information and relegate oppositional sites. Over time, suggests Sunstein (2007), one gets information 'balkanization' (p. 63) that exacerbates fragmentation and isolation. In such circumstances, information abundance may contribute to the diminution of democracy.

Beyond state-centric solutions?

It is also necessary here to reflect on changes in the crucible of democracy, the nation-state. It is in the nation that elections are conducted, debates and programmes scrutinized, and where voters make known their preferences. And it is within the nation-state that the public sphere is institutionalized. At its best, the public sphere would be where debates and discussions would take place amongst citizens engaged in conversations about what would be the most preferable directions of government. In Habermasian terms, it would be here that, following open scrutiny, a national consensus would be created.

There are many difficulties this conception must now face. Amongst them is the objection that the achievement of consensus in democracies has tended towards being discussion amongst privileged élites, in Britain largely one set of Oxbridge men debating with another set of Oxbridge men whose lives in recent decades have been wholly dedicated to politics. Furthermore, questions need to be asked regarding the feasibility of nation-state-organized democracies in an era of intensive globalization. On the one hand, this is to query the capacity of the nation to exercise the influence it was once capable of, sovereignty weakening in contending with real-time currency trading, transnational corporations' dominance of the world economy, and persistent calls for the devolution of power. In addition, there are other pressing issues that cannot be addressed adequately at the level of the nation – global warming, human rights and refugees.

On the other hand, and directly impinging on the public sphere concept, there is the matter of citizens' informational resources in a globalized era. Whatever its shortcomings in practice, in principle it is possible to argue that public service broadcasting played a privileged and central role in meeting these requirements, enabling audiences to learn more about political affairs. Today, however, this function of public service broadcasting must be open to question when satellite television, cable and the Internet opens viewers and listeners to a galaxy of alternative information sources.

Democracy reconceived?

In light of such challenges, the concept of the public sphere begins to look shaky. Globalization has brought new sources of information that undermine national frontiers; postmodern thinkers reject the élitism of public service systems; new technologies raise questions about established modes of information production, distribution and reception; audience fragmentation and cocooning in the face of information overload suggests new media may stimulate information enclaves rather than enriched debates. There are profound questions that need to be raised about the capacity of the nation-state to match the demands of democracy in a global age.

We need to add here some reconsideration of the meaning of democracy. Democratization is an ongoing process that is subject to extension and redefinition. Illustrative of this, over recent decades there has emerged in Western democracies the notion that democracy entails the tolerance of differences. Where once democracy implied uniformity amongst the majority of citizens, nowadays democracy also evokes the tolerance of differences, an ability to live together in ways that do not exclude those whose lifestyles, preferences and attitudes at one time would not have been tolerated by a democratic majority. Today it can be suggested that democracies are constituted by diverse peoples, such that majority/minority distinctions are problematical, since one might be a minority in one dimension yet a majority in another.

From this perspective, what commentators such as Cass Sunstein see as increasing fragmentation of audiences and producers of information is not a problem since these developments make manifest the profusion of differences found within a healthy democracy in which differentiated peoples rub along together. In addition, writers who celebrate new media's capacity to enable once ignored and marginalized groups to access a platform for their views (Dahlberg, 2007) are quick to criticize the model of democracy used by those who deplore diversity as 'information chaos'. These latter, influenced by Habermasian ideals, presuppose the desirability – and possibility – of democracy entailing debate in a public sphere that works towards consensual resolution through the triumph of superior rationality. Objections to this, however, are, first (as already noted), that in practice the public sphere has almost everywhere been dominated by privileged élites who have managed to establish their hegemony across the wider society, so it is at least arguable how open and rational such democracy has actually been. Second, it is objected that the Habermasian model is out of touch, unable to accommodate the realities of democracies that accept diversity as a distinguishing characteristic. The model of democracy in which citizens and their representatives participate in discussions that consensual decisions about how to live are achieved has difficulty in accepting that an important measure of democracy nowadays is its capacity to include as legitimate incommensurate differences of religion, ethnicity, sexuality, lifestyle and so on (Jacka, 2003).

If one embraces difference as a defining feature of contemporary democracy, then the profusion of information from diverse sources might be celebrated. It may be messy, but it helps identify a vital feature of democracy as an *unfinished project*. Such a way of seeing also allows us to appreciate that democracy cannot be regarded as a straightforward means of deciding upon most rational policies. It is easy enough to understand that rationality cannot be presupposed, as is evident from any number of decisions that become questionable with hindsight (for example, the closure of much of the railway network in the 1960s in Britain). Looking back we can see not only that many previous decisions have been made on grounds of dubious rationality, but also that in arriving at those decisions power differentials were in play (for example, the road building lobby was much favoured when deciding on rail closures).

Such questioning of a conception of democracy that lays stress on 'rationality' allows us to better appreciate that rationality emerges through 'discourses' between and within individuals and groups (Dryzek, 2000). In an era in which we have seen the rapid growth of groups able to find outlets for their views using new media (one thinks here of one-time marginalized actors), a key question then is how these views might be connected with other discourses in society. There can be no ready answer and my aim here is not to provide one. The salient point is that such an approach to democracy recognizes discourses – not an abstract rationality – as essential to its making. From this point of view, an approach to democracy and information begins from democracy being capable of including differences and the fact that there has been an information explosion that has enabled groups to find means of expressing themselves. Seeking not an overall rational answer that homogenizes relationships, but rather accepting diversity while encouraging points of intersection amongst different constituencies, might then be a positive way of advancing an inclusive form of democracy.

This may seem a desirable goal, but we might hesitate before too hurried an acceptance. One reason is that this smacks too much of a consumerist ethos, of the belief that democracy means doing one's own thing and, associated, that just about anything is permissible. Praising diversity can come close to endorsing a watered down view of democracy that regards it as little more than the pursuit of individual (at the least sectional) preferences.

Moreover, one might hesitate here before we abandon the notion of a public sphere dedicated to finding most rational solutions. Diversity may be fine when it comes to questions – important though these are – of sexual orientation, lifestyle choices, perhaps even religious beliefs, but surely, we do need a public sphere, which does strive to reach decisions, after open and rational debate, on matters such as taxation, education provision and welfare. To raise such queries is to insist on prioritizing issues in a democracy. Necessarily, then, one must have concerns about developments that increase information resources and thereby enable the sidelined to gain attention, but which perhaps divert attention from the more important aspects of a democratic society. Michael Edwards (2004) helpfully identifies civil society as 'the land of difference, the place where we find meaning in our lives as people of different faiths, races, interests, perspectives and agendas'. But he distinguishes this from the public sphere that he regards as essential to 'the governance of complex societies and the preservation of peaceful coexistence' since it works 'within a common commitment to the interests of a public'. In short, a public sphere of some sort remains necessary to democracy precisely because 'particularities [must be] surrendered to the common interest' (Edwards, 2004: 61–62) if democracy itself is to prosper.

Over-idealization of the public sphere

There is another charge that may be made against the public sphere notion, that it is priggish in its presumption that worthy citizens ought to be engaged, earnest and well-informed about matters of state. There is around the term a whiff of censure towards those who are less than fully abreast of political circumstances and trends. Put more kindly, one might think of public sphere supporters as presenting politics in an aspirational manner, as an ideal towards which all meritorious democracies might strive.

An objection is that citizens may be concerned democrats, but that this does not call for their whole-hearted engagement with politics. Paediatrician Donald Winnicott (1896–1971) coined the term 'good enough' parenting in response to those who, providing advice on best-available child-rearing, appeared to present an unattainable state of perfection. The notion of 'good enough' democrats might be usefully advanced against those who, personally immersed in political issues, readily condemn those who lack the same zeal. We will all have heard the criticism that those who profess a lack of interest in political machinations are shamefully ignorant, that 'surely you must know' about this or that scandal. To these charges, it needs to be insisted that because people are less than fully engaged in political matters does not mean they are less than wholehearted democrats. It is merely that politics does not consume all of their lives.

Michael Schudson's (1998) conception of the 'monitorial citizen' is helpful here. Conceding that a 'cherished ideal' (p. 6) of democracy is the 'informed citizen', Schudson assesses the record and finds that the connections between information and democracy are not as tight as Habermasians might like to think. As we have noted, the public sphere never functioned quite so well as its adherents might imply and, while there have been measurable declines in political participation over recent years, these have been offset by the spread of 'rights' (of gender and racial equality as well as of welfare) that have come about through political struggles but are now defensible through legal and quasi-legal means. In the round, Schudson judges that the timbre of today's democracy is sounder than ever.

Schudson (2008) continues to observe that, living in complex societies, it is unrealistic to expect everyone to be expert in everything, and this includes being expert in politics. Nowadays politicians are overwhelmingly full-timers who began their careers early and rarely command a serious job outside the polity. The regular citizen cannot hope to possess the knowledge and skills of the career politician. This is not necessarily to be deplored since each of us is dependent, one way or another, on experts (and in turn every expert is dependent on other experts). Such is the condition of living in a complex society. However, this need not disenfranchise citizens and it surely does not mean that we must all become deeply knowledgeable about politics, since citizens today are 'monitorial rather than informed' (p. 310) and thereby able to exercise their influence at decisive moments (obviously at elections, but also through investigative media and other querulous experts who routinely challenge politicians' judgements).

This should not be interpreted as a celebration of ignorance amongst the public that is manifested in expressions of deep distrust of politics and politicians. Rather what it endeavours to capture is the coexistence of public *distrust* and day-to-day *trust* in elected representatives that characterizes contemporary democracy. Each of us will recollect times when people have voiced suspicion that 'politicians are just in it for themselves' or that, whatever politicians promise in election campaigns, in office they compromise and concede. On the other hand, each of us will also be able to acknowledge that there are just too many other things to do for each of us to bone up on the details of the Chancellor's tax budget, still less to immerse oneself in the detail of legislation. As Schudson (2006) puts it, 'none of us is well enough informed to make judgments about every important issue before the public' and, because this is so, 'we all have to trust others' (p. 505). Nonetheless, this does not mean that we prostrate ourselves before expert politicians, since we can and do query them and their actions, not least by drawing on the expertise of others that can challenge policies and practices. It does mean, however, that scholars should acknowledge both 'the complexity of democracy' and the 'democracy of complexity' (p. 504) of the modern age.

Michael Schudson's argument resonates with recent debates over the role of the Internet in democracies. It is often suggested that new media will revitalize democracy because it allows users to command huge resources that will make citizens better informed, because it means citizens are able to respond rapidly to challenge and correct statements courtesy of its interactive properties, or because it enables campaigners to mobilize support much more effectively than in the past. New technologies are granted here a privileged role, being seen as capable of empowering citizens by providing means by which ordinary people may get a more direct and powerful say in public affairs. For Yochai Benkler (2006) the emergence of new technologies brings nothing less than a 'networked public sphere', one vastly superior to what went before since that relied perforce on top-down mass media. A host of developments, from social networking to individual blogs, from email to chat rooms, from websites to citizen journalism, can in this way be regarded as democratizing forces in so far as they allow people down below to put across their views without benefit of 'expert' intermediaries. In these terms one-time consumers of information can become producers thanks to new technologies that bring about *disintermediation* and allow user-generation of content (Castells, 2009).

Much of this is to be welcomed even if the substance of the change may not be as marked as enthusiasts hope. We may strike a note of caution by recalling Schudson's insistence that each of us is dependent on expertise as an inescapable condition of life today. When we look at democracy and information from this angle, we appreciate that the modern world is too complex for any of us as individuals, or even for any one institution, to fully comprehend. It behoves us therefore to acknowledge that an essential feature of democracy is governing through collaborations and compromises, and attendant balances of trust and scepticism that accompany efforts at making decisions about how we might live. We cannot organize the world alone, so we must rely on others' expertise and make necessary adjustments.

Enthusiasts for disintermediation go too far in greeting the Internet and cognate technologies as revolutionary democratizing forces. It is positive that citizens gain improved means of voicing their concerns, but the pendulum swings too far if blogging and social network sites result – as they may – in a cacophony that amounts not to more information but rather to distracting 'noise'. This also recalls a point already made, and it bears repeating, that there are risks to democracy if new media lead to a profusion of information that comes from and goes to only isolated and self-confirmatory groups. For democracy to be effective there must be more than a multitude of individual (and marginally connected) voices.

This is not to deny that some blogs have made useful contributions to democratic discourse. Indeed, there is evidence (Albrecht, 2006) that on the Internet there is a kind of self-policing in that sites can build a reputation for helpfulness that results in the relegation of the idiosyncratic to the periphery. Matthew Hindman (2009) makes a related point when examining actual use of new media. He demonstrates that, while there is much more information flowing around, we cannot assume this translates into increased democracy since most people who use the Internet for information actually visit few sites. Indeed, Hindman shows that, over a five-year period, five sites alone account for about 25 per cent of all Internet traffic, a degree of concentration even higher than found in the traduced 'monopoly' press and television media. Curiously, this refutes the charge that participation through the Internet results largely in disjointed 'noise', but raises the problem of what, then, is new?

There remains concern that blogging tends towards the production of solipsistic opinion that can weaken democracy by encouraging fragmentation and the dissemination of uninformed points of view. We cannot return to an era of deference towards 'superiors' who once conducted politics on our behalf, but Andrew Keen (2008) is right to express concern about the decline of authorities in a period when, instead of using the Internet 'to seek news, information or culture', people appear to use it to 'actually BE the news, information, the culture' (p. 7). Authorities act as gatekeepers and at their best serve to filter reliable and robust information from that which is of little if any use.

It is hard to imagine a genuine democracy where each and everyone provides and accesses whatever information he or she fancies. 'When we are all authors', asks Keen, 'whom can we trust?' (p. 65). At the same time, the extension of opportunities to put over points of view that may have been unjustly marginalized is not to be gainsaid. Nonetheless, while new media promise much wider constituencies a 'voice', Hindman (2009) is correct to query what this might mean in terms of the chances of being 'heard'. A major problem is how to connect these contributions with wider informational resources. A democracy must have means of determining common concerns and this implies the provision of sites for dialogue where views can be exchanged, debate conducted and decisions made. The public sphere has been the established way of thinking about how this might be arranged, but for reasons already elaborated upon, it is now creaking. Nevertheless, democracies do need public places and spaces where this dialogue may take place.

Quality of information

Finally, we need to ask questions of the capability of public sphere institutions to produce the best possible information to nurture democracy. Social democrats have little problem demonstrating the market's inadequacies when it comes to informational matters. This familiar critique is the starting point for insistence on state support for institutions such as libraries, television and museums. While there is some concern about political interference in information where the state does get involved, especially about PR and packaging, the supposition is that public service institutions are favourably situated to develop, consider and disseminate the best possible information that is foundational to democracy. This will involve, as we have been reminded, a wide range of accredited experts (statisticians, journalists, academics, scientists, engineers, planners and so on) as well as professional politicians and concerned citizens, who will originate, assess and debate so as to ensure the information is rigorous and trustworthy.

However, Cass Sunstein (2006) presents reasons for hesitation before accepting this account. Against the presumption that the most robust information comes from deliberation amongst experts in whom the public necessarily invests trust, Sunstein reminds us of the influence of prestige and reputation that can shape relations between experts (and hence the information they generate), of the import of rhetoric when it comes to the weighing of evidence, as well as of the significance of 'informational cascades' when even experts follow opinions that are *à la mode*. The gravamen of Sunstein's case is that deliberation amongst experts does not necessarily lead to production of the best information.

This leads him to express sympathy towards anonymity and openness as a means of ensuring the best possible information availability – practices encapsulated in the wiki phenomenon. It is frequently derided, but wiki practices allow pretty much anyone to participate in the production of information without express involvement of (and restriction to) acknowledged experts. And the results are impressive. Sunstein (2006) is not embracing blogging as a means of vitalizing democracy since in his view this leads to 'a stunningly diverse range of claims, perspectives, rants, insights, lies, facts, falsehood, sense, and nonsense' (p. 187). Blogging allows anyone to say anything; wikis are documents that are subject to correction and editing by any other anonymous contributor at any time. This makes for a high degree of reliability as regards the information created.

Sunstein's interest in wiki practices as a means of achieving the best possible information goes back to Condorcet's Jury Theorem that contends that where the average chance of a member of a voting group making a correct decision is greater than even, then the chance of the group as a whole making the correct decision will increase with the addition of more members to the group. This contention has it that the average decisions of members of a group are more accurate than decisions made by small groups of deliberating experts.

At first glance this may appear counter-intuitive, but examination of Wikipedia finds it generally the equal of the experts-only *Encyclopedia Britannica*.[1] Anecdotal evidence also suggests that it is used as a matter of routine by scholars and journalists, even though the former especially are quick to sneer. The general wiki principles – anonymity of contributions and openness to editing of materials – show signs of offering a viable alternative to an expert-dominated public sphere of ensuring best-possible information is made available.

Conclusion

For decades those who regard the market system as incapable of meeting the informational needs of democracy have recommended state intervention to rectify its inadequacies. The public sphere and its cousin public service institutions have been central to this social democratic perspective.

It can be conceded that the market is imperfect when it comes to fulfilling democracy's needs, yet the public sphere conception, and much that has accompanied it, now looks outdated. Globalization that challenges state-centric practices, new technologies that provide easier access and hugely expanded informational resources as well as ready opportunities to produce as well as receive information, changing meanings of democracy that lay emphasis on toleration of differences, and an over-idealization of the properly informed citizen, all contribute towards questioning the continuing pertinence of the social democratic approach. Extensive use of wikis even leads one to wonder about the presumed superiority in terms of achieving optimal information of democratic deliberation that has to date been limited to accredited experts.

Nevertheless, a democracy must have some means of making decisions in the interests of the majority of its citizens if it is to function effectively. Hence, however diverse the lifestyles and opinions of the people, and however extensive are opportunities for the populace to have their voices heard, still there remains the vital issue of bringing these together, even if imperfectly, in ways that allow decisions to be made in the common interest on the basis of the best-possible information availability. Connecting diverse sites so that citizens have access to heterogeneous information to which they may also contribute is surely essential to advancing these goals. Such an imperative prevents us from jettisoning entirely the public sphere concept, though it may mean that we can do with considerably reduced state support.

Note

1   See 'Wikipedia survives research test', *BBC News*, 15 December 2005. Available at http://news.bbc.co.uk/1/hi/technology/4530930.stm

References

Albrecht, S. (2006) 'Whose Voice is Heard in Online Deliberation?' *Information, Communication and Society*, 9 (1): 62–82.

Benkler, Y. (2006) *The Wealth of Networks: How Social Revolution Transforms Markets and Freedom*, New Haven: Yale University Press.

Castells, M. (2008) 'The New Public Sphere: Global Civil Society, Communication Networks and Global Governance', *ANNALS of the American Academy of Political and Social Science*, 616: 78–93.

Castells, M. (2009) *Communication Power*, Oxford: Oxford University Press.

Dahlberg, L. (2007) 'Rethinking the fragmentation of the cyberpublic: from consensus to contestation', *New Media and Society*, 9 (5): 827–47.

Dryzek, J.S. (2000) *Deliberative Democracy and Beyond*, Oxford: Oxford University Press.

Edwards, M. (2004), *Civil Society*, Cambridge: Polity.

Habermas, J. (1989 [1962]), *The Structural Transformation of the Public Sphere: An Inquiry into a Category of Bourgeois Society* (Trans. Thomas Burger with the assistance of Frederick Lawrence), Cambridge: Polity.

Hedges, C. (2008) 'America the Illiterate', *Truthdig*. Available: http://www.truthdig.com/report/item/20081110_america_the-illiterate/ Accessed 1 December 2008.

Hindman, M. (2009) *The Myth of Digital Democracy*, New Haven: Princeton University Press.

Jacka, E. (2003) '"Democracy as Defeat": The Impotence of Arguments for Public Service Broadcasting', *Television & New Media*, 4(2): 177–191.

Jackson, M. (2001) 'Channel 4: The Fourth Way', *New Statesman Media Lecture*, 31 October.

Jacoby, S. (2008) *The Age of American Unreason: Dumbing Down and the Future of Democracy*, London: Old Street Publishing.

Keane, J. (1991) *The Media and Democracy*, Cambridge: Polity.

Keen, A. (2008) *The Cult of the Amateur*, new edition, London: Nicholas Brealey.

Levitas, R. and Guy, W. (eds) (1996) *Interpreting Official Statistics*, London: Routledge.

Lim, E.T. (2008) *The Anti-Intellectual Presidency: The Decline of Presidential Rhetoric from George Washington to George W. Bush*, New York: Oxford University Press.

McNair, Brian (2006) *Cultural Chaos: Journalism, News and Power in a Globalised World*, London: Routledge.

Miliband, R. (1969) *The State in Capitalist Society*, London: Weidenfeld and Nicolson.

Nagourney, A. (2008) 'After Epic Campaign, Voters Go to Polls', *New York Times*, 4 November.

Popkin, S.L. (1994) *The Reasoning Voter: Communication and Persuasion in Presidential Campaigns*, Chicago: University of Chicago Press.

Schudson, M. (1998) *The Good Citizen: A History of American Civic Life*, Boston: Harvard University Press.

Schudson, M. (2006) 'The Trouble with Experts – and why democracies need them', *Theory and Society*, 35: 491–506. Reprinted in Schudson (2008).

Schudson, M. (2008) *Why Democracies Need an Unlovable Press*, Cambridge: Polity.

Sunstein, Cass R. (2006), *Infotopia: How Many Minds Produce Knowledge*, New York: Oxford University Press.

Sunstein, Cass R. (2007) *Republic.com 2.0*, New Haven: Princeton University Press.

Sunstein, Cass R. (2009) *Going to Extremes: How Like Minds Unite and Divide*, New York: Oxford University Press.

Webster, F. (2006), *Theories of the Information Society,* 3rd edn, London: Routledge.

2 The transformation of political communication

*Ralph Negrine and
Stylianos Papathanassopoulos*

In reviewing the literature in the field of political communication produced in the last half-century, one is inevitably struck by the speed, intensity and depth of change in the structures of communication and in the ways in which political communication is carried out. In the case of the former, we have seen the Internet force the older media of communication – television, the printed press, radio – to adapt their styles and contents to a new environment. In the case of the latter, we have seen the emergence of 'spin' and the birth of the 'spin doctor', the growth of the 'public relations state' and the growing interest amongst political parties in 'political marketing'. In these and other ways it is abundantly clear that things are not what they were and that new arrangements, structures, practices and ways of thinking abound. In other words, the nature of political communication – understood here as incorporating the means and practices whereby the communication of politics takes place – has been *transformed* and there has been 'a marked change in its nature, form or appearance'.

The aim of this chapter is to explore the meaning of that transformation and to consider some of the consequences of that transformation.

Transformations

Western societies have become increasingly mediated and the media are no longer simply channels for transmitting messages. They are autonomous mediators in society and they follow their own rules, aims, constraints and production logic (Altheide and Snow, 1979). But the media do not work in a social vacuum and they respond to changing technical, social and political circumstances (see, for example, Blumler and Kavanagh, 1999). The centrality of the media in contemporary societies and the subsequent rise of 'media logic' have taken several forms. According to Denis McQuail (2005: 526) these include:

- the diversion of time from political participation to watching television (video malaise);
- the negative effects of political marketing on voter trust and goodwill;
- the increasing negativity of campaigning and campaign reporting;

- the rising costs and bureaucratization of campaigning;
- the loss by parties of their own channels for reaching a mass following and increased dependence on media channels and gatekeepers.

In effect, what we see in Western democratic societies, then, is not only a move away from traditional forms of political communication (in and outside election periods) to more modern ways and means, but also changes within the political system and media which had in the past sustained other forms and means of political communication. So, for example, increased competition across 'old' and 'new' media potentially impacts on the ability of 'old' and 'new' media to cover politics as in the past. To argue that the media now work in a changed context is also to argue that societies have themselves changed dramatically: things are no longer what they were and 'almost everything to do with political communication seems to be in flux these days: social formations and lifestyle, strategies of persuasion, politician-journalist relations, media technology, organisation and finance' (Coleman and Blumler, 2009: 43). Everything, in other words, is no longer as it was and the relationships between elements have also been reconfigured. The changes often noted in the context of discussions such as these can usefully be subsumed within a broad understanding of the modernization of societies (see Swanson and Mancini, 1996). In such societies, there is an increased 'functional differentiation', and an emergence of specialist interest groups and 'social sectors' – as well as 'secularization', a growing importance of individualism, and so on – all of which undermines 'the traditional aggregative structures ... producing social fragmentation and exclusion. In turn, political parties tend to become segmented, pluralistic, catch-all confederations with weak or inconsistent ideological bases, whose links to voters are fragile and inherently unstable' (Swanson and Mancini, 1996: 253).

Apart from the fact that societies are no longer as they were, these processes point the way to societies being increasingly composed of shifting alliances, groupings and collaborations. In such societies, the media become even more important as mechanisms of communication and mediators – of the political system, of values, of individuality, and so on. Media, in this understanding of the processes of modernization, become critical central features in the political process too because the older ties no longer bind ... and those who seek power are forced to use the media to reach individuals who are no longer in their 'traditional aggregative structures'.

It is thus possible to see many of the changes taking place in the conduct and content of political communication as coming out of the *interaction* between emerging and/or maturing media and emerging and/or maturing political parties within continually changing and modernizing societies. For students of political communication, the most dramatic changes have involved changes in the forms of political parties, changing practices in political communication and, lastly, changes in media (both structures and systems). Whether this amounts to a 'crisis of public communication' (Coleman and Blumler, 2009: 45) or not is entirely a matter of perspective. What is less a matter of perspective is the fact that change has taken place which, in due course, encourages us to re-think the meaning, forms and nature of political communication for the twenty-first century.

In the next section we will deal briefly with some of the key aspects of the changes that we are all currently experiencing. As will emerge most clearly, the two areas that require consideration – and link us to the past and to the future – are those that relate to the changing nature of media and the changing nature of political parties. More than this, it is possible to see many of the changes taking place in the conduct and content of political communication as coming out of the *interaction* between emerging 'new' media and maturing 'old' media and maturing political parties within continually changing and modernizing societies. Widespread social change, in this view, is a backdrop to the changes taking place wherein media and political parties also undergo change.

Framing the discussion in this way, unfortunately, hides from view a consideration of the public or publics and public and civic engagement in the political process and in political communication. Identifying this limitation goes a very little way to acknowledge the need for a deeper discussion of the connections between politics, media *and* public which, in its own way, throws up a myriad of issues about such things as inequalities, cultural capital, civic engagement, participation, etc. Curiously, the emergence of the 'new' media has occasioned much discussion about the public's re-engagement with politics through new means of communication, new facilitates and new ways to be heard and not only by those in power. The 'new' media offers up the possibility of 'peer-to-peer' communication and hence the creation of communities of interest that are independent of those in power but not themselves without power. These are some of the key issues that need to be explored in the future.

Changes in media

Since the mid-1980s, the media sector in most Western European democracies has been in a state of constant change. Processes of deregulation, privatization, and the rapid commercialization of the audiovisual media have led to the explosion of TV outlets providing more choice to the citizens and much more competition among the media channels. The further and recent convergence and digitalization of the communications sector have created a new landscape across the media sector as a whole. By and large, there have been changes as new media of communication have replaced older ones in importance (e.g. radio to television, the onset of new media) but also changes in the *ways* the media work. So, for example, commercialization privileges 'media logic' over 'political logic' (Mazzoleni, 1987) with the effect of forcing those in politics to become aware of the needs of the media. Thomas Meyer (2002) has described the process as the colonization of politics by media logic resulting in what he calls a 'mediocracy' and this gives a proper sense of the ways in which politics has altered and those who practise it have come to deal with the media, and 'feeling increasingly under pressure' (Meyer, 2002: 71). In reviewing the Swedish scene, for example, Lars Nord (2007) has noted that:

> recent years have seen dramatic changes on the national media scene where deregulations and technological advances have introduced more market-oriented broadcast media companies. At the same time there have been enormous changes in the newspaper market, which has seen a market-driven development ... Thus, a party-related media system has to a large extent been replaced by an independent and market-oriented media system. All the main actors in the Swedish political communication system now have to adjust to new conditions where marketing logic and highly volatile public opinion are distinctive features (Nord, 2007: 83).

The above description illustrates how change at the level of media can result in *change at the level of media practice* whereby individual political actors – and individuals who are strategically placed in organizations – not only learn to respond to the prerequisites of 'media logic' but also learn to use the media to their advantage. Though political actors may have lost direct control over the media as journalism becomes more independent and critical, they can often find other and different ways to exert their control over the media. To paraphrase Leon Mayhew, we are currently experiencing a 'rationalization of persuasion' where the intent on the part of political actors as a broad category is to find and utilize 'effective means of persuasion based on research on audiences and the organization of systematic campaigns' (1997: 190). Political actors, in other words, become more professional too (see Negrine, 2008; Negrine *et al.*, 2007)

But both political actors and 'old' media have had to adapt to the emergence of 'new' media. Prior to the rise of the Internet as a mass phenomenon, other information and communication technologies (ICTs) such as cable and satellite television also began to challenge the hegemony of earlier forms of broadcast communication. By the early 1990s, for example, cable and satellite television had created a television of abundance where there was once scarcity. Equally important, these newer forms of television gave rise to round-the-clock services, such as in news provision, that forced politicians amongst others to re-think their communication strategies.

Whilst the newer ICTs brought about what Seymour-Ure (1996) called 'electronic glut' and others have referred to as the 'third age' of political communication (Blumler and Kavanagh, 1999), it could be argued that the emergence of the Internet pushed all these developments in a direction that had hitherto only been dreamt of. Henceforth, political communication would no longer need to be *mass* communication: it could be targeted to individuals as well as groups; it could be direct and not mediated by traditional professional journalists; it could be interactive; it could be plentiful since there was no restriction on supply; it could be peer-to-peer, and so on. This was the era of digital communication in which all forms of communication – visual or audio or text – could be converted into a digital format, processed by computers and pushed (or pulled) around the globe with the greatest of ease.

Although we still live in an age of *mass* media – television and newspapers continue to be important players within the political system– the digital age creates different conditions for political communication. As Slavko Splichal notes: 'With the new interactive virtual spaces it has created, the Internet, in particular, substantially increased the feasibility of citizens' participation in public discourse beyond national boundaries' (2009: 392). At one level, the digital media complements and supplements the older forms of communication by creating other sources of information, but, at another level, the Internet becomes a means of communication *per se* connecting peoples in different and complex ways.

In the digital age, political parties have to consider new ways of gaining a presence in the communications universe. With the Internet in place, political parties have, it seems, an even more limited power to exercise control over the mainstream media. This argument is captured in Brian McNair's analysis of news and journalism in the twenty-first century. In the introduction to his book *Cultural Chaos* (McNair, 2006) he writes that:

> while the desire for control of the news agenda, and for definitional power in the journalistic construction of meaning, are powerful and ever-present... the capacity of elite groups to wield it effectively is more limited than it has been since the emergence of the first news media in the sixteenth century.... The chaos paradigm does not abolish the desire for control; it focuses on the shrinking media space available for securing it ideologically (2006:4).

Whilst it is true that there is a 'shrinking media space for securing it ideologically', when applied to the digital era – or to the Internet more specifically – this argument is only partially correct. To understand why this should be so, we need to look more closely at how élites (of which political parties are a prime example) work with the media generally.

In the case of the mainstream media – principally television and the press – élites seek to control the agenda through a series of well-established tactics. Often the positions of élites can be challenged because of the ways in which the media work (Schlesinger and Tumber, 1994; Davis, 2002) so that in the pursuit of the newsworthy, élite positions and counter positions usually sit side-by-side on news broadcasts or on the pages of daily newspapers. It follows from this that attentive viewers and readers will be exposed to a range of sometimes conflicting views. With the Internet developing rapidly in most modern societies, there are countless ways in which connections between organizations and people can be made. Yet in respect of the communication of politics, it is worth noting that the mainstream news media are still dominant as sources of news and though élites can create and control their own media space (their websites, blogs, etc.) these are of little use unless they are accessed. However, the potential for interactivity exposes élites to interrogation and contradiction as there now is a greater potential for scrutiny and supervision of the political process. We can see this in the ways in which websites release information (e.g. wikileaks) and link to other websites, so creating a network of information leading to greater transparency and scrutiny. Also, with many sites on the Internet providing tools for interactivity, individuals can not only feed back comments but also create their own networks of information, so extending networks. Lastly, networks of information can open up discussions beyond what is made available through élite or traditional media outlets.

As John Keane has argued, 'communicative abundance permits of greater scrutiny of those who are in power or who seek power':

> All institutions in the business of scrutinising power rely heavily on these media innovations (of the Internet); if the new galaxy of communicative abundance suddenly imploded, monitory democracy would not last long (Keane, 2008: 739).
>
> Elected and unelected representatives routinely strive to define and to determine who gets what, when and how; but the represented, taking advantage of various power-scrutinising devices, keep tabs on their representatives (Keane, 2008: 743).

Nonetheless, the fact that the Internet is a 'pull' technology – we have to 'pull' the information contrary to the 'push' of traditional technologies where the content is pushed to us in digestible chunks whether we wish it or not – is both its strength and its weakness. It can give rise to millions of websites (its strength) but if no one accesses them, they are of little use (its weakness). This is why the digital era has not completely eroded the strength of the mainstream media for day-to-day coverage of events and opinions: political debate is still debate that takes place in traditional media, augmented perhaps by the presence of conversation on the web.

So, while the argument that 'media space' has shrunk is valid, it is valid up to a point in that it does not explore the details of how different media work and how traditional media remain dominant despite the erosion of their pre-eminence. Equally, it does not explore the extent to which élites will try to control their own media space through the creation of their own websites. Finally, it does not consider the extent to which élites will shift their efforts away from mediated communication via mainstream media to unmediated communication via the Internet.

All this suggests, therefore, that when we speak of the digital age or the Internet age in the context of politics and political communication, we need to be aware of the interaction and adaptation of media to other media and of élites adapting their own practices to the newer media. Once again, élites and political parties will need to adapt to newer media in order to gain advantage from them and to gain any advantage they can over their rivals. This suggests that it is not the development of new technologies *per se* that brings about change but the development of new technologies within particular structures and frameworks that may have consequences.

The extent to which the entry of the Internet has transformed and professionalized the nature and content of political communication is another question. While it has certainly led to the creation of more outlets and more outlets run by more professional webmasters, we need to explore in greater depth how the Internet is used in politics and to return to the question of how we can study the 'impact' of the new media.

Clearly, there is no shortage on the Internet of political and governmental (institutional) information. Much of it is produced by individuals, groups and institutions but established political parties are by no means absent from the web. Simple or raw numbers, however, do not necessarily translate into significance. Although numbers do begin to indicate the extent to which use of the Internet has begun to re-shape patterns of communication and political activity, on their own they are unlikely to resolve the question of how significant the Internet has been, or is, in major political struggles. For example, many more Americans turned to the Internet for campaign news in 2008 as the web had become a key source of election news; for some it was the 'Facebook election'. However, according to the Pew Research Center (2008), television remains the dominant source, since the percentage of Americans relying on TV and newspapers for campaign news has remained relatively flat since 2004.

Reviewing the experience of the 2004 presidential election, Cornfield (2006) conceded that the Internet's distinctive role in politics has arisen because it can be used in multiple ways. Part deliberative town square, part raucous debating society, part research library, part instant news source, and part political comedy club, the Internet connects voters to a wealth of content and commentary about politics. At the same time, campaigners learned a great deal about how to use the Internet to attract and aggregate viewers, donors, message forwarders, volunteers and voters during the 2003–2004 election cycles (Cornfield, 2006:1). These lessons came into their own in the 2008 US presidential elections.

In this respect, communication increasingly takes place without mediation: governments, political parties, social movements, political leaders and actors can bypass traditional media outlets (see also Porta and Mosca, 2009) and this gives them the power to communicate directly with individuals or each other. Perhaps more significantly, political parties can also interact continually with their supporters, as well as with other citizens, and they can consult and so be better placed to create or modify policies in line with what citizens wanted.

The architecture of the Internet thus creates numerous possibilities for citizens and voters to play a part in politics, policy-making and in the decision-making process itself. Political communication need no longer be from government or party to the citizen or voter via the mass media; it could include elements of feedback, response, discussion and so on. Equally important is the possibility of interaction taking place amongst citizens or voters themselves with scant reference to those who are in government or politics. Social movements, for example, have found the Internet useful as a means of building support and encouraging direct action (Bennett, 2003).

What all these different ways of connecting peoples and organizations means is that 'political communication' in the modern age can take many forms and be looked at from a number of different perspectives. But as a recent research study conducted by the Pew Internet & American Life Project indicates (quoted in Smith *et al.*, 2009):

> Whether they take place on the Internet or off, traditional political activities remain the domain of those with high levels of income and education. Contrary to the hopes of some advocates, the Internet is not changing the socio-economic character of civic engagement in America. Just as in offline civic life, the well-to-do and well-educated are more likely than those less well off to participate in online political activities such as emailing a government official, signing an online petition or making a political contribution.

The task, as we alluded to above, and which is discussed more fully elsewhere (Couldry *et al.*, 2006; Coleman and Blumler, 2009) is how to widen the base of that civic engagement and participation.

Changes in, and to, political parties

Changes in media have occasioned responses in political parties and in the ways in which they have come to use the media for their own ends, be it electoral campaigning or forms of public communication. As has been argued elsewhere (see Negrine, 2008), there has been a greater degree of professionalism in the ways in which all organizations have sought to deploy the media for their uses. A more proactive media strategy is probably typical of all such organizations as they continue to employ armies of public and media relations professionals to mediate (control, 'spin', 'leak', spread) content.

Although this suggests that the balance of power has shifted towards those in the world of politics and away from media and publics, there are a range of factors that have conspired against the exercise of *total* control over media. *At the media–politics juncture* – where the 'negotiation of newsworthiness' takes place (Cook, 1998) – it is no longer the case that politicians and the media are the only participants in the negotiation process.

A range of other intermediaries – consultants, spin doctors, advisers – have been placed at the political end of the spectrum to deal with, that is, manage and control, political communication on the part of political actors, but the media – now including bloggers, tweeters, and so on – have pulled in other participants from a spectrum of non-governmental but interested bodies who can provide the scrutiny that is often necessary.

Yet such changes are themselves a reflection of a detachment between parties and their members or, perhaps more correctly, a disconnect between parties and their former mass membership base. The trans-formation of parties into electoral professional political parties has had numerous consequences and is probably responsible for the emergence of a different approach to the practice of political communication, political advocacy and political engagement. Much of this is common across Europe where political parties have witnessed a decline in their membership (see also Mair and Biezen, 2001) and a changed relationship between parties and the public and/or voters. The most often referred-to trend is one of de-alignment, whereby voters are no longer making political decisions on the basis of traditional allegiances (such as class or religion) and are more prepared to switch votes, and hence are more open to persuasion. This has major implications for the political process. Political parties must therefore turn their attention to how they can more effectively communi-cate with the public and/or voters, how they can get their messages across, how they can persuade and mobilize voters. Furthermore, in a situa-tion where citizens have become less supportive of political parties, less trusting of the political system and more likely to abstain, there is likely to be a greater incentive to employ those skilled in the arts of commu-nication and marketing – the 'professional' consultants, communicators and organizers – to help the political parties to position themselves in the minds of the citizen and/or voter. 'Western European parties' according to Plasser and Plasser 'have responded to dealignment tendencies within the electorate with a strategy of professionalization of party management and reliance on modern campaign techniques' (2002: 307).

These changes have led to considerable organizational change within political parties ranging from a greater centralization of operations to a re-assessment of the role of members, the relationship of the centre to the periphery (e.g. constituencies, local campaigns) as well as a persistent focus on the political leaders leading to a further personalization of the campaigning and of the political scene (Brettschneider, 2008). There have also been changes in views about how such organizations should act. Some of these, such as the view that organizations should operate with a single vision and should communicate that throughout, have infected political parties and the ways in which they interact with their members, the media and others; others, such as the need to act in a 'professional' way, have also entered the vocabulary and the practice of organizations, as well as those of individuals. Another indication of these changes is the process of centralization, both within political parties but also in government, that has created a tight framework for the control and conduct of communication functions. In probably all cases, more care has been taken to deal with communication, and to reflect on and alter the processes and content of communication to meet the challenges that have arisen from the changing nature of media, changing nature of government and the changing nature of the parties themselves.

A creeping danger in all these changes is that political parties become no more than small, unrepresentative bodies seeking power but without a real organic power base to voters. In this scenario, voters are nothing more than individuals to be courted at irregular intervals for their (limited) consent without a continuing process of engagement for policy-making, consultations and involvement. Attempts to create a framework for greater involvement – in e-democracy projects, e-consultations, e-forums, and the like – have had, by and large, limited successes though they do exploit the potential of the new media to connect people in different ways. That such attempts should continue, there is no doubt, but that they should also address deeper issues about the reasons for disengagement is also imperative. Couldry *et al.* (2006: 3) have pointed out that the media are important enablers of greater engagement:

> Media consumption (of old and new media) contributes importantly to people's possibilities for public connection and engagement in the democratic process. Yet important recent research gives limited emphasis to media consumption's specific contribution to democratic engagement. Our [research findings] illustrate the multiple ways in which media consumption contributes to public connection, while our survey shows news engagement contributes significantly to explaining political interest – itself a major predictor of voting. *Encouraging a broad range of public-oriented media consumption, and the growth of related media literacy, should be central to wider strategies for reversing political disengagement* (emphasis in original).

But inequalities and differential experiences, knowledge and capacities must not be forgotten in any strategy that seeks to deepen engagement since 'traditional media must be given as much weight as new media and habits of news-oriented Internet use must be prioritized over general Internet use' (Couldry *et al.*, 2006: 3).

Political communication in the twenty-first century

In modern mediated societies, politics has come to depend more and more on the media in its central function (Schulz, 2008). This situation has led to a transformation of politics, as those engaged in politics come to learn to cope, deal with and match the growing power of the media. For some, as noted above, we are in nothing more than a 'crisis' (Coleman and Blumler, 2009); others, in other contexts, have seen 'breakdowns' between politics and media and between politics, media and the public. As Flinders (2010) has recently argued, modern politics and government – in no small measure egged on by simplified, exaggerated and crisis-infused media coverage of politics – have failed to manage public expectations because our expectations of what can be achieved have outstripped what can in reality be achieved. With politics mediated by a super-adversarial media, it is little wonder that versions of breakdowns and crises abound.

How to row back from this situation must surely be one of the key research topics in political communication in the twenty-first century. The new media, as Coleman and Blumler (2009) and others have argued, offer one way out. By opening up communication in numerous ways, by offering the potential for interactivity, peer-to-peer communication, deliberation and the like, the new media does introduce different elements into the mix. How this will significantly transform the nature of political communication – practices, language, styles – is a question for the future. There is, as yet, an insufficient body of research to indicate the path of future change.

What is perhaps clear at the moment is that whilst different forms of the new media are increasingly being used, including by the people's representatives, they are still at the margins. They have yet to move to centre-stage – to become ingrained and fundamentally central – in the activities of key players in society. When that happens, as happened when television became central to political communication in the late 1960s, then we can truly speak of a transformation from old, traditional to new, modern media. Charting that transformation is a further topic for a research agenda for the future. At present, though, the overall mix of mediated politics remains unsatisfactory:

> Although users have more content to choose from, more channels and platforms from which to receive it, and more opportunities than ever before to comment upon the political events and issues of the day, the overall amount and quality of in-depth, thought provoking, deliberative, or investigative political news and analysis is atrophying in a media landscape that is increasingly dominated by a focus upon celebrity, rumor, and attack. Politics is presented to the public as a cynical game (Gurevitch, Coleman and Blumler, 2009: 176).

Citizens, often at the fringes of discussions of political communication, have more media choices but those are not necessarily any better than what had gone before; those who support the tabloidization thesis would argue that, in fact, things have got worse. How to re-engage the citizen, to create a better informed citizenry and a more active citizenry must be one other item on a research agenda for the future. Citizens should no longer be – or be seen to be – talked down to by political parties, or to be persuaded by parties, or to simply consume politics. Citizens ought to be brought back into the political communication process and citizens ought to want to come back into that process. Furthermore, the traditional mass audiences will not only be fragmented into smaller groups, they will also get their political information from various media, mass or individual alternatives.

For some of these 'desired' changes to happen – maybe for all of them to happen – we might need a reformed media landscape and a media system that is less commercially driven, less crisis-ridden. How this will ever come about is by no means clear and suggestions for change can often appear idealistic and unrealistic (see, for example, Coleman and Blumler, 2009) For their part, political parties must also change in some way and re-connect with citizens. The financial crisis of 2008–2010 has drawn attention to the need for a new political environment in Western democracies. To date, new communication practices combined with the professionalization of political communication have widened the gap between politicians and citizens in terms of the capacity to manipulate political messages, perceptions and opinions, contributing to the development of 'democracy without citizens' (see Hamelink, 2007: 182–185). It is not, perhaps, a surprise that governments can no longer easily 'communicate' their policies to their citizens. Political parties and politicians may have paid too much attention to how to communicate their messages rather than to communicating substantive messages, good and bad. The media may also have played a part in furthering interest in 'image' politics rather than in 'real' politics, promoting celebrity politicians and indulging in revelatory stories rather than pursuing their traditional 'watchdog' and 'surveillance' functions. For some commentators, these tendencies have left the public less well informed and consequently less involved in politics (Prior, 2007).

Broadly speaking, though representative democracies have succeeded in creating stable democratic systems, it is possible that a new more active citizenship is waiting in the wings. Political parties should therefore seek ways of engaging citizens in an intelligent way, build on citizen knowledge, and see citizens less as election fodder and more as stakeholders in the future. Moreover, political parties should challenge the output of media rather than simply bow down to those who raise expectations and eagerly dissect problems in the pursuit of stories and profit. That too is a topic for a future agenda.

The outcome of all these changes is a growing complexity in the terms of engagement and a changing political and media landscape which give rise to multiple sets of relationships. What has not changed, though, is the continuing need for politicians to find ways to communicate in an effective and persuasive way with voters as citizens. What has changed is that citizens can now communicate more easily and effectively and organize their political activities, if not actions, in better ways, as well as 'survey' politicians much more easily than ever before. In the Internet age, the 'monitorial citizen' (Schudson, 1998: 310–311) is 'media savvy' and better able to verify information and less likely just to absorb it uncritically.

In essence, that is still the core interest of political communication. The transformation of political communication in democratic societies merely points to the ways in which the fragmentation of the media landscape, the growth of knowledge about how best to communicate, better understanding of what motivates citizens/voters, better ways of identifying the needs and wishes of citizens/voters and an expansion of political citizens/ actors in a host of new media have added layers of complexity to the essentially simple matter of winning votes. At the same time, it has introduced the possibility that politics is no longer simply about winning votes but about better forms of engaged governance and a new relationship between those in power and citizens, with the role of the media – old and new – not diminished but better managed. In this perspective we may need to rethink our theoretical approaches to media politics, media effects and of course to our theories of democracy.

References

Altheide, D.L. and Snow, R.P. (1979) *Media Logic*, Beverly Hills, CA: Sage.

Bennett, L.W. (2003) 'Communicating Global Activism: Strengths and vulnerabilities of networked politics', *Information, Communication and Society*, 6: 143–168.

Blumler, J.G. and Kavanagh, D. (1999) 'The Third Age of Political Communication: Influences and Features', *Political Communication*, 16: 209–230.

Blumler, J.G. and Coleman, S. (2008) *The Internet and Democratic Citizenship; Theory, Practice and Policy*, Cambridge: Cambridge University Press.

Brettschneider, F. (2008) 'Personalization of Campaigning', in Donsbach, W. (ed.) *The International Encyclopedia of Communication*, Blackwell Publishing. Blackwell Reference Online. Available: <http://www.communicationencyclopedia.com/ subscriber/ tocnode?id=g9781405131995_chunk_g978140513199521_ss29-1>

Cook, T.E. (1998) *Governing with the News: The News Media as a Political Institution*, Chicago: University of Chicago Press.

Cornfield, M. (2006) *The Internet and Campaign 2004: A Look Back at the Campaigners*, Pew Internet and American Life Project. Available: <http://pewresearch.org/ odfs/Cornfield-commentary.pdf>

Couldry, N., Livingstone, S. and Markham, T. (2006) *Media Consumption and the Future of Public Connection*, London: ESRC Report, LSE.

Davis, A. (2002) *Public Relations Democracy. Public Relations, Politics and the Mass Media in Britain*, Manchester: Manchester University Press.

Flinders, M. (2010) 'In defence of politics', Inaugural lecture delivered at the University of Sheffield on 5 May 2010.

Gibbins, J.R. and Reimer, B. (1999) *The Politics of Postmodernity: An Introduction to Contemporary Politics and Culture*, London: Sage.

Gibson, R. and Römmele, A. (2001) 'Changing Campaign Communications: A Party-Centered Theory of Professionalized Campaigning', *Press/Politics*, 6: 31–44.

Gurevitch, M., Coleman, S. and Blumler, J.G. (2009) 'Political Communication: Old and New Media Relationships', *Annals of the American Academy of Political and Social Science*, 625: 164–181.

Hallin, D.C. and Mancini, P. (2004) *Comparing Media Systems; Three Models of Media and Politics*, Cambridge: Cambridge University Press.

Hamelink, C. (2007) 'The Professionalisation of Political Communication: Democracy at Stake?', pp. 179–188, in Negrine, R.M., Mancini, P.,

Holtz-Bacha, C. and Papathanassopoulos, S. (eds) *The Professionalisation of Political Communication*, Bristol: Intellect.

Keane, J. (2009) *The Life and Death of Democracy*, London: Simon & Schuster.

Mair, P. and Biezen, I.V. (2001) 'Party Membership in Twenty European Democracies, 1980–2000', *Party Politics*, 7: 5–21.

Mayhew, L. (1997) *The New Public*, Cambridge: Cambridge University Press.

Mazzoleni, G. (1987) 'Media Logic and Party Logic in Campaign Coverage: The Italian General Election of 1983', *European Journal of Communication*, 2: 81–104.

McNair, B. (2006) *Cultural Chaos. Journalism, News and Power in a Globalised World*, London: Routledge.

McQuail, D. (2005) *McQuail's Mass Communication Theory*, London: Sage.

Meyer, T. with Hinchman, L. (2002) *Media Democracy: How the Media have Colonized Politics*, Oxford: Polity.

Negrine, R. (2008) *The Transformation of Political Communication; Continuities and Changes in Media and Politics*, Basingstoke: Palgrave.

Negrine, R., Mancini, P., Holtz-Bacha, C. and Papathanassopoulos, S. (eds) (2007) *The Professionalisation of Political Communication*, Bristol: Intellect.

Nord, L. (2007) 'The Swedish Model Becomes Less Swedish', pp. 81–95, in Negrine, R. M., Mancini, P., Holtz-Bacha, C. and Papathanassopoulos, S. (eds) *The Professionalisation of Political Communication*, Bristol: Intellect.

Pew Research Center (2008) 'Internet Now Major Source of Campaign News', Press Release, 31 October 2008. Available: <http://pewresearch.org/pubs/1017/Internet-now-major-source-of-campaign-news

Plasser, F. and Plasser, G. (2002) *Global Political Campaigning; A Worldwide Analysis of Campaign Professionals and their Practices*, London: Praeger.

Porta, D.D. and Mosca, L. (2009) 'Searching the Net', *Information, Communication & Society*, 12 (6): 771–792.

Prior, M. (2007) *Post-Broadcast Democracy: How Media Choice Increases Inequality in Political Involvement and Polarizes Elections*, Cambridge: Cambridge University Press.

Schlesinger, P. and Tumber, H. (1994) *Reporting Crime. The Media Politics of Criminal Justice*, Oxford: Oxford University Press.

Schudson, M. (1998) *The Good Citizen*, New York: The Free Press.

Schulz, W. (2008) 'Political communication', in Donsbach, W. (ed.) *International Encyclopedia of Communication*, Blackwell Publishing. Blackwell Reference Online. Available: <http://www.communicationencyclopedia.com/subscriber/tocnode?id= g9781405131995_chunk_g978140513199521_ss51-1>

Seymour-Ure, C. (1996, 1st edition 1991) *The British Press and Broadcasting since 1945*, Oxford: Blackwell.

Smith, A., Lehman-Schlozman, K., Verba, S. and Brady, H. (2009) *The Internet and Civic Engagement*. Available: <http://pewInternet.org/Reports/2009/15--The-Internet-and-Civic-Engagement.aspx>

Splichal, S. (2009) '"New" Media, "Old" Theories: Does the (National) Public Melt into the Air of Global Governance?', *European Journal of Communication*, 24 (4): 391–405.

Swanson, D.L. and Mancini, P. (1996) 'Patterns of modern electoral campaigning and their consequences', pp. 247–276, in Swanson, D.L. and Mancini, P. (eds) *Politics, Media and Modern Democracy; An International Study of Innovations in Electoral Campaign and their Consequences*, New York: Praeger.

3 What does information technology imply for media effects research?

Shanto Iyengar

The principal impact of the revolution in information technology has been the exponential increase in the supply of information. Today, citizens interested in the American presidential election have access to thousands of online sources ranging from well-established news organizations to relatively unknown bloggers whose reports and views are widely circulated through email, viral videos and other forms of content sharing.

Given the imminent prospects of information overload, a basic question for communication researchers concerns consumers' coping strategies; that is, just how do they sort through this vast array of news sources? The question is particularly challenging because the use of newer forms of information is correlated not only with demographic attributes (e.g. age), but also with levels of political motivation and political preference. It is well established, for instance, that younger media users disproportionately avoid conventional news channels and choose instead to congregate in online interactive environments where they are not merely consumers, but co-producers of messages. Similarly, the people who seek out news on the Internet are much more involved in political life than their counterparts who spend their time online shopping for travel bargains or long-lost relatives.

The fragmentation of the audience

Fifty years ago, voters depended primarily on television news to keep up with events. In the United States, the dominant sources of public affairs information were the daily evening newscasts broadcast by the three major networks. The norms of objective journalism meant that no matter which network voters tuned in to, they encountered the same set of news reports, according balanced attention to parties, candidates, or points of view (see Robinson and Sheehan, 1983). In the era of 'old media', it made little difference where voters obtained their news. The offerings of all news organizations were sufficiently homogeneous and standardized to represent an 'information commons'. Americans of all walks of life and political inclinations were exposed to the same stream of information.

The development of cable television in the 1980s and the explosion of media outlets on the Internet more recently both created a more fragmented information environment in which political commentary, talk radio, twenty-four hour news outlets, and myriad non-political outlets all competed for attention. The rapid diffusion of new media has made available a wider range of media choices, providing much greater variability in the content of available information. On the one hand, the attentive citizen can – with minimal effort – access newspapers, radio and television stations the world over. On the other hand, the typical citizen – who is relatively uninterested in politics – can avoid news programming altogether by tuning into ESPN or the Food Network. Thus, fragmentation means the disappearance of the apathetic voter from the news audience and, among those interested in politics, the greater exercise of discretionary or selective exposure to political information.

The demise of the inadvertent audience

Political theorists and mass communication researchers agree that some minimal level of information facilitates the exercise of citizenship. The acquisition of information depends not only on the context (the availability or supply of news), but also on individual-level attentiveness or demand. At some level, citizens must consider it important to be informed. It is the demand or motivational side of the information function that is most affected by changes in the media landscape.

During the heyday of network news, when the combined audience for the three evening newscasts exceeded 60 million, exposure to political information was less affected by the demand for information because many Americans were exposed to television news as a simple byproduct of their loyalty to the sitcom or other entertainment programme that immediately followed the news (Robinson, 1976; Prior, 2007). These viewers may have been watching television rather than television news. Although precise estimates are not available, it is likely that this 'inadvertent' audience may have accounted for half the total audience for network news.[1]

One major consequence of the massive size of the broadcast news audience was that television had a levelling effect on the distribution of information. The evening news reached not only those motivated to tune in, but also people with generally low levels of political interest, thus allowing the latter group to 'catch up' with their more attentive counterparts. But once the networks' hold on the national audience was loosened, first by the advent of cable, then by the profusion of local news programming, and eventually by the Internet, some minimal exposure to news was no longer a given for the great majority of Americans. Between 1968 and 2003, the total audience for network news fell by more than 30 million viewers. The decline in news consumption occurred disproportionately among the less politically engaged segments of the audience thus making exposure to information more closely correlated with the demand for news programming. Since exposure to news was now more contingent on motivational factors, the knowledge gap between the 'haves' and 'have nots' expanded. Paradoxically, just as technology has made possible a flow of information hitherto unimaginable, the size of the total audience for news has shrunk substantially.

In any given society, the knowledge gap is mainly a reflection of differing levels of demand for information (see Tichenor *et al.*, 1970; Genova and Greenberg, 1979; Graziano 1983; Kwak, 1999; Eveland and Scheufele, 2000). Demand for information, in turn, is contingent on basic cultural norms such as a sense of community identity and civic pride or duty. As these norms have weakened, so too have the psychological incentives for acquiring political information. The principal implication is that under conditions of enhanced consumer choice, the knowledge gap between more and less motivated citizens widens (see Prior, 2003, 2005; for a contrary view, see Baum, 2003).

Interestingly, the increased knowledge gap does not appear to be a universal phenomenon (see Curran *et al.*, 2008a, 2008b). As shown in Figure 3.1, a citizen's level of education is a powerful predictor of both international and domestic affairs knowledge in the United States, but proves significantly less consequential in Finland or Denmark. In Scandinavia, where 'public service' requirements continue to be imposed on the broadcast media including commercial broadcasters, the flow of news programming is more extensive and occurs at multiple points during the programming day making it more likely that relatively apolitical viewers will manage to encounter public affairs information at least on a sporadic basis.

It is not merely the availability of news that explains the reduced scale of the knowledge gap in public service-oriented media systems. In these nations, television is more successful in reaching disadvantaged groups because public broadcasters, who are financed by a licence fee or public grant, are under continuous pressure to connect to all sections of society in order to justify their public funding. By contrast, commercial media prioritize affluent, high spending audiences in order to maximize advertising revenue.

As a consequence of their social inclusion and information commitments, public service broadcasters have been relatively successful in getting disadvantaged groups to join in the national ritual of watching the evening news. Much higher proportions of the less educated and less affluent watch television news on a regular basis in Finland or Denmark than in the United States (see Curran *et al.*, 2008). Thus, the knowledge gap between more and less educated citizens may be reduced in public service-oriented systems because public broadcasters make greater attempts to reach all educational levels.

In short, it is the interaction of technology, the media system and cultural norms that drives exposure to news. However, even in strong public service systems such as Germany and Britain, growing competition

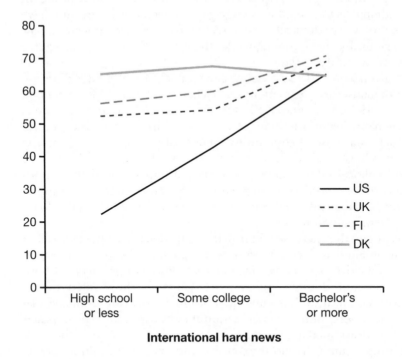

International hard news

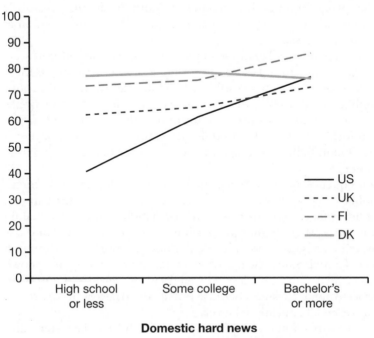

Domestic hard news

Figure 3.1 Knowledge gaps associated with level of education

has diluted the supply of political information (through the infusion of vast amounts of soft news); commercial news programmes increasingly resemble the mix of sports, fashion, celebrity lifestyles and mayhem depicted in US local television news programming.

To reiterate, the increased availability of media channels and sources makes it possible for people who care little about political debates to avoid news programming altogether. As a result, this group is likely to possess very little information about political issues and events, thus increasing the size of the knowledge gap.

Selective exposure among information seekers

The demise of the inadvertent audience is symptomatic of one form of selective exposure – avoidance of political messages among the politically uninvolved members of the audience. But technology and the increasing quantity of news supply also make it necessary for the politically attentive to exercise some form of choice when seeking information. As I outline below, there are two principal forms of selective exposure mechanisms reflecting either partisan predispositions or issue salience.

Partisan selectivity

Ever since the development of consistency theories of persuasion and attitude change in the 1950s, communications researchers have hypothesized that a person's exposure to political information will reflect individual partisan leanings. In other words, people will avoid information that they expect will be discrepant or disagreeable and seek out information that is expected to be congruent with their pre-existing attitudes (see, for instance, Mutz, 2006).

In the days of old media, selecting conventional news sources on the basis of partisan preference was relatively difficult given the demise of the partisan press in the nineteenth century. But during campaigns, voters could still gravitate to their preferred candidate, and several studies documented the tendency of partisans to report greater exposure to appeals from the candidate or party they preferred (Lazarsfeld *et al.*, 1948; Schramm and Carter, 1959; Sears and Freedman, 1967). Early voting researchers deemed this preference for in-party exposure antithetical to the democratic ideal of reasoned choice. As Lazarsfeld *et al.* put it,

> In recent years there has been a good deal of talk by men of good will about the desirability and necessity of guaranteeing the free exchange of ideas in the market place of public opinion. Such talk has centered upon the problem of keeping free the channels of expression and communication. Now we find that the consumers of ideas, if they have made a decision on the issue, themselves erect high tariff walls against alien notions (Lazarsfeld *et al.*, 1948: 89).

Initially, research on selective exposure to information in the era of mass media yielded equivocal results. In several instances, what seemed to be motivated or deliberate selective exposure turned out to occur on a de facto or byproduct basis instead: for instance, people were more likely to encounter attitude congruent information as a result of their social milieu rather than any active choices to avoid incongruent information (see Sears and Freedman, 1967).

It is not a coincidence that the increased availability of news sources has been accompanied by increasing political polarization. Over time, polarization appears to have spread to the level of mass public opinion (Abramowitz and Saunders, 2006; Jacobson, 2000, 2006; for a dissenting view, see Fiorina *et al.* 2005). For instance, Democrats' and Republicans' negative evaluations of a president of the other party have steadily intensified (Jacobson, 2006; Abramowitz and Saunders, 2006). The presidential approval data reveal a widening chasm between Republicans and Democrats; the percentage of partisans who respond at the extremes ('strong approval' or 'strong disapproval') has increased significantly over time. In fact, polarized assessments of presidential performance are higher today than at any other time in recent history, including the months preceding the resignation of President Nixon.

Given the intensification of partisan animus, it is not surprising that media choices increasingly reflect partisan considerations. People who feel strongly about the correctness of their cause or policy preferences are more likely to seek out information they believe is consistent with their preferences. But while as recently as 25 years ago, these partisans would have been hard pressed to find overtly partisan sources of information, today the task is relatively simple. In the case of Republicans, all they need to do is tune in to Fox News or the *O'Reilly Report*.

The new, more diversified information environment not only makes it more feasible for consumers to seek out news they might find agreeable, but also provides a strong economic incentive for news organizations to cater to their viewers' political preferences (Mullainathan and Schleifer, 2005). The emergence of Fox News as the leading cable news provider is testimony to the viability of this 'niche news' paradigm. Between 2000 and 2004, while Fox News increased the size of its regular audience by some 50 per cent, the other cable providers showed no growth (Pew Center, 2004). There is a growing body of evidence suggesting that politically polarized consumers are motivated to exercise greater selectivity in their news choices. In the first place, in keeping with the well-known 'hostile media' phenomenon (Vallone *et al.*, 1985; Gunther *et al.*, 2001), partisans of either side have become more likely to impute bias to mainstream news sources (Smith *et al.*, 1997). Cynical assessments of the media have surged most dramatically among conservatives; according to a Pew Research Center for the People and the Press survey, Republicans are twice as likely as Democrats to rate major news outlets (such as the three network newscasts, the weekly news magazines, NPR, and PBS) as biased (Pew Center, 2004). In the aftermath of the *New York Times'* front-page story on Senator McCain's alleged affair with a lobbyist (Rutenberg *et al.*, 2008), the McCain campaign was able to use this 'liberal attack' as a significant fund-raising appeal (Bumiller, 2008). Given their perceptions of hostile bias in the mainstream media environment, partisans of both sides have begun to explore alternative sources of news. During the 2000 and 2004 campaigns, Republicans were more frequent users of talk radio, while Democrats avoided talk radio and tuned in to late night entertainment television (Pfau *et al.*, 2007: 36–38).

Experimental studies of news consumption further confirm the tendency of partisans to self-select into distinct audiences. In one online study administered on a national sample, the researchers manipulated the source of news stories in five different subject matter areas ranging from national politics and the Iraq War to vacation destinations and sports (Iyengar *et al.*, 2008). Depending on the condition to which participants were assigned, the very same news headline was attributed either to Fox News, National Public Radio, CNN, or BBC. Participants were asked which of the four different headlines they would prefer to read, if any. The results were unequivocal: Republicans and conservatives were much more likely to select news stories from Fox, while Democrats and liberals avoided Fox in favour of NPR and CNN. What was especially striking about the pattern of results was that the selection applied not only to hard news (national politics, the war in Iraq, healthcare), but also to soft news stories about travel and sports. The polarization of the news audience extends even to non-political subject matter. The partisan homogenization of the Fox audience is also confirmed in a Pew national survey reported in Bennett and Manheim (2006: 224).

Some implications of these trends are important to consider. First, the partisan polarization among some (but not all) segments of the public offers audiences greater choice over what information, whether true or false, to use to ornament their opinions. This raises the question of the value of information itself in this information age. In the case of information about Iraq following the invasion in 2003, Fox audiences acquired a far greater level of factually incorrect information than, for example, PBS audiences, with other TV and radio sources arrayed in between (Bennett *et al.*, 2007: 120; Iyengar and McGrady, 2007).

There is reason to think that the interaction between increasingly individualized reality construction and proliferating personal media platforms has accelerated in just the last few years. For example, the news selection study reported earlier revealed strong evidence of partisan polarization in news selection, yet seven years earlier, in a similar study of exposure to campaign rhetoric, the researchers could detect only modest traces of partisan selectivity (see Iyengar *et al.*, 2008). In this study, the investigators compiled a large selection of campaign speeches by the two major presidential candidates (Al Gore and George W. Bush) along with a full set of the candidates' television advertisements. This material was assembled on an interactive, multimedia CD and distributed to a representative sample of registered voters with Internet access a few weeks before the election. Participants were informed that they were free to use the CD as they saw fit and that their usage would be recorded on their computer. Following the election, they were provided instructions for downloading and transmitting the data to the market research firm from which they received the CD.

The CD tracking data in this study showed only modest traces of a preference for information from the in-party candidate. Republicans and conservatives were significantly more likely to seek out information from the Bush campaign, but liberals and Democrats showed no preference for Gore over Bush speeches or advertisements. These findings suggest either that the intensity of partisan identity is higher among Republicans, or that selective exposure has become habitual among Republicans because they were provided earlier opportunities than Democrats (with the launch of the Fox Network in 1986) to engage in biased information seeking. The news selection study, conducted in 2007, suggests that Democrats are now keeping pace; in 2000, very few Democrats in the CD study showed an aversion to speeches from Governor Bush, but by 2007 hardly any Democrats selected Fox News as a preferred news source.

Issue salience as a basis for selective exposure

People may respond to the problem of information overload by paying particular attention to issues they most care about while ignoring others. Given that citizens' vote choices are based, at least in part, on their perceived agreement–disagreement with the candidates on salient issues, it is likely that they will seek out information that reveals the candidates' attitudes on those same issues. Thus, members of an issue public will be especially motivated to encounter information on 'their' issue.

Price and Zaller (1993) tested the issue salience-based exposure hypothesis, although only indirectly. They examined whether people whose characteristics suggested they might belong to a particular issue public were more able to recall recent news on the issue. They found support for the issue public hypothesis in about half of their tests. In another related investigation, Iyengar (1990) found that recall of news reports about social security and racial discrimination increased significantly among older and minority viewers, respectively. This study found other evidence consistent with the issue public hypothesis as well: African Americans, for instance, though less informed than whites on typical 'civics knowledge' questions, proved more informed on matters pertaining to race and civil rights (Iyengar, 1990). Burns *et al.* (2000) reported parallel findings on gender and information about women's issues: women knew more than men. The most direct evidence concerning the effects of issue salience on information-seeking behaviour is provided by the CD study described earlier. The authors tested the issue public hypothesis by examining whether CD users with higher levels of concern for particular issues also paid more attention to the candidates' positions on those issues. In terms of their design, the key outcome measure was amount of CD usage: did issue public members register more page visits for issues of interest? The findings supported the hypothesis in multiple policy domains including healthcare, education and abortion. In terms of CD usage, members of issue publics registered between 38 and 80 per cent more usage than non-members (see Iyengar *et al.*, 2008).

In summary, a media environment featuring an abundance of consumer choice implies first, that we will witness increasing inequality in the acquisition of political information. The 'haves' will find it easier to keep abreast of political events and the 'have nots' will find it easier to ignore political discussion altogether. Second, the increased availability of information implies an important degree of selective exposure to political information. Among the relatively attentive stratum, partisans will gravitate to information from favoured sources, while ignoring sources or arguments from the opposing side. Information seekers also limit their attention span to issues that affect them most directly. Meanwhile, the large ranks of inadvertent citizens remain disconnected from the political world, frustrating those who attempt to communicate with them, fueling the costs of political communication, while diminishing the effects.

General implications

As part of the American audience polarizes over matters of politics and public policy, it is possible that rational media owners stand to gain market share by injecting more rather than less political bias into the news (Gentzkow and Shapiro, 2006). The emergence of Fox News as the cable ratings leader suggests that in a competitive market, politically slanted news programming allows a new organization to create a niche for itself.

Recent theoretical work in economics shows that under competition and diversity of opinion, newspapers will provide content that is more biased: 'Competition forces newspapers to cater to the prejudices of their readers, and greater competition typically results in more aggressive catering to such prejudices as competitors strive to divide the market' (Mullainathan and Schleifer, 2005: 18). The recent efforts of MSNBC to emulate Fox are revealing. The network's most popular evening programme – *Countdown with Keith Olbermann* – conveys an unabashedly anti-Republican perspective. The network now plans to 'to showcase its nighttime lineup as a welcome haven for viewers of a similar mind' (Steinberg, 2007).[2] When the audience is polarized, 'news with an edge' makes for market success.

More generally, the evidence on partisan bias in news consumption is consistent with the argument that technology will narrow rather than widen users' political horizons. Over time, avoidance of disagreeable information may become habitual so that users turn to their preferred sources automatically no matter what the subject matter. By relying on biased but favoured providers, consumers will be able to 'wall themselves off from topics and opinions that they would prefer to avoid' (Sunstein 2001: 201–202). The end result will be a less informed and more polarized electorate, with the political communication game aimed at those who have largely tuned out.

The increasingly self-selected composition of audiences has important consequences for those who study media effects. Survey researchers, who rely on self-reported measures of news exposure, will find it increasingly difficult to treat exposure as a potential cause of political beliefs or attitudes. Those who say they read a particular newspaper or watch a network newscast are likely to differ systematically in their political attitudes, and it will be imperative that survey-based analyses disentangle the reciprocal effects of media exposure and political attitudes or behaviours (see Iyengar, 2009; Iyengar and Vavreck, 2010).

Self-selection also has consequences for experimental research. Actual exposure to political messages in the real world is no longer analogous to random assignment. As we have noted, news and public affairs information can easily be avoided by choice, meaning that exposure is limited to the politically engaged strata. Thus, as Hovland (1959) pointed out, manipulational control actually weakens the ability to generalize to the real world where exposure to politics is typically voluntary. Accordingly, it is important that experimental researchers use designs that combine manipulation with self-selection of exposure.

In substantive terms, we anticipate that the fragmentation of the national audience reduces the likelihood of attitude change in response to particular patterns of news. The persuasion and framing paradigms require some observable level of attitude change in response to a media stimulus. As media audiences devolve into smaller, like-minded subsets of the electorate, it becomes less likely that media messages will do anything other than reinforce prior predispositions. Most media users will rarely find themselves in the path of attitude-discrepant information.

The increasing level of political polarization will further bring into question findings of significant media effects. Findings suggesting that audiences have been persuaded by a message will be suspect because discrete media audiences will tend to self-select for preference congruence. Further, media users will be more attuned to resisting any messages that prove discrepant; thus, we would expect to observe reinforcement effects *even when voters encounter one-sided news at odds with their partisan priors*. For example, after the revelations in the news media that the Bush administration's pre-war intelligence claims were ill-founded, the percentage of Republicans giving an affirmative response when asked whether the US had found WMD in Iraq remained essentially unchanged, while at the same time the percentage of Democrats giving a 'no WMD' response increased by about 30 percentage points (Kull *et al.*, 2003). In short, the Republicans remained unaffected by a tidal wave of discrepant information.

The increasing level of selective exposure based on partisan preference thus presages a new era of minimal consequences, at least insofar as persuasive effects are concerned. But other forms of media influence, such as indexing, agenda-setting or priming may continue to be important. Put differently, selective exposure is more likely to erode the influence of the tone or valence of news messages (vis-à-vis elected officials or policy positions), but may not similarly undermine media effects that are based on the sheer volume of news.

Notes

1 In Robinson's words (1976: 426), the inadvertent audience consists of those who 'fall into the news' as opposed to the more attentive audience that 'watches for the news'.
2 More recently, the network attempted to extend this model of partisan style reporting to the Democratic and Republican nominating conventions. MSNBC coverage was anchored by Chris Mathews and Keith Olbermann, both of whom are commentators rather than 'objective' reporters. The more interpretive coverage provided by the MSNBC anchors clashed with the more mainstream norms of the NBC correspondents (such as Tom Brokaw) leading to periods of tension and disagreement during the convention coverage. Tom Brokaw went so far as to publicly distance himself from the views of Olbermann and Mathews. In the aftermath of the controversy, NBC announced that their debate coverage would be anchored by David Gregory – a reporter from the news division – rather than Mathews or Olbermann.

References

Abramowitz, A.I., and Saunders, K.L. (2006) 'Exploring the bases of partisanship in the American electorate: Social identity vs. ideology', *Political Research Quarterly*, 59: 175–187.

Baum, M. (2003) 'Soft news and political knowledge, evidence of absence or absence of evidence?', *Political Communication*, 20: 173–190.

Bennett, W.L. and Manheim, J. (2006) 'The one-step flow of communication', *The Annals*, 608: 213–232.

Bumiller, E. (2008) 'McCain Gathers Support and Donations in Aftermath of Article in The Times', *New York Times*, 23 February, p. A13.

Burns, N., Schlozman, K.L. and Verba, S. (2000) 'What if politics weren't a man's game? Gender, citizen participation, and the lessons of politics', Unpublished manuscript, Princeton University.

Curran, J., Iyengar, S., Lund, A. and Morin, I. (2008) 'Media systems, public knowledge and democracy: A comparative study', *European Journal of Communication*, 24: 5–26.

Eveland, W.P. and Scheufele, D.A. (2000) 'Connecting news media use with gaps in knowledge and participation', *Political Communication*, 17: 215–237.

Fiorina, M.P., Abrams, S.J. and Pope, J.C. (2005) *Culture Wars? The Myth of Polarized America*, New York: Pearson Longman.

Genova, B.K. and Greenberg, B. (1979) 'Interests in news and the knowledge gap', *Public Opinion Quarterly*, 43: 79–91.

Gentzkow, M. and Shapiro, J.M. (2006) 'Media bias and reputation', *Journal of Political Economy*, 114: 280–316.

Graziano, C. (1983) 'The knowledge gap: An analytical review of media effects', *Communication Research*, 10: 447–85.

Gunther, A.C., Christen, C.T., Liebhart, J.L. and Chia, S.C-Y. (2001) 'Congenial public, contrary press, and biased estimates of the climate of opinion', *Public Opinion Quarterly*, 65: 295–320.

Hovland, C. I. (1959), 'Reconciling Conflicting Results Derived from Experimental and Survey Studies of Attitude Change', *The American Psychologist*, 14: 8–17.

Iyengar, S. (1990) 'Shortcuts to political knowledge: Selective attention and the accessibility bias', in Ferejohn, J.A. and Kuklinski, J.H. (eds) *Information and the Democratic Process*, Champaign, IL: University of Illinois Press.

Iyengar, S. (2010) 'Laboratory experiments in political science', in Drucknan, J., Green, D., Kuklinski, J. and Lupia, A. (eds) (forthcoming) *Handbook of Experimentation in Political Science*, New York: Cambridge University Press.

Iyengar, S. and Vavreck, L. (2010) 'Online panels and the future of political communication research', in Semetko, H. and Scammell, M. (eds) *Handbook of Political Communication*, Thousand Oaks, CA: Sage Publications, forthcoming.

Iyengar, S., Hahn, K., Krosnick, J. and Walker, J. (2008) 'Selective exposure to campaign communication: The role of anticipated agreement and issue public membership', *Journal of Politics*, 70: 186–200.

Iyengar, S. and McGrady, J. (2007) *Media Politics: A Citizen's Guide*, New York: Norton.

Jacobson, G.C. (2000) 'Party polarization in national politics: The electoral connection', in Bond, J.R. and Fleisher, R. (eds) *Polarized Politics*, Washington, DC: CQ Press.

Jacobson, G.C. (2006) *A Divider, not a Uniter: George W. Bush and the American People*, New York: Pearson.

Jerit, J, Barabas, J. and Bolsen, T. (2006) 'Citizens, knowledge, and the information environment', *American Journal of Political Science*, 50: 266–282.

Kull, S., Ramsay, C. and Lewis, E. (2003) 'Misperceptions, the media, and the Iraq war', *Political Science Quarterly*, 118: 569–98.

Kwak, N. (1999) 'Revisiting the Knowledge Gap Hypothesis: Education, Motivation, and Media Use', *Communication Research*, 26: 385–413.

Lazarsfeld, P.F., Berelson, B.R. and Gaudet, H. (1948) *The People's Choice*, New York: Columbia University Press.

Mullainathan, S. and Shleifer, A. (2005) 'The market for news', *American Economic Review*, 95: 1031–1053.

Mutz, D.C. (2006) *Hearing the Other Side: Deliberative vs. Participatory Democracy*, New York: Cambridge University Press.

Pew Center (Pew Research Center for the People and Press) (2004) 'Online news audience larger, more diverse: News audience increasingly polarized', Washington, DC.

Pfau, M.J., Houston, B. and Semmler, S.M. (2007) *Mediating the Vote: The Changing Media Landscape in U.S. Presidential Campaigns*, Lanham, MD: Rowman and Littlefield.

Price, V. and Zaller, J.R. (1993) 'Who gets the news: Alternative measures of news reception and their implications for research', *Public Opinion Quarterly*, 57: 133–64.

Prior, M. (2003) 'Any good news in soft news? The impact of soft news preference on political knowledge', *Political Communication*, 20: 149–171.

Prior, M. (2007) *Post-Broadcast Democracy*, New York: Cambridge University Press.

Robinson, M.J. (1976) 'Public affairs television and growth of political malaise: The case of the "selling of the Pentagon"', *American Political Science Review*, 70: 409–32.

Robinson, M.J. and Sheehan, M. (1983) *Over the Wire and on TV: CBS and UPI in Campaign '80*, New York: Basic Books.

Rutenberg, J., Thompson, M.W. and Kirkpatrick, D.D. (2008) 'For McCain, Self-Confidence on Ethics Poses Its Own Risk', *New York Times*, 21 February, p. A1.

Schramm, W. and Carter, R.F. 1959. 'Effectiveness of a Political Telethon', *Public Opinion Quarterly*, 23(1): 121–126.

Sears, D.O. (1968) 'The paradox of *de facto* selective exposure without preference for supportive information', in Abelson, R.P., Aronson, E., McGuire, W.J., Newcomb, T.M., Rosenberg, M.J. and Tannenbaum, P.H. (eds) *Theories of Cognitive Consistency: A Sourcebook*, Chicago, IL: Rand McNally.

Sears, D.O. and Freedman, J.F. (1967) 'Selective exposure to information: A critical review', *Public Opinion Quarterly*, 31: 194–213.

Smith, T.J. III, Lichter, S.R. and Harris, T. (1997) *What the People Want from the Press*, Washington, DC: Center for Media and Public Affairs.

Steinberg, J. (2007) 'Cable channel nods to ratings and leans left', *New York Times*, November 6: A1.

Stone, W.J., Rapoport, R.B. and Abramowitz, A.I. (1990) 'The Reagan revolution and party polarization in the 1980s', in Maisel, L.S (ed.) *The Parties Respond: Changes in the American Party System*, Boulder, CO: Westview Press.

Sunstein, C.R. (2001) *Republic.com*, Princeton, NJ: Princeton University Press.

Tichenor, P.J., Donohue, G.A. and Olien, C.N (1970) 'Mass media flow and differential growth in knowledge', *Public Opinion Quarterly*, 34: 159–170.

Vallone, R.P., Ross, L. and Lepper, M.R. (1985) 'The hostile media phenomenon: Biased perception and perceptions of media bias in coverage of the "Beirut massacre"', *Journal of Personality and Social Psychology*, 49: 577–585.

4   Infotainment Inc.: the ascent of a global ideology

Daya Kishan Thussu

This chapter focuses on the growth of infotainment as a result of the worldwide commercialization of broadcast journalism, arising from the combined processes of privatization, deregulation, digitization and the opening up of new markets, which has led to a marked shift from a public-service to a ratings-conscious television news. The proliferation of all-news channels, broadcasting to a heterogeneous global audience and dependent on corporate advertising has encouraged a tendency among broadcasters to move away from a socially relevant news agenda – privileging information and education over the entertainment value of news – to a more market-led, 'soft' version of news, with its emphasis on consumer journalism, sports and entertainment. I discuss these changes in a global context and relate this to the specific case of television news in India – home to one of the world's most complex media landscapes. Finally, I explore the key implications of such trends for news agendas and editorial priorities, and, more broadly, for public media, arguing that infotainment is emerging as an ideology for legitimizing US-led free-market capitalism.

In the age of Twitter, Facebook, YouTube and MySpace and other such wonders of modern communication, it is easy to be swayed by the potential for growing multimedia convergence, reshaping global media production, distribution and consumption. There is no doubt that these apparently free media provide extraordinary possibilities to study globalization of media, culture and communication. Nevertheless, television still remains by most accounts the premier medium, especially in a global context. According to Internet World Stats, by the end of 2009 only 26 per cent of the world's population had access to the Internet – and this was skewed in favour of a few mostly rich countries. In the developing world, the Internet remains largely an élite medium – in Africa just 7 per cent of the population has access, as against nearly 75 per cent in the USA (Internet World Stats, 2010).

Television has a much wider reach than the Internet, already an established global mass medium, whose moving images and dynamic visuals have a big impact on viewers and are powerful tools for persuasion. It is therefore vital for those who consume or produce television news to

understand the significance of the shift away from purveying public information, as news is not merely a media product but a vehicle for engagement in domestic politics and international relations.

The proliferation of news channels internationally is an indication of
how corporations and governments are developing a visual presence
in a global media sphere, increasingly using English, the language of
global commerce and communication. Even outside the Anglophone
world, there has been a spate of launches of English-language networks:
Russia Today, France 24, NDTV 24x7, Press TV, CCTV-9, and Al-Jazeera
English, to name a prominent few.

It is fair to say that in the battle between public-service and private,
commercially driven television, the commercial model of broadcast journalism has won, a phenomenon that Hallin and Mancini have characterized as the 'triumph of the liberal model' (Hallin and Mancini, 2004: 251).
They have argued that 'differences among national media systems are
clearly diminishing. A global media culture is emerging, one that closely
resembles the Liberal Model', which is represented by central features of
the American media system (ibid: 294). The 'liberal model' is likely to be
adopted across the world 'because its global influence has been so great
and because neo-liberalism and globalization continue to diffuse liberal
media structures and ideas' (ibid: 305).

The liberal model privileges a commercial model of television news,
where news becomes like any other tele-visual commodity that needs to
be sold in a competitive and crowded news marketplace (McChesney,
1999; Barkin, 2002; Baker, 2007). Such a market-driven, 24/7 broadcasting ecology, I argue, forces television news to privilege 'soft' news, in
which lifestyle and consumer journalism become more prominent, at the
expense of public-interest news. The question arises whether such 'infotainment' operates as a conduit for the corporate control of consciousness,
thus legitimizing a neo-liberal ideology predicated on the superiority of
the free market.

Anchored in American news culture

It is important to remind ourselves that the liberal model has its roots in
the United States, where broadcasting – both radio and television – had
a commercial remit from its very inception. As McChesney has noted, the
US Radio Act of 1927 defined radio broadcasting as a commercial enterprise, funded by advertising. It was argued then that public interest would
be best served by largely unfettered private broadcasting and therefore
the Act made no provision for supporting or developing non-commercial
broadcasting (McChesney, 1993). The precedent established by radio
was enthusiastically followed by television, where the trio of networks
– CBS (Columbia Broadcasting System), NBC (National Broadcasting
Corporation) and ABC (American Broadcasting Corporation) – provided
both mass entertainment and public information.

The entertainment element was strong in all three networks, with game and talent shows, as well as glamour and celebrity programming, becoming the staple diet: the *Miss America* pageant was broadcast for the first time in 1954, while the celebrity chit-chat *The Tonight Show* has been successfully running on NBC since 1954.

With the creation of a multi-channel broadcasting environment during the 1990s, the networks started to lose audience and advertising revenue. As a consequence there was a growing number of infotainment features on television news, including the framing of news stories as dramatic events to retain audience interest. A major example of the encroachment of entertainment into news was the 1995 O.J. Simpson story, which Douglas Kellner defined as a 'mega spectacle', in a nation 'hooked on infotainment and tabloid culture' and marking the 'shift from journalism to infotainment.' Kellner noted: 'For TV news, 1995 was the year of the Simpson spectacle, thus making clear that the priorities of corporate journalism are infotainment and profits, merging news into entertainment and journalism into business' (Kellner, 2003: 100–101).

Evidence of such trends was found in a study conducted in 1997 by the Project for Excellence in Journalism, which examined the US mass media over the previous two decades. The study reported:

> The greatest new shift in emphasis of network news was a marked rise in the number of stories about scandals, up from just one-half of one per cent in 1977 to 15 per cent in 1997. The next biggest shift in emphasis in network news is a rise in human interest and quality of life stories. On network TV, human interest and quality of life stories doubled from 8 per cent of the stories that appeared in 1977 to 16 per cent in 1997 (Project for Excellence in Journalism, 1998).

One major recent development has been the acquisition of key news networks by conglomerates whose primary interest is in the entertainment business: until recently Viacom-Paramount owned CBS News; ABC News has been part of the Disney empire for more than a decade; CNN is a key component of Time-Warner (one of the world's biggest media and entertainment conglomerates), and Fox News is owned by Rupert Murdoch's News Corporation. This media concentration has contributed to a tendency in journalism towards a 'socially dysfunctional' focus on the 'bottom line' (Baker, 2007: 28–29). The ownership structure is reflected in the type of stories, for example, about celebrities from the world of entertainment thus promoting corporate synergies.

These are supplemented by the new genre of reality TV and its relatives – docudramas, celebrity talk shows, court and crime enactments, and rescue missions. In the process, symbiotic relationships between the news and new forms of current affairs and factual entertainment genres, such as reality TV have developed, blurring the boundaries between news, documentary and entertainment. Such hybrid programming feeds into and benefits from the 24/7 news cycle: providing a feast of visually arresting, emotionally charged infotainment which sustains ratings and keeps production costs low. The growing global popularity of such infotainment-driven programming indicates the success of this hybrid formula (Thussu, 2007a).

One result of the proliferation of news outlets is a growing competition for audiences and, crucially, advertising revenue, at a time when interest in television news, especially among the young, is waning. In the US, audiences for network television peak-time news bulletins have declined substantially, from 85 per cent of the television audience in 1969 to 29 per cent in 2005, partly as a result of many, especially younger, viewers opting for online news sources. 'Since 1980 network evening newscasts have lost an average of one million viewers a year', says the *2010 State of the News Media* report. 'We estimate', it adds, 'that network news staffs had already been cut by roughly half from their peak in the 1980s' (Project for Excellence in Journalism, 2010).

Television news-gathering, production and reporting is an expensive operation requiring high levels of investment and, consequently, media executives are under constant pressure to deliver demographically desirable audiences for news and current affairs programming to contribute to profits or at least avoid losses. Under such structural constraints, the need to make television news entertaining has become a crucial priority for journalists and news managers as they are forced to borrow and adapt characteristics from entertainment genres and modes of conversation and communication that privilege an informal style with its emphasis on story-telling skills and spectacle.

The undermining of journalism as a profession – partly because of the growing availability of 'free' user-generated content on the Internet – has contributed to a tabloid approach to broadcast journalism – one which is predicated on infotainment. Though used widely, infotainment – a neologism – is a relatively new term, emerging in the late 1980s. It grew in popularity to become a buzzword by the 1990s, having found a mention in *Roget's Thesaurus* in 1992. The *Oxford English Dictionary* defines infotainment as 'broadcast material which is intended both to entertain and to inform.'

The phenomenon denotes a kind of television news where style triumphs over substance and thus the mode of presentation becomes more important than the content. This new news cannibalizes visual forms and styles borrowed from postmodernist TV commercials and an MTV-style visual aesthetics, including fast-paced visual action, a postmodern studio, computer-animated logos, eye-catching visuals and rhetorical headlines from an often glamorous anchor person. Such news, particularly on the rolling 24/7 channels, appears to be the answer to attracting the 'me' generation of media users, prone to channel hopping and zapping as well as more inclined towards online and mobile news (Thussu, 2007a).

Global infotainment

This style of news production and presentation, with its epicentre in the ratings-driven commercial television news culture of the US, is becoming increasingly global, as news channels attempt to reach more viewers and keep their target audiences from switching over. Elsewhere I have defined 'global infotainment' as 'the globalization of a US-style ratings-driven television journalism which privileges privatized soft news – about celebrities, crime, corruption and violence – and presents it as a form of spectacle, at the expense of news about political, civic and public affairs' (Thussu, 2007a: 8).

With the globalization of television news, in parallel with the 'triumph' of market capitalism during the 1990s, the state-driven model of public broadcasting was inevitably undermined. As communism fell, state broadcasters in Eastern Europe and part of the former Soviet Union were exposed as propaganda networks, losing all credibility. With the rapid privatization of the airwaves across the region, public-service as well as state-run broadcasting was threatened. The journalism that emerged in post-Cold War Russia had acquired a new function, as one commentator noted:

> entertaining its audience to promote goods and services in a consumer-driven marketplace. The media sector has turned into a battlefield for audiences and advertisers and is proposing a new role for its workers – as organizers of leisure for the masses (Pasti, 2005: 99).

Even in Britain, home to the BBC, the role of entertainment – the last of the Reithian triad of 'informing, educating and entertaining' the public – gained greater prominence during the 1990s. Following the US experience, British television programming was increasingly affected by the trend to infotainment. Bob Franklin, a seasoned observer of the British journalism scene, noted:

> journalism's priorities have changed. Entertainment has superseded the provision of information; human interest has supplanted the public interest; measured judgment has succumbed to sensationalism; the trivial has triumphed over the weighty; the intimate relationships of celebrities, from soap operas, the world of sport or the royal family, are judged more 'newsworthy' than the reporting of significant issues and events of international consequence. Traditional news values have been undermined by new values; 'infotainment' is rampant (Franklin, 1997:4).

The BBC's flagship current affairs series *Panorama*, broadcast since 1953, had set the standards for current affairs reporting for half a century, with a dedicated audience of up to 10 million in its heyday in the late1950s (Lindley, 2002). It was shifted to a late weekend slot, though later moved back to weekday prime time but shortened and its content diluted to retain steadily declining viewership. Britain's other major broadcaster, ITV, also seemed to have abandoned such hard-hitting and well-respected current affairs programming as *World in Action* (1963–65 and 1967–98) and *This Week* (1955–1992) and replaced them with docudramas and programmes about consumerism and lifestyle.

In the rest of Western Europe too the deregulation and privatization of the European airwaves, which started in the late 1980s, undermined public-service monopolies with an explosion of new private channels. In Germany, one study noted, 'the information programmes on television have become more tabloidized with more emphasis on conflict and drama, on soft news and infotainment formats' (Schulz *et al.*, 2005: 65).

Infotainment-led personality-driven television has also benefited political leaders: Silvio Berlusconi, sometimes referred to as 'Mr Broadcasting', is a prominent example; control of television networks helped him to transform himself from a businessman to the Prime Minister, elected first in 1994 (for seven months); in 2001; and then again in 2008. The incessant coverage of the private lives of the French President Nicolas Sarkozy and his wife Carla Bruni have continued to bring audience to television news channels in France – especially those run on commercial lines.

Such trends are contrary to the public-service ethos of broadcasting, which shaped electronic journalism in Western Europe. According to a UNESCO definition:

> Public Service Broadcasting (PSB) is broadcasting made, financed and controlled by the public, for the public. It is neither commercial nor state-owned, free from political interference and pressure from commercial forces. Through PSB, citizens are informed, educated and also entertained. When guaranteed with pluralism, programming diversity, editorial independence, appropriate funding, accountability and transparency, public service broadcasting can serve as a cornerstone of democracy (UNESCO, 2006).

In the new media and communication ecology, public-service broadcasters in Europe had to adjust to the market pressures as well as technological challenges to reinvent themselves (Iosifidis, 2010).

Unlike Europe, in much of Latin America, the commercial model of TV news has been dominant since the beginning of television, exemplified by such multimedia infotainment conglomerates as Brazil's Globo and Mexico's Televisa. News on these networks is heavily focused on *telenovelas* and soccer matches and more recently, reality TV. In the Arab world, where television news has traditionally been controlled by often unrepresentative governments, globalization of infotainment has brought a 'liberal commercial television' exposing viewers to 'the American-style news formats and orientations that draw on sensational and technically alluring features' (Ayish, 2002: 151). As Arab news channels have proliferated, especially after the 2003 US invasion of Iraq, the competition has also risen, with such networks as Al-Jazeera. In China, where the transition from Mao to market has its own Chinese characteristics, the still state-controlled media have softened their 'propagandist edges' and replaced it with 'soft', entertaining and apolitical news, which is perceived to be particularly appealing to a mass audience and 'sets the stage for profit' (Chan, 2003).

Infotainment in India

Arguably, one of the most dramatic changes in television news has occurred in India, the world's largest democracy and one which, until 1991, had a highly regulated state broadcasting monopoly with Doordarshan (Thussu, 2007b). By 2009, 461 channels were in operation – 44 of which were broadcasting in English, making India one of the world's largest English-language television markets – in a country with 500 million TV viewers (FICCI-KPMG, 2010).

Unlike in the Western world, the media and cultural industries in India are growing rapidly and the news genre is particularly popular. Moreover, Western investment is increasing in India's media sector as cross-media ownership rules are relaxed. Conversely, Indian media companies are also investing outside the national territories, as a recent report noted: 'Aspirations of Indian players to go global and foreign players entering the industry are likely to help the industry target a double digit growth in next five years' (FICCI-KPMG, 2010: 15).

By 2010, there were more than 70 dedicated news networks – unrivalled by any other country in the world. As the networks have proliferated, the audience has fragmented, forcing journalists to constantly lower the threshold of taste and decorum, invoking popular and populist tropes in order to survive in an extremely competitive marketplace.

There is little surprise then that cinema and sport dominate most of the content on Indian television news programmes. Prominent among these, and one which reflects infotainment trends elsewhere in the world, is the apparent obsession of almost all news channels with celebrity culture, which in India centres on Bollywood, the world's largest film factory which is increasingly integrating into a global media sphere, shaped and dominated by the US conglomerates.

Rupert Murdoch, the doyen of global media, was instrumental in popularizing Bollywoodized infotainment on Indian television when, in 2000, he employed the superstar Amitabh Bachchan as the host of *Kaun Banega Crorepati*, an Indian version of the successful British game show *Who Wants to be a Millionaire?* on his Star Plus channel. He also promoted the show by providing extensive coverage on Star News, India's first 24/7 news channel, then part of News Corporation. Since then, the infotainment quotient of news channels across the board has increased substantially – with such examples as *Nightout* (on NDTV 24x7) and *After Hours* (on Zee TV) – regularly broadcasting gossip from the glitterati (Thussu, 2007b). Bollywood, which defines popular culture in India and among the Indian diaspora, seems to have colonized the airwaves, with many leading stars hosting their own shows during prime-time television (see Table 4.1), and as a replication of the American media conglomerates, promoting synergies by extensive coverage on news channels.

Another major obsession of Indian television news is with cricket – the most popular sport in India which was introduced by the British. In a spectacular case of the Empire striking back, cricket is now far more popular a sport in dusty streets and by-lanes of India than on the village greens of England. It is also much more prosperous in the former colony: more than 60 per cent of global broadcasting revenue for cricket emanates from India. The 5-day traditional test match has been drastically altered, primarily for television, to a 4-hour game – the so-called 20/20 format – and the Indian Premier League (IPL), launched in 2008, has emerged as the richest league for the sport in the world, valued at $4 billion (Burke, 2010).

Moreover, the infotainment element in the form of Bollywood celebrities has transformed the sport into an entertainment spectacle for television, receiving prime-time coverage on all news networks (Chattopadhyay and Subramanian, 2010). Three of the eight IPL league teams are actually majority-owned by prominent Bollywood stars – Shah Rukh Khan, Priety Zinta and Shilpa Shetty – herself an example of celebrity swamping of news with the *Celebrity Big Brother* scandal in 2007 when she won the British contest. They provide the glamour and glitz to the sport – cheering their respective teams, their smiles and shouts beamed across giant TV screens in the field, as well as shown live on television around the globe.

Prior to the start of the third season of the IPL in 2010, a Hindi-language general entertainment channel, Colors (partly owned by the

Table 4.1 Celebrity shows on Indian TV in 2009

Title of show	Bollywood host
Big Boss 2	Shilpa Shetty
Big Boss 3	Amitabh Bachchan
Bingo	Abhishek Bachchan
Dance Premium League	Rani Mukherjee
Fear Factor	Akshay Kumar
Kya Aap Panchvi Pass Se Tez Hain	Shah Rukh Khan
Lift Kara De	Karan Johar
Roadies 7	Irfaan Khan

Source: Industry data

US giant Viacom), filmed a reality show called *IPL Rockstar* in the cricket grounds before the match with the aim, in the words of the chief executive of Colors, 'to get that Superbowl-style entertainment atmosphere.' 'Bollywood is a passion and cricket a religion', he told the *Guardian* newspaper (quoted in Burke, 2010).

The nexus between Bollywood, Bollywoodized television news and televised sport and their corporate clients has generated a great deal of controversy in the media itself. Allegations of 'match-fixing' and tax evasion by politicians and industrialists who hold shares in IPL have sullied the reputation of the sport. In April 2010, one prominent minister in the national government was forced to resign when it was revealed that his friends and associates had lobbied for a new IPL cricket team consortium. As one of India's leading media commentators noted:

> With the IPL comes the convergence of the most important media trends: the ABC of Media – Advertising, Bollywood and Corporate Power. Corporate barons and Bollywood stars own cricket teams. One IPL team is owned by a newspaper. Other dailies have become 'media partners' of IPL teams. Some Bollywood stars have 'promotional agreements' for their films with TV channels who disguise their paid-for gushing over those films as 'news' (Sainath, 2010).

Infotainment as a global ideology

The example of India is indicative of what excessive marketization can do to the news media in a rapidly changing society and a fast-growing economy. The media economy is particularly dependent on the advertising industry. In India as in many other countries, television takes a large share of advertising revenue: in 2009, TV share of ad-spend was 40 per cent of the total, while 9,400 advertisements were aired in the course of the year; during prime-time slots, 17 minutes in an hour was pure advertising (FICCI-KPMG, 2010). But who are the big advertisers? As the data from *Advertising Age* demonstrates, the top ten in 2009 were transnational conglomerates (see Table 4.2).

An advertisement-driven media ecology is inevitably more susceptible to commercial imperatives, as Michael Tracey suggests: 'In a public system, television producers acquire money to make programmes. In a commercial system, they make programmes to acquire money' (Tracey, 1998: 18). Are the 'public' aspects of news being taken over by private corporate interests? Does a celebrity-cricket-centred news play an ideological role in a country where despite impressive economic growth more than 400 million people remain illiterate? As Castells has suggested: 'Audiovisual media are the primary feeders of people's minds, as they relate to public affairs' (Castells, 2004: 372).

Table 4.2 Top ten global advertisers in 2009

Company	Worldwide measured media spending $ billion
Procter & Gamble	9.73
Unilever	5.72
L'Oreal	4.04
General Motors	3.67
Toyota Motor	3.20
Coca-Cola	2.67
Johnson & Johnson	2.60
Ford Motor	2.45
Reckitt Benckiser	2.37
Nestle	2.31

Source: http://adage.com/globalmarketers09/

Fierce and growing competition between proliferating news networks for ratings and advertising has prompted news managers to provide news in an entertaining manner. Broadcasters have adapted their news operations to retain their viewers or to acquire them anew. Adapt or perish appears to be the motto: it is indicative that even well-established brands such as Britain's ITN had to close down ITV News in 2005, a round-the-clock digital news channel, for lack of sufficient ratings.

Supporters of popular communication have tended to valorize the rise of infotainment, suggesting that it expands and democratizes the public debate (Hartley, 1999). It has been argued that news about sex, scandal and celebrity have been intrinsic to journalism since its inception and therefore news as commodity is as old as modern journalism, with varying degrees of competition endemic to the news market (Mott, 1962). Arguably, the US was the inventor of the infotainment industry, starting with the penny press in the 1830s. These pioneering popular newspapers provided diversions for working people, as Gabler has noted:

> For a constituency being conditioned by trashy crime pamphlets, gory novels and overwrought melodramas, news was simply the most exciting, most entertaining content a paper could offer, especially when it was skewed, as it invariably was in the penny press, to the most sensational stories. In fact, one might even say that the masters of the penny press *invented* the concept of news because it was the best way to sell their papers in an entertainment environment (cited in Gitlin, 2002: 51).

Later, the so-called 'yellow journalism' was characterized by intense competition between newspaper magnates of the period: Joseph Pulitzer (after whom the prestigious Pulitzer Prize in US journalism is named) and his rival William Randolph Hearst, both indulging in sensationalist and scandalous reporting as well as covering 'staged' and invented events, part of what has been called a 'journalism of entertainment' (Schudson, 1978: 89).

In his influential book *Amusing Ourselves to Death*, Neil Postman argued that the 'epistemology of television' militated against deeper knowledge and understanding since television's conversations promoted 'incoherence and triviality' as television speaks in only one persistent voice – the voice of entertainment' (Postman, 1985: 84).

Is this emphasis on entertainment contributing to what Tracey has called 'the trivialization of public discourse, an evangelism of the ephemeral, the celebration of the insignificant, and the marginalization of the important' (Tracey, 1998: 264)? I would argue that global infotainment entails more than just 'dumbing down'. It can work as a seductive discourse of diversion, in the sense both of taking the attention away, and of displacing from the airwaves such grim realities as the excesses of neo-liberalism, notably the global banking crisis of 2008, as well as neo-imperial adventures, witnessed most blatantly in the US invasion and continued occupation of Iraq.

The global economic crisis is an excellent example of the irresponsibility of television news to inform and educate its audience. McChesney has rightly argued that the corporate media system 'is not only closely linked to the *ideological* dictates of the business-run society, it is also an integral element of the economy' (McChesney, 1999: 281, emphasis in original). In this sense, the words of the veteran economist John Kenneth Galbraith are very relevant. In one of his last treatises before his death, Galbraith noted that in a 'market system' the transnational corporations set the public discourse, and mainstream economists, the policy élite and the media are party to what he termed an 'innocent fraud'. Since these groups have the 'respectability and authority' and little sense of 'guilt or responsibility', such fraud enters the public discourse and is becoming public knowledge (Galbraith, 2004). The Enron scandal and the more recent global banking crisis which wiped out trillions of dollars from the international economy spring to mind as exemplars of a perhaps less than innocent 'fraud' being perpetuated by an infotainment-driven media.

Herbert Schiller had argued that Western media corporations are integral to the capitalist system and play a core role as ideological agents: 'They provide in their imagery and messagery, the beliefs and perspectives that create and reinforce their audiences' attachments to the way things are in the system overall' (Schiller, 1976: 30).

In an age of ever-shortening sight-bites, the average consumer of the 24/7 infotainment bombardment may not be able to differentiate between public information and corporate propaganda. Jacques Ellul distinguishes between an overtly political and a more subtle conception of propaganda – a propaganda of 'integration' which unconsciously moulds individuals and makes them conform to the dominant ideas in a society. In the long run, popular cinema, television, advertising and public relations, Ellul has argued, can be more effective in reinforcing the official political agenda than control or manipulation of news (Ellul, 1965 [1962]). With the blurring of boundaries between news, advertising and entertainment, Ellul's formulation of propaganda gains contemporary relevance and added significance.

The diversion of infotainment can distract attention away from corporate control of public information, as well as displacing alternative views and information that are essential for public debate. Given the growing power of global infotainment conglomerates and their local clones, there is a danger that the existence of an informed citizenry, essential for genuine democratic discourse, is undermined, while corporate propaganda masquerading as infotainment reaches billions of people in their living rooms. Adorno warned that the mechanisms of television, 'often operate under the guise of false realism' (Adorno, 1991: 158). Are they creating a false global 'feel good' factor, predicated on the supremacy of the market as defined by the West, led by the United States? Guy DeBord in his 1967 book referred to the 'society of the spectacle', defining the spectacle as 'the existing order's uninterrupted discourse about itself, its laudatory monologue' (DeBord, 1977 [1967]: 24).

DeBord claimed that the imagery devised and shaped by television and the advertising industry masks social reality: 'the spectacle is capital to such a degree of accumulation that it becomes an image' (DeBord, 1977 [1967]: 34). Are we moving towards a global spectacle society in which neo-liberalism has become a hegemonic discourse with pervasive effects on ways of thought and political-economic practices, making it part of the commonsense view of the world (Harvey, 2003)? In this common-sense view of the world is the image replacing reality? With the rapid circulation of what I have elsewhere called 'glocal Americana' the capacity to divert and deflect attention from vital concerns has in fact increased many-fold (Thussu, 2007c).

While infotainment conglomerates entertain and engage the masses by various versions of 'reality TV' and Hollywoodized or Bollywoodized news, the 'global pax-Americana,' with its 'empire of bases' scattered around the world and the US control of 'the global commons' continues to grow, despite economic downturn (Johnson, 2004; Posen, 2003). More than the Pentagon's 'total spectrum dominance', it is the US cultural hegemony 'from Hollywood to Harvard' which 'has greater global reach than any other', in the words of Joseph Nye (2004: 7).

Underpinned by enormous hard military power, this soft power, represented globally by infotainment conglomerates, effectively legitimizes neo-liberal ideology as a precursor to a postmodern free-market utopia. Given the semiotic and symbolic power of television news, it is a crucial element in promoting this ideology. The globalization of neo-liberal ideology and the near-global reach and circulation of televised infotainment has provided neo-liberalism with a powerful opportunity to communicate directly with the world's populace, as more and more global infotainment conglomerates are localizing their content to reach beyond the 'Westernized' élites.

Infotainment conglomerates are part of the dominant economic force in neo-liberal societies and operate within what Ellul refers to as a 'total' and 'constant' propaganda 'environment', which can render the influence of propaganda virtually unnoticed (Ellul, 1965 [1962]). The ideology of neo-liberalism has been embraced, almost universalized, by dominant sections of the transnational capitalist class – in its infancy in many developing countries and in transition economies such as in China and India. The new élite benefits from having closer ties with the powerful core of this tiny minority, largely based in the West, as the annual *Fortune 500* listings attest. Governments across the globe are less perturbed by the growth of infotainment, as it can keep the masses diverted with various versions of 'reality TV' and consumerist and entertaining information, displacing serious news and documentaries. Unlike news and current affairs, the Chinese communist party machinery is not as sensitive to infotainment programming – one of the most popular recent television shows in China has been *Super Girl*, a Chinese version of *American Idol*.

The Indian example discussed above demonstrates that the new Bollywoodized media élite does not particularly care about rural poverty (more than 100,000 small farmers in India committed suicide between 1993 and 2003, the period of neo-liberal 'reform', according to government figures) or the rise of so-called Maoist violence (associated with left-wing extremists, which the Indian Prime Minister has described as the greatest threat to the Indian state). Unfortunately, such grim stories do not translate into ratings for urban, Westernized viewers and are displaced by the diversion of infotainment.

The ideological contours of infotainment can be deciphered in news rooms across the globe. As television news loses its younger audience to online news outlets and as the liberal model of broadcast journalism itself is threatened by new technologies, fragmenting audiences and increasing competition, infotainment-driven news is likely to be visible with greater regularity and rigour. And while the ever more 'active' and connected audiences are regaled with the next big scandal of a celebrity or a cricketing lifestyle, the globalizing corporate media will ensure that attention will be skillfully and seductively diverted from the real scandals inflicted by neo-liberalism.

References

Adorno, T. (1991) *The Cultural Industry: Selected Essays on Mass Culture*, London: Routledge.

Ayish, M. (2002) 'Political Communication on Arab World Television: Evolving Patterns', *Political Communication*, 19: 137–154.

Baker, C.E. (2007) *Media Concentration and Democracy: Why Ownership Matters*, Cambridge: Cambridge University Press.

Barkin, S. (2002) *American Television News: The Media Marketplace and the Public Interest*, New York: M.E. Sharpe.

Burke, J. (2010) 'Not just cricket – Bollywood treatment gives India its very own "Superbowling"', *Guardian*, March 10.

Castells, M. (2004) *The Information Age: Economy, Society and Culture*, vol. 2: The Power of Identity, 2nd edn, Oxford: Blackwell.

Chattopadhyay, D. and Subramanian, A. (2010) 'SRK Inc', *Business Today*, March 2.

Chan, J.M. (2003) 'Administrative Boundaries and Media Marketization: A Comparative Analysis of the Newspaper, TV and Internet Markets in China', in Lee, C.C. (ed.) *Chinese Media, Global Contexts*, London: Routledge.

DeBord, G. (1977) *The Society of the Spectacle*, Detroit: *Black and Red*. (First published in 1967 as *La société du spetacle* by Buchet-Chastel, Paris.)

Ellul, J. (1965) *Propaganda: The Formation of Men's Attitudes*, New York: Knopf. (Originally published in French as *Propagandes* in 1962.)

FICCI-KPMG (2010) *Back in the Spotlight – FICCI-KPMG Indian Media and Entertainment Report*, 2010, Federation of Indian Chambers of Commerce and Industry, Mumbai.

Franklin, B. (1997) *Newszak and News Media*, London: Arnold.

Galbraith, J.K. (2004) *The Economics of Innocent Fraud: Truth For Our Time*, New York: Houghton Mifflin.

Gitlin, T. (2002) *Media Unlimited: How the Torrent of Images and Sounds Overwhelms Our Lives*, New York: Metropolitan Books.

Hallin, D. and Mancini, P. (2004) *Comparing Media Systems*, Cambridge: Cambridge University Press.

Hartley, J. (1999) *Uses of Television*, London: Routledge.

Harvey, D. (2003) *The New Imperialism*, Oxford: Oxford University Press.

Internet World Stats (2010) *Usage and Population Statistics*. Available: <http://www.internetworldstats.com/>.

Iosifidis, P. (ed.) (2010) *Reinventing Public Service Communication: European Broadcasters and Beyond*, London: Palgrave/Macmillan.

Johnson, C. (2004) *The Sorrows of Empire: Militarism, Secrecy, and the End of the Republic*, New York: Metropolitan Books.

Kellner, D. (2003) *Media Spectacle*, New York: Routledge.

Lindley, R. (2002) *Panorama: 50 Years of Pride and Paranoia*, London: Politico's.

McChesney, R. (1993) *Telecommunications, Mass Media and Democracy: The Battle for the Control of US Broadcasting, 1928–1935*, New York: Oxford University Press.

McChesney, R. (1999) *Rich Media, Poor Democracy – Communication Politics in Dubious Times*, Champaign, IL: University of Illinois Press.

Mott, F.L. (1962) *American Journalism: A History: 1690–1960*, 3rd edn, New York: Macmillan.

Nye, J. (2004) *Power in the Global Information Age: From Realism to Globalization*, New York: Routledge.

Pasti, S. (2005) 'Two Generations of Contemporary Russian Journalists', *European Journal of Communication*, 20(1): 89–115.

Posen, B. (2003) 'Command of the Commons: The Military Foundation of U.S. Hegemony', *International Security*, 28(1): 5–46.

Postman, N. (1985) *Amusing Ourselves to Death: Public Discourse in the Age of Show Business*, New York: Viking.

Project for Excellence in Journalism (1998) *Changing Definitions of News*, March 6. Available: <http://www.journalism.org/resources/research/reports/>.

Project for Excellence in Journalism (2010) *The State of the News Media: An Annual Report on American Journalism, 2010. Journalism.org.* Available: <http://stateofthemedia.org/2010>.

Sainath, P. (2010) 'How to feed your billionaires', *The Hindu*, April 17.

Schiller, H. (1976) *Communication and Cultural Domination*, New York: International Arts and Sciences Press.

Schudson, M. (1978) *Discovering the News: A Social History of American Newspapers*, New York: Harper.

Thussu, D.K. (2007a) *News as Entertainment: The Rise of Global Infotainment*, London: Sage.

Thussu, D.K. (2007b) 'The "Murdochization" of News? The Case of Star TV in India', *Media, Culture & Society*, 29 (3): 593–611.

Thussu, D.K. (2007c) 'Mapping Global Media Flow and Contra-Flow', in Thussu, D.K. (ed.) *Media on the Move: Global Flow and Contra-Flow*, London: Routledge.

Tracey, M. (1998) *The Decline and Fall of Public Service Broadcasting*, Oxford: Oxford University Press.

UNESCO (2006) *What is Public Service Broadcasting?* Paris: United Nations Educational, Scientific and Cultural Organization. Available: <http://portal.unesco.org/ci/en/ev.php>.

5 Emotions in the media and the mediatization of traumas

Nicolas Demertzis

Introduction

This chapter draws on work on the analysis of emotions in sociology and seeks to do two things. First, it seeks to provide a brief assessment of the status of emotions in communication and media studies by drawing attention to over-researched and under-researched areas; second, it delves into a particular topic where media studies, cultural studies, media ethics and the sociology of emotions intersect, namely mediatized traumas and the moral dilemmas they convey for members of the audiences.

Emotions and the media: a short outline

If not a paradigmatic shift, during the last decade or so, sociology has taken a major turn towards the analysis and understanding of emotions' impact on societal processes (Turner and Stets, 2005; Stets and Turner, 2006; Clough *et al.*, 2007). This turn is rooted in the early 1970s when the field of the sociology of emotions started to grow, so putting an end to the 'non-emotion period of sociology' (Barbalet, 1998: 19–22). To be sure, the discussion of 'affect' or emotions has always been present, occupying a crucial place in the works of prominent figures in the sociological tradition such as Weber, Simmel, Durkheim, Mead and Cooley. Yet, for several decades, the domination of structural-functionalism and rational choice theory pushed the analysis of emotions in the understanding of social action to the margins. Rooted in the Enlightenment dichotomy between Reason and Passion, the marginalization of emotions in sociological analysis was part and parcel of the 'normal science' of academic sociology (Kemper, 1990: 3; Williams, 2001: 1–15). Emotions were assessed as the property of quasi-scientific disciplines such as cultural anthropology and psychoanalysis, treated obliquely and unsystematically. For a number of societal, cultural and epistemic reasons constitutive of late modernity (the demise of logocentric knowledge, feminist studies, body studies, consumer culture, individualism, informalization of social manners) emotions have re-emerged as a fully legitimate and much demanding topic of inquiry. Far from being the opposite of reason, emotions are absolutely essential for sociology because 'no action can occur in a society without emotional involvement' (Barbalet, 2002:2, 2009). Therefore, as a separate field, the sociology of emotions is growing steadily, and it includes a variety of competing perspectives and different research agendas (Kemper, 1991; Hopkins *et al.*, 2009).

For all their links and conceptual contiguities with sociology, it seems that nothing similar has ever taken place in the field of communication and media studies. Unlike sociological literature, emotions and affect have not re-emerged as a normal and legitimate subject matter; from the very beginning, in one way or another, they were to be found in the earliest studies of human communication and mass communication. As early as the first quarter of the twentieth century, American scholars conducted psychological research on film and radio broadcasting which were moving beyond audience ratings and coverage, and extended to emotional aspects of reception, emotional gratifications, and the impact of film and radio usage. With the advent of television, emotional-psychological research expanded and flourished so that gradually, from the 1960s onwards, a sustainable theoretical body with different conceptualizations and methodologies emerged under the rubric of 'media and emotions' (Wirth and Schramm, 2005)[1].

The topic of the media and emotions is not restricted to media psychology where an impressive body of theoretical and empirical research has been produced over the last twenty years or so; as I shall try to show in this chapter, the media–emotions nexus can be found in many other areas of academic and public concern. Moreover, not all fields and sub-fields in communication studies treated emotions equally; in fact, there are areas of importance, such as communication policy and media economics, where the analysis of emotions is virtually absent. To take two more examples from political communication, much remains to be done in the areas of agenda setting and media framing. Traditionally, the agenda building of an issue has been studied as comprising three main components:

1   the media agenda, which influences
2   the public agenda, which in turn may influence
3   the policy agenda, i.e. political élites' opinions and attitudes (Dearing and Rogers, 1996).

In this tradition, the emphasis has been given to cognitions, issue attention and awareness with the affective component being effectively absent from the researchers' priorities. Nevertheless, the media do not only prioritize certain issues but also call attention to some emotions while ignoring others (Doeveling, 2009).

By the same token, the research tradition of news framing has been cognitively oriented as well, to the extent that it focuses on interpretation and schemes of perception conveyed by the news media. According to Entman (1993: 52):

to frame is to select some aspects of a perceived reality and make them more salient in a communicating text, in such a way as to promote a particular problem definition, causal interpretation, moral evaluation, and/or treatment recommendation for the item described.

Studies leaning on the framing hypothesis have shown that the way news is framed may dramatically alter opinions among readers, and news frame studies have also shown that certain standard frames tend to appear in political reporting (e.g. thematic, episodic, conflict orientation, game, and so on). Moral evaluations have been present as an undercurrent in earlier research; yet, their affective pair, i.e. emotions, have either, at best, been inferred indirectly, or, at worst, totally ignored. Nonetheless, taking emotions seriously would enhance agenda-setting and frame analysis in tandem with qualitative audience research by understanding not only what news consumers think but also what they feel about news items, and consequently under which frame of reference they may form political judgements and take decisions over disputed public issues. It is indicative that although Kinder (2007) has recently pointed out that frames include metaphors, exemplars, catchphrases, visual images, rhetorical flourishes and justifications, which in politics bring about emotional arousal, he emphatically claims that from this point of view, 'research on framing has so far explored just a small patch of the whole territory'. From a different theoretical tradition, Nabi (2003) maintains that rather than considering how emotions function within traditional paradigms of attitude change, communication scholars should explore the possibility that emotions serve as frames for issues, privileging certain information in terms of accessibility and thus guiding subsequent decision-making.

Yet, one could argue that the inclusion of affect and emotions in most fields of communication studies would not pass unnoticed; directly or indirectly, the affective dimension has important consequences for our understanding of the relation between media and society. At the risk of oversimplifying, I would argue that the areas of study in which emotions have been (or should be) taken into consideration include: propaganda, persuasion, advertising/political advertising, risk communication, uses and gratification, media violence/children, news analysis, journalism, film studies, audience ethnography, and new media. The paradox is that some of these areas are quite over-researched (e.g. media violence, advertising, persuasion) while others are under-researched (e.g. media framing, agenda setting).

Conceptualizing emotions in communication and media studies

By and large, and given the absence of any major affective turn in communication and media studies, scholars have tended to deal with emotions in three different ways: metaphorically, metonymically, and denotatively. Below I provide a few examples of these conceptualizations.

Metaphoric conceptualizations

In many cases, communication scholars have treated emotions evoked by or imputed to the media by placing them metaphorically at a different level of abstraction; in the first place, metaphor is commonly classified as a trope in which one entity is described by comparing it to another but without directly asserting a comparison. For Lacan, who was heavily influenced by Jakobson in this respect, metaphor is the substitution of one signifier for another. In an analogous parlance, metaphor corresponds to Saussure's paradigmatic relations which hold *in absentia* (Evans, 1996: 111). Ever since advocates of the uses and gratification theory(ies) referred to 'escapism' they have treated emotions *in absentia* because under this signifier a number of different emotions may have been accommodated: calmness, tranquility, joy, hope, delight, contentment, elation, worship, mindfulness, fascination, amazement, astonishment or even gloominess. More than this, the rubric 'gratifications' itself, in the name of this theory, serves as a metaphor of multiple and co-current emotions experienced by media users in real time. The most that scholars in this tradition are willing to admit is that the 'affective needs' the users seek to gratify are needs relating to aesthetic experiences, love and friendship (Rayburn, 1996). The same holds true for 'sensationalism' and 'info-tainment' in news analysis (Schudson, 1997; Postman, 1985: 87), 'the symbolic power of the media' in the sociology of communication (Thompson, 1995), and 'meaning' and 'identification' in audience ethnography (Wilson, 1993). No doubt, all these narrative tropes are indices of emotions and affective states of mind which, nonetheless, remain indeterminate; or, to be more precise, these tropes are substitutes for emotional terms due to the metaphoric discursive context in use.

Metonymic conceptualizations

Not infrequently, scholars refer to emotions metonymically by using a combinatorial (syntagmatic) axis of theoretical language (Evans, 1996: 113–4). In this respect, they do not substitute (as in metaphoric conceptions) but link emotional terms to one another. Yet this combinatorial link involves a perpetual deferral of meaning in the sense that emotional terms are not equated but connected to each other according to the logic of the parts–whole relationship. Hence, elements of vagueness and imprecision come to the fore. An examplary metonymic use of emotions can be found in Fiske's analysis (1987: 224–239) of television's discourse where he emphatically registers 'pleasures' instead of more distinct emotions like joy, happiness, surprise, astonishment, love and so on. Similarly, Massumi (2002) refers generally to 'affect' not only as the primary feature for the understanding of the user's experience in the new media environments but as a central 'medium' for the understanding of our information- and image-based late capitalist culture.

Inspired by Spinoza's notion of passion, as something which acts upon the body and as something which is acted upon by consciousness, Massumi assumes that 'affect' is a pre-social and never fully conscious nonlinear complexity, prior to passivity and activity, which makes for 'synesthesia', that is, the connections between the senses, and 'kinaesthesia', feelings of movement through moving images and icons on the screen in our computer and media saturated society. Seen in this light, Massumi's affect serves as a whole and overarching emotional climate which is linked metonymically to the particular emotions that can spring from it. In a similar vein, much of the advertising literature abides to such metonymic notions as 'desires', 'emotional appeals' and 'emotional conditioning' that are built in to many ads, or to the 'emotional responses' of consumers (Leiss *et al.*, 1986: 225, 233, 289; Bocock, 1993: 76ff.; Kroeber-Riel, 1998). Clearly, general terms like 'emotional appeals' or 'emotional responses' are conducive to more specific emotions and feelings such as guilt, shame, hope, sadness, trust, confidence, cheerfulness, loyalty, greediness and so on.

Denotative approaches

In contrast to metaphoric and metonymic uses, some communication scholars focus on specific and discrete emotions. This trend does not necessarily coincide with the emotional turn in sociology and in the humanities although it gets certain feedback from this; most notably, the denotative approach is commensurable with the sociology of emotions' preference for the analysis of particular emotions within concrete socio-cultural and relational settings. In this context, one of the most representative cases is the analysis of shame and guilt in public communication, social influence and persuasion processes; in this analysis, strong or weak guilt appeal of messages is related to differential levels of aroused guilt in the recipients and persuasive outcomes (O'Keefe, 2000; Planalp *et al.*, 2000). Similarly, and more recently, Breakwell (2007: 109–172) discusses particular emotions involved in risk communication from a psychological point of view. Provided that risk communication usually takes places in forums that are highly emotionally charged, she offers ample research evidence as to the role of particular emotions in enhancing media messages about risks and hazards. Some of the most prominent emotions in her analysis include:

1   induced fear in communication messages for risk awareness and risk aversion;
2   trust and distrust towards public institutions regarding the willingness to undertake a specific risk such as hosting a nuclear waste repository in one's community;
3   worry, regret, anger, outrage, terror, and panic as to the understanding of the public's perception of risk.

More generally, in media psychology, there has been an on-going tendency to see emotions as explanatory mechanisms within established media effects theories and as outcomes of audiences' interactions with media content. In this context, Robin Nabi (1999) has been giving particular attention to discrete, message-induced negative emotions that influence attitudes in persuasion processes in the sense that emotion type, emotional intensity, and emotion placement within a message are expected to mediate information processing depth, message acceptance or rejection, and information recall. She (Nabi, 2002) has also developed a theory or model of coping with discrete emotions in media use such as regret, jealousy, sadness and anxiety so as to predict selection and perception of media content based on the individual's need to reframe the person–environment situation. Recently, within the context of media psychology, Vorderer and Hartmann (2009) have delved into the research and theoretical agenda of media entertainment pointing out particular positive and negative emotions experienced by the users of media content.

A first round appraisal

All three approaches have their pros and cons as they build on different levels of abstraction. Metaphoric approaches offer broad-spectrum explanations about people's reactions to and people's uses of media, but sweep aside proper analysis of particular emotions. Metonymic approaches to emotions bring the affective dimension much more effectively to the fore, yet they still lack specificity and concreteness. Finally, administrative or critical research of discrete emotions (such as fear, cynicism, shame and so on), though more concrete, offers a compartmentalized account and fails to recognize that emotions are experienced in a complex and/or flow-like manner rather than one at a time.

By and large, in the media effects literature the media are seen as causes of emotions. Less research has been done the other way around; namely, to see specific emotions as predictors of the selection of media content, particularly in entertainment television. Another prominent feature in media and emotions research is its almost one-sided emphasis on negative emotions and the neglect of positive ones in analysing various aspects of human and mass communication like social influence, persuasion, decision-making, attitude formation, watching television, consuming news, vote preference and so on.

As noted earlier, there are a number of extensively researched, and other less researched areas of investigation, in communication studies in the field of media and emotions. In the rest of this chapter, I shall deal with an issue that broadens the theoretical agenda and straddles media studies, cultural studies and media ethics on the one hand, and the sociology and, to a lesser degree, the psychology of emotions on the other; I am referring to the mediatization of traumas.[2] As I shall show, analysing this issue entails the analysis of both negative and positive emotions, and a double understanding of the media as both causes and instances of audience's affective responses.

Mediatization of traumas: an emotionally charged topic

As a fresh object of theoretical scrutiny, the mediatization of traumas springs from the novel field of trauma studies. Concurrently with memory studies, trauma studies has developed in a steadfast way. Due to the horrific mass experiences of various collectivities in the twentieth century it is not accidental that a number of scholars talk about our times and culture as 'trauma time' (Edkins, 2003: xiv) and 'the culture of trauma' (Miller and Tougaw, 2002: 2) upgrading 'trauma' into a central imaginative signification and a master signifier of contemporary risk society. The preoccupation with trauma might possibly have not happened unless the media played a decisive role.

Trauma, and cultural-social trauma for that matter, is a metaphor that we live with in the contemporary era. Its metaphorical meaning is constantly under negotiation and therefore gives rise to an ambivalent attitude: on the one hand, trauma can activate the logic of self-fulfilling prophecy, victimizing the subject and cultivating a fatalistic culture of risk and helplessness (Žižek, 1997: 136). This kind of victimization is accompanied and supported by the breaking of bonds of trust and confidence (interpersonal, political, and so on). An event is called traumatic not only when it offends the subject's capabilities, but when at the same time it implies the betrayal and breaching of relations of trust and rattles default notions of what it means morally to remain part of a collective (Edkins, 2003: 4; Zelizer, 2002).

On the other hand, it is also argued that traumas have the capacity to widen the field of social understanding and sympathy. They imply the designation of victims, the attribution of responsibility and the allocation of material and symbolic consequences. The strong feelings that accompany trauma entail the identification with the victims not only of those who suffer from it in the first place (inner group), but also of the wider public. Here, a crucial (although often ambivalent) role is played by the media. In the information society, awareness and evaluation of others' traumas are largely accomplished through the means of communication and journalism (Eyerman, 2008: 21, 168–9; Zelizer and Allan, 2002; Andén-Papadopoulus, 2003; Tenenboim-Weinblatt, 2008).

A common wisdom in the critical media debate is that suffering is commodified chiefly by the electronic media and the members of the audience become passive spectators of distant death and pain endowed with no moral commitment. Thus mediatization of traumas leads to quasi-emotions; namely, emotions, which do not motivate, do not endure and mortify or numb our sensitivities (Meštrović, 1997) contributing, according to Robins (2001), to the 'social production of indifference' premised on the capacity of the television to screen the suffering of the world and at the same time the capacity to screen out the brutal reality of that suffering. Spectators see the faces of those who are suffering, but they do not necessarily feel any moral obligation. Therefore, a mediatized trauma is seen as mere entertainment and gives rise to a detached curiosity (Kansteiner, 2004). Yet, it is also argued that due to the extended availability of their messages about people's suffering, the media allow forms of sympathy with distant others (Thompson, 1995: 258ff.; Baer, 2001; Sontag, 2003). The mediated participation in the pain of others can lead to new forms of social interaction (Alexander, 2004: 22, 24) and it may initiate what Luc Boltanski (1999: 3–19) calls 'the politics of pity' premised on strong moral sentiments and public action in favour of the unfortunates.[3] Among others, this is possible because often media content is linked to memory and offers opportunities for bearing witness which may establish moral accountability by moving individuals from the personal act of seeing to the adoption of a public point of view (Zelizer, 2002; Coonfield, 2007; Tenenboim-Weinblatt, 2008).

Though it is not compulsory for someone to adopt either an ungrounded optimism or an unnecessary pessimism in the debate under consideration (Chouliaraki, 2004), the crucial question is to what extent can the media eradicate the natural disposition of the human being to sympathize with other people, a disposition much praised by moral philosophers like Hume and Smith. It is my opinion that it would be too harsh to exclude moral sensibility from the mediated quasi-interaction (Thompson, 1995: 87ff.). The electronic media of mass communication do help the politics of pity and global compassion to emerge, as the immediate speed in the transmission of distant others' traumas and suffering facilitates recipients to identify somehow with the visualized victims. That was the case, for instance, with the so-called 'Kosovocaust', an aftermath of the 'CNN effect'; footage and news photos articulated in reference to the 'lessons of the Holocaust' provoked intense moral outcries among Western public opinion, thus affecting to a considerable degree international decision-making. Yet, identification with the victims can be accomplished retroactively as well; for instance, the film *Schindler's List* and almost two decades earlier the TV drama *The Holocaust* (not to mention a host of other products of popular culture on Jews' cultural-social trauma) greatly contributed to the formation of a global awareness and a strong moral stance. Through real-time transmission or retroactively, or both, the media build up a sort of 'cosmopolitan memory' sustained by the universal language of emotions; the visualization of others' pain – say, for instance, the Rwanda genocide, the atrocities in Somalia, the Khmer Rouge's extermination of one-third of Cambodia's population, the famine in Darfur, and Ground Zero – triggers in the spectators the expression of some of the most basic emotions recognizable by everyone: disgust and anger at the perpetrators, sadness and fear for the victims.

Willy-nilly the spectator is addressed as a witness of the evil and while viewing it she/he is interpellated as a moral subject; as long as this interpellation takes place, new loci of global solidarity and ethical universality are carved out (Levi and Sznaider, 2002: 88), fuelled, to say the least, by the above mentioned emotions. It is precisely through these emotions that television becomes 'an agent of moral responsibility' (Chouliaraki, 2004:186) and, consequently, a facilitator of the 'democratization of responsibility' (Thompson, 1995: 263–4). Needless to say, much depends on whether the drama of the depicted traumas is represented in the media as tragedy or as melodrama (Eyerman, 2008: 17).[4]

It can be argued that time–space compression is a sufficient condition for the rising of cosmopolitan memories and the global spreading of responsibility; the ultimate necessary condition, though, is guilt. It is guilt that allows the spectators to engulf the suffering of the distant others and their traumatic history; but why is this so? Attempting an interpretation – and here I am using a simplified psychoanalytic perspective though not so closely as it deserves – I would claim that this is so because the 'average' person is endowed with unconscious guilt due to the Superego's imperatives (Freud, 1930/2001). The paradox Freud underscores is that the more ethical the subject is, the more guilty he/she feels. Ambivalence towards the father (or everyone who assumes the role of the father) as well as the subsequent repressed aggression return to the Ego through the Superego. This is so, because it is not only that the subject has repressed the forbidden drives before an external authority, i.e. the father; what counts more is that the subject feels anxious in front of the internal authority, the Superego. This internal authority monitors all forbidden desires so that intention becomes equivalent to wrongdoing. That is why many people feel guilty without prior wrongdoing.

Yet, it is not only the severe and punishing Superego that elicits guilt; it is also the symbolic Law underlying all social relations, that is, the Law of the signifier, which according to Lacan commands that not everything is possible in human affairs. The prohibition of incest is an example of the symbolic Law which actually 'superimposes the kingdom of culture on that of nature' (Lacan, 1977: 66). It seems to me that somehow the *Lacanian* account of the Law, closely related to Kant's Categorical Imperative, is linked to the normative vulnerability Velleman (2003) speaks about. Normative vulnerability is the sense of being unjustified and defenceless against negative reactions and responses addressed by the other(s) in a warranted way. Thus, even if one commits no wrongdoing one may feel guilty upon the imaginary anticipation that there is somewhere someone else suffering who resents or envies one's good fortune. So, whenever a spectator is in front of a horrendous mediatized event, for example the collapse of the twins towers on 11 September or the Rwanda genocide or the Katrina hurricane, not only does she/he feel that the symbolic order, represented by the Law, is violated by the intrusion of pure negativity (or Evil, one could say) evading any discursive intermediation; what is more, he/she experiences that his/her secure state and wellbeing are unacceptable and unjustified before the victims' tragic plight. In virtue of unconscious guilt, the spectator feels that the violation of the Law is somehow her/his responsibility. Besides, I would also claim that the spectator of the pain of Third World distant others on Western television and the Internet may also experience a preconscious guilt in line with the following logic: although I as a person have done nothing for their suffering, somehow I am guilty because I enjoy the goods of the capitalist centre which exploits and dominates countries in the periphery.

In one way or another, therefore, guilt is an ontogenetic moral ground for the development of the politics of pity, precisely because it is rooted deep in the human psyche. It is not accidental or contingent but an immanent moral stance. Yet, the crucial point in the information age is the degree of its universalizability against the grammar of the media; apart from redefining the interplay between distance and proximity, the latter systematically promote particularity over universality through personalization, dramatization and episodic coverage of traumatic situations.

As ambivalent as their moral impact might be, and irrespective of the compassion fatigue and the routinization of the others' traumas they produce (Tester, 2001: 13; Alexander, 2003:103), observing the pain of others through the media cannot totally shield spectators from moral interpellation, from their direct or indirect moralization. It is certainly true that media reporting on distant suffering serves cynical commercial interests; telethons dedicated to the alleviation of Third World suffering and misfortunes are part of entertainment programming and offer ample opportunities for humanitarian sponsoring and image making. It is true that frequently the politics of pity or compassion is reduced in giving money for charity just in order to keep the distant other at an arm's length. It is also true that mediatized cosmopolitan memories buttress the post-democratic ideological discourse on 'human rights' which provides moral grounds to international interventions described euphemistically as 'humanitarian interventions' which of course create new victims, as was in fact the case when NATO and the US dropped bombs over Kosovo and Serbia in the spring of 1999.

All these are true, but they are not the whole truth. It seems to me that there is always a moral remainder, a sort of unconscious or preconscious guilt, which escapes the commercial logic of the medium (Bennet, 2003) and under certain circumstances overwhelms quasi-emotions leading to autonomous public action. This virtual moral stance has a neurobiological origin that actually sets the conditions of possibility for its emergence; neuro-scientific evidence suggests that clusters of 92 neurons in the premotor cortex have the ability to represent the action or experience of another and produce the same emotional energy as if this action or experience was performed by oneself (Williams, 2009: 255). Therefore, 'the same neurons are activated when I feel fear as when I observe you feeling fear' and 'when I am performing the action and when I am observing you performing the action' (Schreiber, 2007: 52–53). Far from endorsing a sort of neuro-scientific determinism, it seems to me that herein lies a non-reversible neurobiological substratum of empathy and sympathy precisely because mirror neurons facilitate mental representations of how other people think and feel. Different from emotional contagion, in this context I define empathy as an other-oriented emotion that stems from the apprehension of another's condition, and that is identical or almost identical to what the other person feels or would be expected to feel. Rather than feeling the same emotion as the other person, sympathy is defined as an involving other-oriented affective response that consists of feeling sorrow for the needy other (Eisenberg, 2004). Well before the discovery of mirror neurons, research in twins evidenced a biological basis of empathy.

Luckily, the function of mirror neurons provides a firm basis for the validation of Adam Smith's programmatic statement:

> How selfish so ever man may be supposed, there are evidently some principles in his nature, which interest him in the fortune of others, and render their happiness necessary for him, though he derives nothing from it except the pleasure of seeing it. Of this kind is pity or compassion, the emotion which we feel for the misery of others, when we either see it, or are made to conceive it in a very lively manner (1759/1976: 9).

For Smith this ability to put ourselves in the place of the other is elementary in everyone, not confined to the virtuous and the humane: 'the greatest ruffian, the most hardened violator of the laws of society, is not altogether without it' (ibid).

Though he had not anticipated this link between classic moral philosophy and modern neuro-science, it is actually this which provides ground for the surfacing of those rare cases where the public media assume the role of the 'mediapolis' Silverstone (2006) spoke so passionately about: as a space of socio-political dialogue and deliberation of moral significance with remote others, precisely because they contribute to the keeping of the proper distance from the victims, bringing them neither too close nor keeping them too far. Here I would claim that in virtue of mediapolis, though fragile and precarious, the feelings of guilt, indignation and sadness aroused while watching the unpleasant plight of distant others can be a stimulating condition for alternative moral-practical thinking. Despite the reluctance people experience to interpret their concerns and sentiments into determinate courses of action, the mediatized trauma of the distant other could give rise to a sense of responsibility for his/her life and to a sense of dignity. It prompts what Hans Jonas (1984) regards as the attribute that differentiates par excellence humans as a species: the undertaking of substantive responsibility towards the entire Being and the other human being. Perhaps the mediatization of traumas is unable to mobilize the *Levinasian* ethics of being for the other instead of being simply with the other. The likelihood is that time–space compression is conducive to the moral stance of being with the other, due to the disguised proximity of the sufferers on the screen. Yet, as long as this takes place, it is already too much; one can maintain, therefore, that, serving as carrier groups, the media make possible an ethics of care and responsibility in our age where care seems impossible. This is accomplished, inter alia, through the social construction of 'moral universals', that is, generalized symbols of human suffering and moral evil (Alexander, 2003: 27ff.). By the same token, I would even argue that the media may make our direct or indirect encounter with the suffering of the others easier and mobilize that sort of moral minimalism that Walzer (1994) was writing about: a moral minimum, a 'thin morality', which does not serve any particular interest but instead regulates everyone's behaviour in a mutually beneficial way. Isn't this, after all, the meaning of the international mobilizations against the war in Iraq and the solidarity that was expressed for the people in South East Asia after the tsunami of 26 December 2004?

Conclusion

Academic wisdom suggests that in the media-saturated postmodern society 'the grand narrative has lost its credibility' bringing on de-legitimation and radical suspicion towards 'pre-established rules' (Lyotard, 1984: 37, 81; Rosenau, 1992: 133–137). As individuals become all the more aporetic and distrustful of the offered truth of the 'mutual spying of ideologies' and the fragmentation of societal and political reality, there is no reasonable basis to support their choices. Consequently, in the absence of moral parameters, the moral situation of postmodernity is that 'yesterday's idealists have become pragmatic' (Bauman, 1993: 2) and that 'liars call liars liars' (Sloterdijk, 1988: xxvii).

Another common wisdom, both academic and mundane which is nonetheless related to the first, maintains that, due to the aesthetization of public discourse conferred by the hyper-mediation of still and moving images, most people get satiated when encountering mediatized traumas. In a media-saturated society the intimate spectacle of others' suffering, it is said, makes for denial and unfeelingness and/or quasi-emotionality; to this end, traumas become anaesthetized banalities. Technologies of spectacle 'permeate the body and are articulated as forms of memory, experience, belonging, emotion, and ethics' in such a way that 'the fundamental link between life and death and conceptions of ethics and justice are progressively eroded' (Lafleur, 2007: 225).

To a certain extent, the argument I put forward in this paper attempted to challenge these wisdoms by suggesting that the media may assume the role of a quasi-transcendental moral claimer when it comes to the representation of others' traumas and suffering. Representation of others' traumas brings forth emotional shock and a process of interpretation as to who the victims and the perpetrators are, initiating, by the same token, moral judgement and active solidarity premised on the universal feeling of guilt and the neuro-biological ground of sympathy and empathy. Also, one should take note that when representing our own traumas the media may contribute to the healing process and working through; this is accomplished through the definition of the trauma (by transforming via signification a traumatogenic event into a public, or cultural trauma), its narration and its articulation into collective memory. In a way, this threefold process contributes to successful mourning and reconnection to ordinary life (Herman, 1992; Zelizer, 2002; Wastell, 2005). It is perfectly accepted that media outlets are perceived and appropriated in social-cultural contexts which often leave room for alternative de-codifications (Hall, 1980) that do not always create representations that contribute to ideological views of what is socially and culturally acceptable and desirable; consequently, the effects elicited from observing others' trauma as well as ours may not necessarily serve as a commodity (emotional capital) in the media market, and may not unavoidably lead to sentimentalism.

Arguably, there is not much evidence as to the ethical role of the media in the spirit of Silverstone's *Mediapolis*; most of the works conducted in this field opt for a pessimist interpretation premised on the legacy of the Frankfurt School. Yet, a lot remains to be done towards the analysis of media morality in view of the forthcoming bridging between the sociology of emotions, media psychology, and media ethics, especially when it comes to the interpretation of traumas, either collective or cultural. To this end, of absolute necessity is the combination of quantitative and qualitative methodologies of all kinds and the scrutinizing of theoretical questions such as the media's impact on emotional reflexivity, the relation and/or distinction between media morality and ideology(ies)[5] on the one hand, and the articulation of collective memory(ies) with ideological discourses on the other. Other relevant issues include the analysis of the code of ethics in covering others' traumas, be it interstate armed conflicts, natural catastrophes, civil wars, terrorist attacks, crises of public health and so on; the tension between spectators' anaesthesia and the politics of pity; the zone of indistinction between humanitarian tele-marathons and active solidarity and critical responsibility for distant others; and the over-anaesthetization and over-emotionalization of political traumas.

Notes

1   Though in a rather restricted manner, in an attempt to delineate the sub-field of the sociology of emotions, four chapters of a recent reader focus on the relations between the media and emotions. See Greco and Stenner (2008).
2   From a different perspective directed by the premises of war studies Carpentier's edited volume (2007) touches upon a number of issues raised in this chapter.
3   These issues refer to the essentials of moral philosophy and entail a host of conceptual controversies as to the meaning of compassion, pity, fellow-feeling and the like. See: Scheler (1954), Sznaider (1998), Hoggett (2006), Nussbaum (2001) and Höijer (2003).

4   September 11 made clear that when it comes to 'our' trauma, American media and journalists adopt a much less melodramatic and entertaining stance (Rosen, 2002).
5   Something related, in my view, to the way American media and journalism coped with September 11 succumbing almost entirely to nationalism.

References

Alexander, J. (2003) *The Meanings of Social Life. A Cultural Sociology*, Oxford: Oxford University Press.

Alexander, J. (2004) 'Toward a Theory of Cultural Trauma', in Alexander, J. *et al.* (eds) *Cultural Trauma and Collective Identity*, Berkeley: University of California Press.

Andén-Papadopoulus, K. (2003) 'The Trauma of Representation. Visual Culture, Photojournalism and the September 11 Terrorist Attack', *Nordicom Review* 24(2): 89–104.

Baer, A. (2001) 'Consuming History and Memory through Mass Media Products', *European Journal of Cultural Studies*, 4(4): 491–501.

Barbalet, J. (1998) *Emotion, Social Theory, and Social Structure; A Macrosociological Approach*, Cambridge: Cambridge University Press.

Barbalet, J. (2002) 'Introduction: Why emotions are crucial', in Barbalet, J. (ed.) *Emotions and Sociology*, Oxford: Blackwell.

Baudrillard, J. (1983) *In the Shadow of the Silent Majorities*, New York: Semiotext(e).

Bauman, Z. (1993) *Postmodern Ethics*, Oxford: Blackwell.

Bennett, L. (2003) *News. The Politics of Illusion*, 5th edn, New York: Longman.

Bocock, R. (1993) *Consumption*, London: Routledge.

Boltanski, L. (1999) *Distant Suffering. Morality, Media and Politics*, Cambridge: Cambridge University Press.

Breakwell, G. (2007) *The Psychology of Risk*, Cambridge: Cambridge University Press.

Carpentier, N. (ed.) (2007) *Culture, Trauma, and Conflict. Cultural Studies Perspectives on War*, Newcastle: Cambridge Scholars Publishing.

Chouliaraki, L. (2004) 'Watching 11 September: the Politics of Pity', *Discourse and Society*, 15(2–3): 185–198.

Clough, P.T. with Halley, J. (eds.) (2007) *The Affective Turn. Theorizing the Social*, Durham, NC: Duke University Press.

Coonfield, G. (2007) 'News Images As Lived Images: Witness, Performance, and the U.S. Flag After 9/11', in Carpentier, N. (ed.) *Culture, Truma, and Conflict. Cultural Studies Perspectives on War*, Newcastle: Cambridge Scholars Publishing.

Dearing, J.W. and Rogers, E.M. (1996) *Agenda-Setting*, London: Sage Publications.

Doeveling, K. (2009) 'Mediated Parasocial Emotions and Community: How Media May Strengthen or Weaken Social Communities', in Hopkins, D. *et al.* (eds) *Theorizing Emotions: Sociological Explorations and Applications*, Berlin: Campus.

Edkins, J. (2003) *Trauma and the Memory of Politics*, Cambridge: Cambridge University Press.

Eisenberg, N. (2004) 'Empathy and Sympathy', in Lewis, M. and Haviland-Jones, J.M. (eds) *Handbook of Emotions* (2nd paperback edn), New York/London: The Guilford Press.

Entman, R.M. (1993) 'Framing. Toward Clarification of a Fractured Paradigm', *Journal of Communication*, 43(4): 51–58.

Evans, D. (1996) *An Introductory Dictionary of Lacanian Psychoanalysis*, London: Routledge.

Eyerman, R. (2008) *The Assassination of Theo Van Gogh; From Social Drama to Cultural Trauma*, Durham and London: Duke University Press.

Fiske, J. (1987) *Television Culture*, London: Methuen.

Freud, S. (1930/2001) *Civilization and its Discontents*. In *The Standard Edition of the Complete Psychological Works*, Vol. XXI. London: Vintage, The Hogarth Press.

Greco, M. and Stenner, P. (eds) (2008) *Emotions: A Social Science Reader*, London, New York: Routledge.

Hall, S. (1980) 'Encoding/decoding', in Hall, S., Hobson, D., Lowe, A. and Willis, P. (eds) *Culture, Media, Language*, London: Hutchinson.

Herman, J. (1992) *Trauma and Recovery*, New York: Basic Books.

Hoggett, P. (2006) 'Pity, Compassion, Solidarity', in Clarke, S., Hoggett, P. and Thompson, S. (eds) *Emotion, Politics and Society*, New York: Palgrave MacMillan.

Hopkins, D., Kleres, J., Flam, H. and Kuzmics, H. (eds) (2009) *Theorizing Emotions: Sociological Explorations and Applications*, Berlin: Campus.

Höijer, B. (2003) 'The Discourse of Global Compassion and the Media', *Nordicom Review*, 24 (2): 19–29.

Jonas, H. (1984) *The Imperative of Responsibility: In Search of an Ethics for the Technological Age*, Chicago: University of Chicago Press.

Kansteiner, W. (2004) 'Genealogy of a Category Mistake: A Critical Intellectual History of the Cultural Trauma Metaphor', *Rethinking History*, 8(2): 193–221.

Kemper, Th. (ed.) (1990) *Research Agendas in the Sociology of Emotions*, New York: State University of New York Press.

Kemper, Th. (1991) 'An Introduction to the Sociology of Emotions', in Strongman, K. (ed.) *International Review of Studies on Emotion*, Vol. 1, New York: John Wiley.

Kinder, D.R. (2007) 'Curmudgeonly Advice', *Journal of Communication*, 57: 155–162.

Kroeber-Riel, W. (1998) *Strategy and Technique in Advertising*, Athens: Ellinika Grammata.

Lacan, J. (1977) *Ecrits. A Selection*, London: Tavistock/Routledge.

Lafleur, M. (2007) 'Life and Death in the Shadow of the A-Bomb: Sovereignty and Memory on the 60th Anniversary of Hiroshima and Nagasaki', in Carpentier, N. (ed.) (2007) *Culture, Trauma, and Conflict; Cultural Studies Perspectives on War*, Newcastle: Cambridge Scholars Publishing.

Leiss, W., Kline, S. and Jhally, S. (1986) *Social Communication in Advertising. Persons, Products, and Images of Well Being*, Toronto: Methuen.

Levy, D. and Sznaider, N. (2002) 'Memory Unbound. The Holocaust and the Formation of Cosmopolitan Memory', *European Journal of Social Theory*, 5(1): 87–106.

Lyotard, J.-F. (1984) *The Postmodern Condition: A Report on Knowledge*, Manchester: Manchester University Press.

Massumi, B. (2002) *Parables for the Virtual; Movement, Affect, Sensation*, Durham, NC: Duke University Press.

Meštrović S. (1997) *Postemotional Society*, London: Sage Publications.

Miller, N.K. and Tougaw, J. (eds.) (2002) *Extremities. Trauma, Testimony, and Community*, Urbana and Chicago: University of Illinois Press.

Nabi, R.L. (2003) 'Exploring the Framing Effects of Emotion', *Communication Research*, 30(2): 224–247.

Nabi, R.L. (1999) 'A Cognitive-Functional Model for the Effects of Discrete Negative Emotions on Information Processing, Attitude Change, and Recall', *Communication Theory*, 9: 29.

Nabi, R.L. (2002) 'Discrete emotions and persuasion', in Dillard, J. and Pfau, M. (eds) *Handbook of Persuasion*, Thousand Oaks, CA: Sage.

Nussbaum, M.C. (2001) *Upheavals of Thought. The Intelligence of Emotion*, Cambridge: Cambridge University Press.

O'Keefe, J.D. (2000) 'Guilt and Social Influence', in Roloff, M. (ed.) *Communication Yearbook 23*, London: Sage Publications.

Planalp, S., Hafen, S. and Adkins, A.D. (2000) 'Messages of Shame and Guilt' in Roloff, M. (ed.) *Communication Yearbook 23*, London: Sage Publications.

Postman, N. (1985) *Amusing Ourselves to Death. Public Discourse in the Age of Show Business*, London: Penguin Books.

Rayburn, J.D. II (1996) 'Uses and Gratifications', in Salwen, M. and Stacks, D. (eds) *An Integrated Approach to Communication Theory and Research*, New Jersey: Lawrence Erlbaum Associates.

Robins, K. (2001) 'Seeing the world from a safe distance', *Science as Culture*, 10(4): 531–539.

Rosen, J. (2002) 'September 11 in the Mind of American Journalism', in Zelizer, B. and Allan, S. (eds) *Journalism After September 11*, London: Routledge.

Rosenau, P.M. (1992) *Post-Modernism and the Social Sciences. Insights, Inroads, and Intrusions*, Princeton/New Jersey: Princeton University Press.

Scheler, M. (1954) *The Nature of Sympathy*, London: Routledge & Kegan Paul.

Schreiber, D. (2007) 'Political Cognition: Are We All Political Sophisticates?', in Neuman, R. *et al.* (eds) *The Affect Effect. Dynamics of Emotion in Political Thinking and Behavior*, Chicago: The University of Chicago Press.

Schudson, M. (1997) 'The Sociology of News Production', in Berkowitz, D. (ed.) *Social Meanings of New; A Text-Reader*, London: Sage Publications.

Silverstone, R. (2006) *Media and Morality; On the Rise of Mediapolis*, London: Polity Press.

Smith, A. (1759/1976) *The Theory of Moral Sentiments*, Indianapolis: Liberty.

Sontag, S. (2003) *Regarding the Pain of Others*, New York: Farrar, Straus and Giroux.

Stets, J.E. and Turner, J.H. (2006) *Handbook of the Sociology of Emotions*, New York: Springer.

Sznaider, N. (1998) 'The Sociology of Compassion: A Study in the Sociology of Morals', *Cultural Values*, 2(1): 117–139.

Tenenboim-Weinblatt, K. (2008) '"We will get through this together". Journalism, Trauma and the Israeli Disengagement from the Gaza Strip', *Media, Culture and Society*, 30(4): 495–513.

Tester, K. (2001) *Compassion, Morality and the Media*, Buckingham: Open University Press.

Thompson, J.B. (1995) *Media and Modernity; A Social Theory of the Media*, Oxford: Polity Press.

Turner, J. and Stets, J. (2005) *The Sociology of Emotions*, Cambridge: Cambridge University Press.

Velleman, J.D. (2003) 'Don't Worry, Feel Guilty', in Hatzimoysis, A. (ed.) *Philosophy and the Emotions*, Cambridge: Cambridge University Press.

Vorderer, P.A. and Hartmann, T. (2009) 'Entertainment and Enjoyment as Media Effects', in Bryant, J. and Oliver, M.B. (eds) *Media Effects. Advances in Theory and Research*, 3rd edn, New York: Taylor & Francis.

Walzer, M. (1994) *Thick and Thin. Moral Argument at Home and Abroad*, Notre Dame: University of Notre Dame Press.

Wastell, C. (2005) *Understanding Trauma and Emotion*, Berkshire: Open University Press.

Williams, J.S. (2001) *Emotion and Social Theory*, London: Sage Publications.

Williams, J.S. (2009) 'A "Neurosociology" of Emotion? Progress, Problems and Prospects', in Hopkins, D. *et al.* (eds) *Theorizing Emotions: Sociological Explorations and Applications*, Berlin: Campus.

Wilson, T. (1993) *Watching Television; Hermeneutics, Reception and Popular Culture*, Cambridge: Polity Press.

Wirth, W. and Schramm, H. (2005) 'Media and Emotions', *Communication Research Trends*, 24: 3–39.

Zelizer, B. (2002) 'Finding aids to the past: bearing personal witness to traumatic public events', *Media, Culture and Society*, 24(5): 697–714.

Zelizer, B. and Allan S. (eds) (2002) *Journalism After September 11*, London: Routledge.

Žižek, S. (1997) *The Plague of Fantasies*, London: Verso.

6 Media, migrations and transnational cultures

Tristan Mattelart

The literature on migrations and on diasporas has become, in the Anglo-Saxon academic field, since the end of the 1980s, one of the main places where are studied cultural transformations in times of globalization. In this perspective, contemporaneous identities and cultures tend to be presented as in a state of permanent flux, constantly evolving under the pressure of intercultural encounters. Media flows, along with people flows, are seen in these works as playing a central role: they are described as contributing actively to the advent of new transnational identities and cultures.

This literature has stimulated the rise of a new generation of academic research on media and migration. Breaking with studies analysing the representation of migrants in the main national media of their countries of residence, researchers now increasingly investigate in particular media reception processes among migrant homes and their accompanying transnational cultural practices.

The aim of this paper is to critically assess these new perspectives, by analysing some of the founding works that have given them birth. We will show first how these works, by criticizing the essentialist character of the concepts of national culture and national identity, have stressed the key role that transnational flows play in the reconfiguring of contemporary identities and cultures. And then we will study how these perspectives contributed to bring light to new ways of thinking about the relationship existing between media and migration. Finally, we will address a set of under-researched issues raised by media and migration flows.[1]

Transnational flows and the reconfiguring of cultures

British cultural studies were, from the end of the 1980s, one of the main academic places where concepts of national identity and national culture were deconstructed. One of the seminal books in this respect is Paul Gilroy's *There Ain't No Black in the Union Jack*. Writing in the British context of the late 1980s, where public discourses put the emphasis above all on the English and white components of the national identity, Paul Gilroy denounces in this book the way black minorities are presented as not belonging to the British nation. 'Blacks are represented in contemporary British politics and culture as external to and estranged from the imagined community that is the nation' (Gilroy, 1987: 153).

However, this conception of national culture, explains Gilroy, cannot be sustained in the postcolonial context, a context where people from former colonies settle, with their cultures, in the centre of the former empire. Against national-bounded frameworks used for thinking cultures, Paul Gilroy then puts the emphasis on the crucial role transnational flows have in the formation of these. The transoceanic circulation of black music exemplifies the cultural dynamics Paul Gilroy has in mind. Music coming from black America or the Caribbean offers indeed to the blacks in the United Kingdom, according to Paul Gilroy, 'raw materials for creative processes' during which these cultures are appropriated and adapted to local circumstances, producing 'syncretic' cultures, exerting their influence on British society well beyond British black cultures (Gilroy, 1987: 154–156).

In order to stress the important role transnational mixings play in the elaboration of identities and cultures, Paul Gilroy puts at the heart of his argument the notion of diaspora. A notion he introduces 'as an alternative to the different varieties of absolutisms which would confine culture in "racial", ethnic, or national essences' (Gilroy, 1987: 155). The notion of diaspora is also central to the book he devotes in 1993 to the *Black Atlantic*, whose objective is to produce an explicitly 'intercultural and transnational' research perspective. The 'Black Atlantic' is a metaphor used for describing this complex network of cultural links forged since the slavery days among blacks living in Africa, in Europe, in the Americas and in the Caribbean. And Paul Gilroy recounts 'the histories of borrowing, displacement, transformation, and continual reinscription' that the circulation of black diasporic musical cultures across the ocean encloses (Gilroy, 1993: 102).

These black cultures are diasporic, but they are also protest cultures: they are intimately linked to the fights waged by Blacks on both sides of the Atlantic. If Paul Gilroy condemns national-bounded frames of analysis, it is also because these prevent us from grasping the transnational dimensions of these fights. Indeed, he shows how black American 'struggles for civil rights, black power, racial equality or freedom from police harassment which are celebrated and transmitted by [black American] music' have fed black cultures in the United Kingdom (Gilroy, 1987: 198).

Paul Gilroy's theses have exerted an important influence on Stuart Hall. Writing in the same British context of the late 1980s and early 1990s, Stuart Hall is equally critical of the notion of national cultural identity. He accuses it of being an essentialist notion aiming at imposing a homogeneous dominant representation hiding the cultural diversities that comprise the nation. However, 'the processes of globalization' tend to put, explains Stuart Hall, this notion of national cultural identity 'under considerable pressure'. The advent of 'new global markets', the acceleration of migrations, or the increasingly transnational media flows have indeed eroded 'the nation-state and the national identities which are associated to it' (Hall, 1991a: 22–25). The 'relative decline, or erosion [...] of national identities as points of reference' in times of globalization offers then a favorable context to break with the 'old logics of identity', according to which identity is 'a kind of guarantee of authenticity'. It is time, presses Stuart Hall in the early 1990s, to think 'identities as never completed, never finished', as in process. 'Identity is always in the process of formation', fed as it is by intercultural contacts (Hall, 1991b: 42–47).

In accordance with Paul Gilroy's writings, the concept of diaspora is at the heart of Stuart Hall's theorization of cultural identities. The term diaspora is used here 'metaphorically not literally' to apprehend a conception of 'identity' which would be 'defined not by essence or purity, but by the recognition of a necessary heterogeneity and diversity; [...] by *hybridity*. Diaspora identities are those which are constantly producing and reproducing themselves anew, through transformation and difference'. In proposing this conception of identity, Stuart Hall has clearly in mind, like Paul Gilroy, 'the aesthetics of the "cross-overs", of "cut-and-mix" [...] which is the heart and soul of black music' (Hall, 1990: 235).

These arguments converge with those developed in the late 1980s and the early 1990s by the prominent American anthropologist James Clifford. Echoing the theses put forth by British cultural studies, James Clifford indeed also emphasizes, from another perspective, the need to deconstruct the concepts of identity and culture. The twentieth century 'has seen', he writes in *The Predicament of Culture*, 'a drastic expansion of mobility, including tourism, migrant labor, immigration, urban sprawl. More and more people "dwell" with the help of mass transit, automobiles, airplanes'. And in this 'interconnected world', the nature of culture should be reconsidered. 'Culture is a deeply compromised idea', claims Clifford – even if he admits that he 'cannot yet do without' – because it has too often been thought as a 'transcendent regime of authenticity'. Against this tendency, James Clifford proposes an ethnography 'straining for a concept that can preserve culture's differentiating functions'. 'In an interconnected world, one is always, to varying degrees, inauthentic.' Identity and culture should then be understood as 'conjectural, not essential', as 'inventive and mobile', as 'syncretic', 'mixed', as an 'inventive process' fed by transnational flows (Clifford, 1988: 5–15).

'Practices of displacement' have to be considered 'as constitutive of cultural meanings' pleads James Clifford in a subsequent book, *Routes*, published in 1993. And, in this context, the experiences of diasporas have to be seen as emblematic of the 'transnational identity formations' that are more and more common in an increasingly connected world (Clifford, 1993: 3, 247). This 'syncretic' theorization of identities and cultures has had important consequences on the ways of apprehending cultural contacts in times of globalization. As long as cultures were defined as highly homogeneous entities with fixed contours, transnational cultural flows – including people and media flows – were to be seen as endangering them. Now, with the new perspectives opened by cultural studies and anthropology, transnational flows are more and more seen as participating in the reconfiguring of local identities and cultures.

Another anthropologist, Arjun Appadurai, has been very influential in stressing the role transnational flows play in the elaboration of cultural identities. Transnational flows are indeed at the centre of the 'general theory of global cultural processes' he proposes. Arjun Appadurai is equally critical of nation-bounded categories mobilized for thinking identities and cultures. How could one continue to use those at a time when transnational flows of media and migration daily transcend 'local, national, and regional spaces'? His main hypothesis is that combined flows of media and migration play a central role in the reconfiguration of individuals' imagination. Individuals' imagined worlds are not national imagined worlds any more. Never have 'the images, scripts, models and narratives that came through mass mediation (in its realistic and fictional modes)' circulated so extensively, so quickly, offering 'new resources [...] for the construction of imagined selves and imagined worlds'. Migrations are not new, but when they are 'juxtaposed' with image flows, they create 'a new order of instability in the production of modern subjectivities' (Appadurai, 1996: 3–6).

In this context, 'the imagination has acquired a singular new power in social life'. Indeed, thanks to the 'rich, ever changing store of possible lives' presented by the media or told by migrants, 'more persons in more parts of the world consider a wider set of possible lives than they ever did before'. They are then able to compare their lives with those conveyed by 'moving images'. Imagination, far from being only a means for escaping reality, can then 'become the fuel for action', for contesting 'unjust rule[s]', for defending one's rights, or for finding new jobs in foreign countries, with 'higher wages' (Appadurai, 1996: 7, 53).

From media representation to media negotiation

With these new perspectives, the agenda of research on media and migration has been, at least partly, renewed. One of the main themes of investigation in this field was, in the early 1980s, the study of the representation of immigrants in the main national media of their countries of residence. These studies of representation are of the utmost importance: they unveil the mechanisms through which the media construct a national 'imagined community', to borrow the expression coined by Benedict Anderson (Anderson, 1983), in which the immigrant tends to be described as an Other, foreign to the nation.

Mapping this field, Simon Cottle synthesizes in 2000 some of the 'recurring research findings' from the 'considerable literature existing in both the UK and the US'. Media representations of ethnic minorities are marked, according to these works, by 'under-representation and

stereotypical characterization within entertainment genres and negative problem oriented portrayal within factuality and news forms, and a
tendency to ignore structural inequalities and lived racism experienced
by ethnic minorities in both'. Simon Cottle also stresses the tiny changes
that are occurring in dominant representations, showing for example
how 'the political agendas of "assimilation", "multiculturalism" and "anti-
racism" have informed the development of [new] media representations
across the years' (Cottle, 2000: 7, 9, 16). However, even if we take into
consideration these evolutions, the contrast remains strong between the
perspectives celebrating hybrid cultures and the conclusions of the studies
analysing media portrayals of ethnic populations in Western countries.

Nonetheless, with the new perspectives opened by cultural studies and
anthropology, the agenda of the research on media and migration has
been, at least partly, renewed. Attention of researchers has been more
particularly redirected from the study of the representation of ethnic
populations to the analysis of media consumption practices among
migrant families. The new emphasis put on the issue of diasporas in the
English-speaking academic world has indeed coincided with the development of the researches on active audiences, also largely influenced by
cultural studies.

One of the pioneering studies dealing with this issue is the ethnographic study of media consumption conducted by Marie Gillespie
among Punjabi families living in Southall, in south London. The author
inscribes her work in the continuity of the 'diasporic perspective' offered
by Paul Gilroy, investigating identity transformations under the pressure
of 'cross-cultural exchange and interactions' (Gillespie, 1995: 7).

Doing her fieldwork in the late 1980s and the early 1990s, Marie
Gillespie first analyses how the parents or the grandparents use the
videocassette recorder as a medium to show mainly Hindi films to their
children and thus as a medium through which to reassert the necessity
of conforming to Punjabi cultural traditions. The problem being that
parental efforts 'are subverted and "diverted" by young people' who
also use the television set to watch Western soap operas that convey very
different cultural values and, of course, more dangerous values in the
eyes of their parents. Marie Gillespie analyses then the cultural negotiations of young Punjabis in front of their television sets. She shows more
particularly how they use Western programmes as a 'cultural resource'.
Scrutinizing the moral norms, behaviours or ways of life depicted in these
programmes, young Punjabis exploit them to articulate their own 'aspirations for change'. Soaps 'offer alternative sets of families which young
people use to compare and contrast, judge and evaluate and, in some
cases, attempt to critique and transform aspects of their own family life'
(Gillespie, 1995: 143–162).

Marie Gillespie did her fieldwork just before the outbreak of direct-
to-home satellite television. The rise of satellite dishes constitutes an
important cultural fact for migrants. If, before satellite television, they

had to watch the channels of their country of residence, they can, thanks to its rise, watch the programmes of their countries or their regions of origin. Illustrative of this importance is the fact that, in many European countries, migrant families were among the first to buy satellite dishes. This spread of satellite dishes in migrant homes has raised concerns in different European countries. Indeed, these dishes have often been criticized for nurturing the development of 'parallel societies' and 'ghettos', thus impeding migrants' integration (Hafez, 2007; Hargreaves and Mahdjoub, 1997; Ferjani, 2007). Reception studies carried out in this field have nonetheless come to relativize these fears.

Among the first works studying satellite television reception in migrants' homes, there is the qualitative survey carried out in the mid-1990s by Alec Hargreaves and Dalila Mahdjoub within families of mainly Maghrebi origin in the south of France. In consonance with Gillespie's study, they show that first-generation respondents demonstrate a high 'desire to see more of what was going on in their home country' and that, among all channels available, they prefer those emanating from the country of origin, but that they also 'continue to watch a fair amount of French television, including news broadcasts' (Hargreaves and Mahdjoub, 1997: 473–474).

Interestingly, Alec Hargreaves and Dalila Mahdjoub also stress, following Gillespie, generation gaps. Viewing habits of younger respondents 'remain', they write, 'dominated by French channels', where US programmes abound. As such, young minority ethnic viewers embrace, as millions of other French viewers do, 'popular cultural forms which are at root more American with a French accent than Maghrebi or Turkish' (Hargreaves and Mahdjoub, 1996: 475).

Other reception studies carried out in France subsequently converge with these results. Kamal Hamidou stresses, in his qualitative inquiry conducted in 2003 among viewers of Maghrebi origins living near Paris or in Metz, the fact that 'the French public of Arab satellite channels doesn't constitute a homogeneous whole whose consumption practices would be dictated by community factors'. He distinguishes older viewers (above 45), more inclined to watch exclusively Arab channels, from those aged between 25 and 45, having a 'mixed' consumption of both Arab and French channels, from younger viewers who, mainly, only watch French television. One of the main factors, apart from age, explaining the viewing of Arab channels being, according to Hamidou, 'the position they occupy in [French] society'. Viewers of these channels tend to be more represented 'among those who feel they're rejected by society' (Hamidou, 2005: 101–103; see also Ferjani, 2007).

Kevin Robins and Asu Aksoy have gone a little bit further in deconstructing the idea that transnational television would integrate their 'diasporic viewers' in an isolated media space dominated by the culture of their country of origin. Studying the way transnational Turkish television is received in the homes of Turkish-speaking migrants in London, they show how these channels provide their viewers an ordinary link with Turkey. Television programmes are, they write, 'in a continuum with the (equally common) availability of food, clothes or furnishings from Turkey. [...] Television brings the ordinary, banal reality of Turkish life to the migrants living in London'. And the 'banal' character of this televisual environment is one key to understand its importance (Aksoy and Robins, 2003: 9-10).

Turkish television allows its viewers in London to live in synchrony with Turkish realities. It brings 'the mundane, everyday reality of Turkey' into each migrant home. And this daily televised contact with Turkey prevents its London viewers from developing an idealized image of the country they left, or from developing uncritical nostalgic feelings towards it. As such, 'transnational Turkish television is an agent of cultural de-mythologisation' (Aksoy and Robins, 2003: 10).

Asu Aksoy and Kevin Robins also urge us to break with the idea that television practices of Turkish migrants in London would be dictated by some 'ethno-cultural' belonging. Turkish viewers are looking for the same ordinary pleasures as those pursued by other British viewers. 'Like any other viewers, Turkish speaking viewers in Europe are also in search of broadcast television that is meaningful and effortlessly available. They are also wanting – and to a quite large extent finding – the pleasures of familiarity and confirmation' (Aksoy and Robins, 2003: 16).

But, if they are seeking ordinary pleasures, Turkish migrants live nonetheless a very specific cultural experience. Turkish viewers in London daily 'operate in and across two cultural spaces (at least) – Turkish and British' and, connoisseurs of both television cultures, they are constantly comparing both. As such, they have developed a 'banal transnationalism': 'Turkish migrants cannot recover the simple perspective of monocultural (national) vision. They are compelled to think about Turkish culture in light of other cultural experiences and possibilities' (Aksoy and Robins, 2003: 19).

The scenario sketched by Asu Aksoy and Kevin Robins is not univocally a scenario of ordinary cosmopolitanism. Taking part in a collective research project analysing news reception among migrant homes in the United Kingdom in the aftermath of 11 September 2001, Asu Aksoy shows that Turkish viewers have often been much more active in the decoding of September 11 than 'monocultural' publics. Oscillating between Turkish channels and British ones, Turkish viewers, she explains, have developed, thanks to their 'cultural ambivalence', a highly 'skeptical stance' towards these diverse channels, and have had thus 'to do a lot of thinking by themselves' to give meaning to the events (Aksoy, 2006).

However, all the viewers do not benefit in the same way from this situation of cultural ambivalence. Asu Aksoy indeed opposes the 'flexible thinking' that sustains some viewers, fed by a plurality of information sources, to a 'dogmatic thinking' sustained by other viewers embedded in a cultural environment shaped 'by experiences of persecution and dogmas about persecution'. In this instance, 'the potentially creative possibilities that might emerge from the position of cultural ambivalence are closed down' (Aksoy, 2006: 939–941).

Political economy of hybrid cultures

The importance of the perspectives opened by these works analysing media reception among migrant homes needs to be acknowledged. They have prompted researchers to study the complex processes of cultural negotiations operating within migrant homes. They have succeeded in relativizing the fears of those who think that transnational television could create 'media ghettos' in migrant homes in Western Europe. However, they are not without limits.

Charles Husband has in particular expressed his anxieties in 1994 about the risk, for these studies embedded in 'the vision of the actively hermeneutic audience', of generating 'an overly optimistic vision of the media politics of multiethnic societies'. Indeed, migrant viewers, however active they are in front of their television sets, 'cannot of themselves transcend the pernicious limitations of the structural social spaces that they occupy'. Hence, his call to continue to analyse 'the stereotypical and ideological representation of ethnic minorities in the mass media'. Hence, also, his call for more studies on media production: 'It is now essential that research energies should be applied to examining the situation of ethnic minorities as active agents in media production' (Husband, 1994: 13–14).

These still understudied media produced by and/or for migrants contribute, sometimes in an unnoticeable way, to expand the variety of the media landscape in Western countries. 'The domination that some major media seem to exert' in these countries hides 'the extraordinary complexity and diversity of the media world' created by these 'minority', 'ethnic', 'migrant' or 'community' media (Marthoz, 2001: 189). As implied by the variety of terms used to designate them, these media form a very heterogeneous whole: from the powerful Hispanic network television Univisión to, 'at the other end of the spectrum, [...] indigenous people's media, migrant workers' media, refugees' media', sum up John Downing and Charles Husband. Beyond this variety, these media taken as a whole, each in its own way, offer a plurality of voices that would not otherwise exist. 'In carving out communication spaces specifically targeted at minority-ethnic publics, [...] media with minority-ethnic content significantly complicate the national picture' (Downing and Husband, 2005: 55–56).

In the television field, with the advent of cable and satellite, and its corollary, the increased segmentation of audiences, new minority channels have been created. Hamid Naficy stresses in this context the development of a new model of television, that of 'decentralized global narrowcasting', where he includes the new channels aimed at minorities, largely opposed to the model of 'centralized global broadcasting', represented by private or public channels belonging to 'multinational and transnational media conglomerates and television networks' like ABC, CNN, BBC, or NHK (Naficy, 1998: 51–52).

Studying this 'narrowcasting in diaspora' allows Hamid Naficy to reintroduce political economy in the analysis of the relations between media and migrations, and in the analysis of the hybrid cultures they generate. One of the seminal books in this respect is the one that he devoted to Iranian television in Los Angeles in the 1980s. In *The Making of Exile Cultures*, Hamid Naficy scrutinizes the dynamics through which a 'hybrid' culture is created, borrowing at the same time from the country of origin and from the host country. He shows more particularly how Iranian television in Los Angeles has produced, on one hand, 'a symbolic and fetishized private hermetically sealed electronic *communitas* infused with home, past, memory, loss, nostalgia, longing for return, and the communal self', and how it is, on the other hand, marked by the consumerist culture of the host country. The result of this dynamic is a popular culture that 'is informed by politics, themes, languages, and products of the homeland' and that, at the same time, 'borrows syncretically from the host society's technology, consumer ideology, marketing techniques, and forms and practices of narration and aesthetics'. However, the balance between the two main components of this syncretic culture is unstable. And Hamid Naficy shows how 'the infusion of the host into the syncretic mix becomes stronger, gradually replacing much of the original contents with consumer ideology and products. This is because popular cultures are structurally linked with and promote consumerism' (Naficy, 1993: 58–59). By introducing political economy in the analysis of hybrid cultures, Naficy contributes to a better understanding of the way they operate and offers a more empirically grounded picture of their realities than some of the earlier quoted works.

Transnational television beamed at migrant audiences features prominently among the channels representing this 'narrowcasting in diaspora'. Their number has considerably increased since the 1980s. They do not escape the criticism of commodification either. In an article where he analyses some of these ethnic transnational broadcasters, Karim H. Karim stresses the fact that many of them have adopted 'the market model of mainstream broadcasting'. And he goes as far as saying that 'apart from certain differences in the mode of narrative, the only major difference seems to be in the language and cultures of the content' ... which shouldn't be seen as negligible! (Karim, 1998: 12).

If this commercial model of broadcasting seems to be widespread, its public service counterpart may be less so. In a book devoted to *The Development of Ethnic Minority Media in Western Democracies*, Charles Husband notices that 'the track record of broadcasting media carrying the public service broadcasting imprimatur has been unimpressive'. And, without considering that 'commercial media and the profit motive [are] inimical to ethnic minority media', this situation prompts him to express doubts 'as to the range and quality of media that would be available were purely commercial considerations the sole criteria' (Husband, 1994: 145).

As for transnational television broadcasting to their diasporic publics, they raise other important issues, more particularly for the policies of European public broadcasters. For years, these public broadcasters have tried, not without difficulties, to improve the representation of ethnic minorities on their screens. Nonetheless, migrants' consumption of diasporic channels challenges these policies. Now, they find, as Kevin Robins notes, 'in transnational broadcasting the kinds of services that they have been missing in national broadcasting schedules'. As such, these transnational developments pose a new set of important questions for public broadcasting that remain largely without answers: 'How can these new transnational services be incorporated into models of the public broadcasting sphere? What is the significance of these new media for public service ideals, nationally but also increasingly at a European scale?' (Robins, 2006: 154–155).

Anyway, the fact that many ethnic transnational broadcasters share the same commercial model as mainstream broadcasters leads Karim H. Karim to qualify analyses of the 'resistance cultures' of diasporas. The 'adoption of the market model of mainstream broadcasting' by these minority media appears, he writes, 'to belie the cultural studies view of diasporic media resisting dominant structures and discourses' (Karim, 1998: 8–15).

Hamid Naficy also expresses his doubts about the resistant potential of commercial diasporic media. He considers that even if the television of the Iranian exile in Los Angeles and the popular culture it encloses have been able to produce a 'cultural resistance' for some time, 'their commercially driven nature served ultimately to recuperate their resistive and counterhegemonic spin, turning them chiefly into social agencies of assimilation'. Hamid Naficy stresses then the 'ambivalence' of hybridity, an ambivalence that resides in the fact that hybridity is more a mode of appropriation of dominant cultures than a mode of contestation. What could be seen as hybridity's contestation power erodes over time, argues Naficy, and turns into 'co-optation'. 'To avoid co-optation, opposition must be defined not in terms of or in reaction to that which the dominant has formulated, but in contradiction to it and proactively against it. The problem with hybridity is that it is formulated to be forever reactive, not proactive' (Naficy, 1993: 192–194).

Transnational media, migration and countries of origin

The literature on media and migration, privileging the study of migrants' media consumption, has neglected other important issues. Analysing above all cultural negotiations within ethnic families living in Western countries, it has deprived the study of the combined flows of people and media of one important part of their dynamic. Focusing on migrants' media practices in Northern countries, this literature has largely under-researched the role media can play in Southern countries, prior to the emigration process, in fuelling the desire to emigrate. Indeed, the emphasis Arjun Appadurai has put on 'the force of imagination' nourished by the media, considered as powerful mobility multipliers, has not given rise to much fieldwork.

Among the rare ethnographic studies tackling this question there is the one carried out by Tarik Sabry among young Amazighs living in the Moroccan Atlas. Their 'desire to emigrate to the West', he shows, 'is the product of interplay between socio-economic and symbolic dimensions'. It is of course fed by the harsh economic difficulties young Amazighs daily face, but also by the images of Moroccan television, window on Western realities, and the outward signs of wealth displayed by émigrés coming back to their village. Through these contacts, young Amazighs structure their 'mental geography of the West' in an undeniably positive way, associating life north of the Mediterranean with ideas of happiness, leisure and riches. No matter if these representations work as a 'fetish that conceals the hardship, alienation and exploitation of the Moroccan worker in Europe [...] and acts therefore as myth' (Sabry, 2004).

Another piece of ethnographic research studying the way television can fuel emigration dreams is the one conducted by Nicola Mai among young Albanians. He shows how wealthy public and private terrestrial Italian television, widely received in Albania, spread, for years, in this country, luxuriant images of Western consumer society. It is thus quite natural that in the early 1990s, after the downfall of Tirana's regime, young Albanians, 'driven by economic necessity to be sure, but lured by images of success provided by the imaginary world of television', tried at all costs to reach 'the country that fuelled their hopes and desires'. Disillusions were as high as the illusions created by small screen images. Young Albanians' testimonies gathered by Nicola Mai reveal indeed the violence with which Italian 'television's fairy tale promises' vanished through the contact with reality. As 'the idealised image of Italy as a landscape of material wealth and freedom' recedes, he notes, young Albanians transfer their hopes to new destinations: the USA, Canada or Australia. 'Countries they have come to know once again nearly exclusively through television programmes and in which they are increasingly imagining their futures' (Mai, 2001: 95, 104).

If these studies converge to a certain extent with Arjun Appadurai's analyses emphasizing 'the work of imagination' nourished by the media, they add nonetheless one important element: their mystificatory power that is made evident when migrants land in their 'host' country.

However, if the small screen can fuel migratory projects, it can also dissuade them, since it shows to emigration candidates how migrants are received and treated in destination countries. With the satellite dish, problems raised by the representation of migrants in the media of Western countries become transnationalized. Studying the spread of satellite dishes in Algeria in the 1990s, Lotfi Madani describes in this manner the way main domestic French channels received in North Africa 'not only relay but also reinforce the stereotype of the Muslim-Arab-migrant as an Other, wholly and irremediably different' and potentially dangerous (Madani, 2002: 198).

Another issue that is still under-researched in the field of the studies on media and migration is the issue of the political use of transnational media by exile groups. Yet, communication means have, for a long time, increased exile organizations' ability to influence at distance the political life of their country of origin. In one of the first books analysing this issue, Annabelle Sreberny and Ali Mohammadi stress the changes brought by media transnationalization on the nature of political exile. 'Exiled political activists no longer wait for events to change so that they can return home, but instead can propagandize to change conditions from outside their country, a deterritorialization of politics'. If exiles can organize communication networks to send materials home, they can also use them to 'try to mobilize international public opinion to take up their case in international public forums' (Sreberny-Mohammadi and Mohammadi, 1994: 29).

In their book, where they study media's contribution to the Iranian revolution, Annabelle Sreberny and Ali Mohammadi show how the Ayatollah Khomeini used, in his successive exiles, communication means to address his fellow citizens. They recount how, after he left Najaf, in Iraq, for Neauphle-le-Château, near Paris, in October 1978, he benefitted from better telecommunication infrastructures and how he built, thanks to these, a network through which his speeches were broadcast by telephone to be duplicated in Iran by audio cassette recorders working 24 hours a day, and to be widely circulated (Sreberny-Mohammadi and Mohammadi, 1994: 119).

Linda Basch, Nina Glick Schiller and Cristina Szanton Blanc have for their part documented the increased influence capacity that migrants can have when living in Western countries, in nerve centres of world media.

> Transmigrants [living in the US] are well positioned to challenge leaders in their countries of origin or establish themselves as national leaders because of their ability to wage battles for public opinion that can have international reverberations. In addition to having their own media, transmigrants have access to reporters for US radio, television and newspapers and US media are increasingly global with stations like Cable News Network broadcasting throughout the world (Basch *et al.*, 1994: 274–281).

And the authors stress the way Haitian and Philippine diasporas in the US have succeeded in mobilizing American public opinion against the Duvalier and Marcos regimes, and in establishing communication networks that contributed to the fall of these two dictatorships (Basch *et al.*, 1994: 274).

When examining the way exile groups use resources to influence the politics in their countries of origin, it's important to take into account the role played by the state. In much of the writings devoted to the issue of diasporas, the emphasis is put, above all, on transnational flows. As such, these analyses tend to converge with the theses on cultural globalization that see the state as losing more and more of its relevance. Nonetheless, the stress that is put on transnational flows should not overshadow the enduring importance of the state. The way some Cuban-American exile groups have, in the 1980s and in the 1990s, successfully lobbied the American government to obtain the creation of radio and television broadcasting to Cuba – Radio and Television Martí – to try to undermine the Havana regime exemplifies this (Mattelart, 2002).

Another study illustrating the enduring importance of the state, despite the increasing transnational flows, is the one Amir Hassanpour devoted to the case of transfrontier Kurdish television, where he examines the sophisticated strategies elaborated against it by the Turkish state. There is no doubt that the first Kurdish channel – Med TV, created in 1995 – represented a real danger in the eyes of Ankara: 'Med TV worked as the national television of the Kurds. It threatened the Turkish state's single coherent sovereign presence in politically and culturally significant ways' (Hassanpour, 2003: 81). Accordingly, Ankara responded to this perceived danger with intensive diplomatic activity aimed at European governments that resulted in the closing down of Med TV in 1999, soon replaced by Medya TV ... succeeded in 2004 by Roj TV (Akpinar, 2007).

These studies serve as a useful counterpoint to the writings claiming 'the emergence of an open, fluid, contingent and uncertain world' where hybrid cultures would flourish. 'Much more than a war of meanings and identities', writes Amir Hassanpour about the conflict between the Turkish state and Kurdish TV, 'this was a conflict between two nationalisms – one that achieved state power and one that struggles for statehood' (Hassanpour, 2003: 82). Indeed, far from producing only hybrid cultures, migration can also fuel the development of what Benedict Anderson has called 'long-distance nationalism' (Anderson, 1998: 68–74).

Conclusion

The new perspectives opened by cultural studies and anthropology have been effective in challenging essentialist conceptions of national cultural identities and in stressing the important role transnational flows play in their elaboration. However, these perspectives have also probably gone too far, celebrating the advent of new transnational identities and cultures without sufficiently considering the social, economic and political conditions of their production.

As we have tried to suggest here, for understanding the issues raised by the combined role of transnational media and migration flows in all their complexity, one needs to complement the new insights brought by cultural studies and anthropology with perspectives that should be more informed by social, economic and political structures and realities.

Note

1 For a more exhaustive overview, see Mattelart, 2007.

References

Akpinar, Z. (2007) 'L'État turc face aux télévisions transfrontières kurdes', in Mattelart, T. (ed.) *Médias, migrations et cultures transnationales*, Paris-Bruxelles: Ina-De Boeck.

Aksoy, A. (2006) 'Transnational virtues and cool loyalties: Responses of Turkish-speaking migrants in London to September 11', *Journal of Ethnic and Migration Studies*, 32 (6): 923–946.

Aksoy, A. and Robins, K. (2003) 'Banal transnationalism; the difference that television makes', in Karim, K.H. (ed.) *The Media of Diaspora*, London: Routledge. Available: <http://www.transcomm.ox.ac.uk/working%20papers/WPTC-02-08%20Robins.pdf>.

Anderson, B. (1983) *Imagined Communities*, London: Verso.

Anderson, B. (1998) *The Spectre of Comparisons; Nationalism, Southeast Asia and the World*, London: Verso.

Appadurai, A. (1996) *Modernity at Large. Cultural Dimensions of Globalization*, Minneapolis: University of Minnesota Press.

Basch, L., Schiller, G.N. and Blanc, S.C. (1994) *Nations Unbound. Transnational Projects, Postcolonial Predicaments, and Deterritorialized Nation-States*, Amsterdam: Gordon and Breach Publishers.

Clifford, J. (1988) *The Predicament of Culture. Twentieth-Century Ethnography, Literature, and Art*, Cambridge: Harvard University Press.

Clifford, J. (1997) *Routes. Travel and Translation in the Late Twentieth Century*, Cambridge: Harvard University Press.

Cottle, S. (ed.) (2000) *Ethnic Minorities and the Media: Changing Cultural Boundaries*, Buckingham: Open University Press.

Downing, J. and Husband, C. (2005) *Representing 'Race'. Racisms, Ethnicities and Media*, London: Sage.

Ferjani, R. (2007) 'Les télévisions arabophones en France: une transnationalité postcoloniale', in Mattelart, T. (ed.) *Médias, migrations et cultures transnationales*, Paris-Bruxelles: Ina-De Boeck.

Gillespie, M. (1995) *Television, Ethnicity, and Cultural Change*, London: Routledge.

Gilroy, P. (1987) [2nd edn 1991] *'There Ain't No Black in the Union Jack'; The Cultural Politics of Race and Nation*, Chicago: The University of Chicago Press.

Gilroy, P. (1993) *The Black Atlantic. Modernity and Double Consciousness*, Cambridge: Harvard University Press.

Hafez, K. (2007) *The Myth of Media Globalization*, Cambridge: Polity Press.

Hall, S. (1991a) [2nd edn 1997] 'The local and the global: Globalization and ethnicity', in King, A.D. (ed.) *Culture, Globalization and the World System, Contemporary Conditions for the Representation of Identity*, London: MacMillan.

Hall, Stuart (1991b) [1997] 'Old and new identities, old and new ethnicities', in King, A.D. (ed.) *Culture, Globalization and the World System; Contemporary Conditions for the Representation of Identity*; London: Macmillan.

Hall, S. (1990) 'Cultural Identity and Diaspora', in Rutherford, J. (ed.) *Community, Culture, Difference*, London: Lawrence and Wishart.

Hamidou, K. (2005) 'Médias du cœur et médias de la raison. La socialisation des migrants en question', *Questions de Communication*, 8: 93–112.

Hargreaves, A. and Mahdjoub, D. (1997) 'Satellite television viewing among ethnic minorities in France', *European Journal of Communication*, 12(4): 459–477.

Hassanpour, A. (2003) 'Diaspora, homeland and communication technologies', in Karim, K.H. (ed.) *The Media of Diaspora*, London: Routledge.

Husband, C. (ed.) (1994) *A Richer Vision; The Development of Ethnic Minority Media in Western Democracies*, Paris-London: UNESCO-John Libbey.

Karim, K.H. (1998) 'From ethnic media to global media: Transnational communication networks among diasporic communities'. Available: <http://www.trans-comm.ox.ac.uk/working%20papers/karim.pdf>.

Madani, L. (2002) 'L'antenne parabolique en Algérie, entre dominations et resistances', in Mattelart, T. (ed.) *La mondialisation des médias contre la censure. Tiers Monde et audiovisuel sans frontières*, Paris-Bruxelles: Ina-De Boeck.

Mai, N. (2001) '"Italy is beautiful". The role of Italian television in Albanian migration to Italy', in King, R. and Wood, N. (eds) *Media and Migration; Constructions of Mobility and Difference*, London: Routledge.

Marthoz, J.P. (2001) 'Médias et "va-et-vient" communicationnel des diasporas', in Blion, R. and Rigoni, I. (eds) *D'un voyage à l'autre; Des voix de l'immigration pour un développement pluriel*, Paris: Karthala-Institut Panos.

Mattelart, T. (2002) 'Radio et Télévision Martí: des armes audiovisuelles contre Fidel Castro', in Mattelart, T. (ed.) *La mondialisation des médias contre la censure. Tiers Monde et audiovisuel sans frontières*, Paris-Bruxelles: Ina-De Boeck.

Mattelart, T. (ed.) (2007) *Médias, migrations et cultures transnationales*, Paris-Bruxelles: Ina-De Boeck.

Naficy, H. (1993) *The Making of Exile Cultures. Iranian Television in Los Angeles*, Minneapolis: University of Minnesota Press.

Naficy, H. (1998) [2nd edn 2003] 'Narrowcasting in Diaspora. Middle Eastern Television in Los Angeles', in Karim, K.H. (ed.) *The Media of Diaspora*, London: Routledge.

Robins, K. (2006) 'Transnational media, cultural diversity and new public cultures', in Robins, K. (ed.) *The Challenge of Transcultural Diversities; Transversal Study on the Theme of Cultural Policy and Cultural Diversity*, Strasbourg: Council of Europe Publishing.

Sabry, T. (2004) 'Young Amazighs, the land of Eromen and Pamela Anderson as the embodiment of modernity', *Westminster Papers in Communication and Culture*, 1 (1): 41–48.

Sreberny-Mohammadi, A. and Mohammadi, A. (1994) *Small Media, Big Revolution. Communication, Culture and the Iranian Revolution*, Minneapolis: University of Minnesota Press.

Part II
Communication in the digital era

7 From mass to networked communication

Gustavo Cardoso

This paper argues that one can identify a number of changes in the context of communication in our societies and that those changes can be interpreted in the light of the emergence of a new communication model: a model that is no longer based on the idea of 'mass' but one of 'network'. In addition to the structural change and the forces that shape it, one can also identify a set of contextual changes that are, at times, the result of appropriation of this new networked communication model and, at other times, a manifestation of the very development of a new media system with a new identity. On the following pages I will enumerate the main characteristics of this new communication model (Cardoso, 2008) and also highlight, amongst other things, what are considered to be the main manifestations of change of context or, if we prefer, of present futures, in the context of communication, its technologies, appropriations and uses.

A new communication model

All societies are characterized by communicational models and not just informational models (Wolton, 1999; Colombo, 1993; Himanen, 2006; Castells, 2006; Cardoso, 2006). Our information societies have witnessed the emergence of a new communication model: a fourth model that one can add to the three preceding models and can be put in chronological order in terms of its cycles of social affirmation (Ortoleva, 2004). The first model is defined as interpersonal communication, which takes the form of the two-way exchange between two or more persons in a group. The second model, which is equally deeply rooted in our societies, is one-to-many communication, where an individual sends one single message to a limited group of persons. And the third model, with which we have less experience in historical terms, is mass communication, where, thanks to the use of specific mediation technologies, one single message can be sent to a mass of people: it is forwarded to an audience of an unknown size that is, therefore, unlimited at the outset (Cardoso, 2008; Thompson, 1995). The communication model of our contemporary society is shaped by the capacity of communication globalization, together with the networked interconnection of mass and interpersonal media in what Castells (2007) describes as self–mass communication, and, accordingly, by the emergence of networked mediation. The organization of uses and networked interconnection of the media within this communicational model seem to be directly related to the different degrees of interactivity that our current media allow (Cardoso, 2008).

If it is true that we have built communication models in our societies, it is equally true that the main *communication paradigms* format what a given media system will be (Cardoso, 2008). Our current communication paradigms seem to be built around a rhetoric essentially based on the importance of the moving picture, combined with the availability of the new dynamics of access to information, with the innovating role now also being handed over from the providers, publishers and broadcasters to the users and with profound alterations to the news and entertainment models.

Our contents – be they news, information or entertainment – seem to have changed thanks to the presence of contents provided by the media users and not just the media companies themselves, giving rise to the co-existence of different information models for different audiences. But not only has the news information changed, entertainment has as well. The innovation in the entertainment models is reflected in the availability of user-generated contents and also in the changes introduced by the media companies, namely in their search for new contents and 'formats', their experimentation with the erasure of borders between traditional programme genres and the new approaches to social values such as privacy and reserve, together with changes in the social appropriation of time, space and ethics, all of which are reflected in the way stories are told and scripts written.

The communication model developed in information societies, where the prevailing social organization model is the network (Castells, 2000), is *networked communication*. It is one that does not replace the preceding models, but instead interconnects them, producing new communication formats and also allowing for new forms of facilitating empowerment and, thus, communicative autonomy.

In the information societies, where the network is a central organizational element, a new communicational model has been taking shape. This communicational model is characterized by the fusion of interpersonal and mass communication, connecting audiences, broadcasters and publishers under one networked media matrix.

In a network communication environment, mediation (Silverstone, 2006), the media diets (Aroldi and Colombo, 2003), the media matrixes (Meyrovitz, 1985) and the media system itself (Ortoleva, 2004) have all been transformed. These transformations in the relationships between the different media, which are now more *networked* than they are *converging* – be it in terms of hardware, service or networks – make mediation an integrated experience, combining the use of different media: from the telephone to television, from the newspaper to the video game, from the Internet to radio, from cinema to the mobile phone, and placing the users, their practices and the literacies they need, once again at the centre of analysis (Livingstone, 1999; Cardoso, 2007; Cardoso, 2008).

Given these phenomena, one can affirm that we are dealing with a new media system organized around two networks and their respective central nodes: television and the Internet: television for low interactivity practices and the Internet for high interactivity practices (Kim and Sawhney, 2002). All the other technologies connect to (and interact with) these two networks. Even if this relationship is, at times, established between technologies that share the same technical environments (for example, when someone establishes a link between two webpages), the form it takes depends on the user's choices: when someone votes by SMS message (e.g., to a radio programme or a newspaper) and that choice is read or published in paper form, we have communication established between different media in a network based on the interactions between users, mass media companies and, perhaps, regulators. This example illustrates what network communication is: a constant reformulation of the relations between the media forms, interconnecting interpersonal communication media (such as SMS, the mobile phone and email) and mass media (such as TV, radio, online newspapers and Internet forums).

The network communication model is, thus, shaped by three change-inducing forces, which are:

1   the processes of communication globalization;
2   the networking of the mass and interpersonal media and the consequent emergence of network mediation;
3   the differing degrees of interactivity made available to the users.

In this process of change one can likewise find the emergence of new communication paradigms that comprise a generalizing rhetoric influencing all the media dimensions and levels (Cardoso, 2008). This paper seeks to go beyond a characterization of the emerging communicational model and the forces bringing it about, and the discussion on the new communicational paradigms, to identify the signs of the change of context that may strengthen or reformulate the new emerging *networked communication* structure. In other words, it will deal with *present futures* in the context of communication and its technologies, appropriations and uses.

Hello information, goodbye news!

The first identifiable trend is the change in the public and shared ideal of the 'informed citizen'. The early twenty-first century ideal of the informed citizen is no longer based on reading. This does not mean that we don't read newspapers any more, but that the newspaper is no longer one of the two central nodes in the network communication model, which are now occupied by television and the Internet.

The cultural change in terms of what an 'informed person' is generally considered to be and the consequences of this change are present at all levels in the current media system. Robert Picard (2006) suggests the existence of five major trends that are changing the face of the media in our societies. The abundance of the range of channels, titles and technologies to distribute these contents is one of these trends. Another is a kind of response to the first – the fragmentation and polarization of consumption by audiences, which are distributed across ever-growing numbers of channels, titles and technologies. The third trend is the development of portfolios. Portfolios are developed because the income per unit sold is decreasing and owning just one medium is becoming a problem. Having a range of products reduces the risk and helps achieve economies of scale. The fourth trend is that media companies are steadily falling in the ranking of the largest companies (nowadays, there are no media companies amongst the 100 largest corporations in the USA or amongst the 500 largest in the world). Last, but not least, Picard (2006) suggests that a change in the balance of power between the producer and consumer is taking place. One sign of this trend is the fact that, in general, for every euro that the media companies earn through advertising, three more euros come from direct payments by the consumer (there are many examples of this, from pay-per-view television to products one can buy together with newspapers).

I would suggest a sixth trend, one that is eminently cultural in nature: what is valued today is not access to news (be it in the form of TV news programmes, half-hourly radio news updates or from the newspapers), but information. This is not to say that news is not important, for it continues to be as important as before and will always play a central role in our societies. What we are now witnessing is that we have gone from a world in which we considered it of central importance in the life of citizens that they inform themselves about what goes on in the world (from football to politics and culture) to one where the ideal is that the citizen is informed in order to produce knowledge, so that he can be a better worker, cost the state less and be more socially and politically participative.

One only has to think of the buzzwords we have adopted as central to our societies, such as 'information society' and 'knowledge society'. But buzzwords and slogans are never enough; if they are not put into practice they do not change anything. And things have changed. They have changed because the Internet arrived and, a decade on, has reached between 40 per cent and 90 per cent of the population in the more developed countries (WIP, 2006). The traditional news in the newspapers, and on television and radio, has inherited the notion that it is important to keep abreast of what's going on in the world so as to be not caught off-guard and be able to react accordingly (academics in the field of communication have added to this the idea that one must have mass media to maintain the social union bonds of a population in a given territory, an idea that is open to discussion). The Internet, on the other hand, has inherited another, more academic, tradition – that it is of fundamental importance to be informed so as to be able to anticipate what may happen. In other words, one must produce knowledge (whatever it may be about, from current affairs to the most eccentric tastes and most ethically dubious interests) to understand and anticipate, and to be always one step ahead. Here we are, of course, talking about ideal situations and the reader, viewer or listener of the news or the person consulting information online does not always think in this way. However, we must understand that the emergence of a different technology, with a different way of dealing with information, has led to changes that have in turn given rise to trends, which, in turn, will change the face of the media (in already perceptible ways and other ways not yet foreseeable). We may argue that the gratuity of information on the Internet is also a new development and that this is maybe more important than the cultural idea of the importance of information, but gratuity (based on advertising) already was the most common way of providing news. After all, have television and radio not accustomed us to this for over fifty years? The Internet would not have changed so much the way we perceive the function of information if television itself had not changed so much over the last two decades. If it had not become neo-television (Caseti and Odin, 1990), investing more and more heavily in entertainment, it would be doubtful that the Internet would have been able to so easily change our perceptions. Why? Because television is the most widespread technology and news programmes take up only two to three broadcasting hours a day and are a minority presence during prime time.

So what is the ideal of the informed citizen at the beginning of this century? My suggestion is that an informed citizen is someone who knows how to generate knowledge from all the news information available from the different media, applying differing depths of analysis, and who knows how to cross this information with further-reaching analyses on different matters. In other words, it is someone who knows how to, and can, see the news on different television channels – in his own language and in English – and who surfs the net and reads foreign news on domestic matters and also reads the news produced in his own country online. An informed person is one who can consult media, exchange ideas with friends on these the matters in question, seeking more information, and also consult what others write and publish about those matters elsewhere in his own country and around the world. Obviously, an informed person is one who informs himself on (and normally only on) what he is interested in at a certain moment in time, and that can be a lot of things. In a network society, networked communication prevails – communication that links different media in the search for information and in the exchange of that information with other members in our social networks.

In communication, innovation is (almost always) incremental

Currently, in the field of communication, innovation is almost always incremental. This can be seen as a sign of growing stability of a new model, given that radical innovation tends to characterize the beginning of cycles and not their stabilization (Perez, 2004). Incremental innovation in communication (Bakker, 2002, 2007b) is another identifiable development in the context of the change of communicational models and network communication's assumption of a central position. Eco (2001), for example, suggests that we are no longer in, as suggested by McLuhan (1997), an environment where the media is the message. We could also add that no longer, as Castells argued (Rantanen, 2005), is the message the media. It might be that the media itself precedes the message (Eco, 2001). In other words, innovation in the media sector is focusing more and more on anticipating the contents that the media may end up offering. Accordingly, it will be increasingly up to the consumer to make the final decision as to what the winning standard will be, thus defining the form innovation will take in the media sector. On the other hand, Bakker (2002; Bakker and Van Duijvenbode, 2007) asks the question to what extent innovation in the media is effected not through the best mediation offer – be it related to technology (machines or interfaces), supports or formats – but through worse mediation. By this Bakker means worse in comparison to that which was available before – be it a better image, better definition sound, more pages in the newspapers, more in-depth treatment of matters or more complex texts.[1] The analyses by Bakker (2002, 2007) and Eco (2001) at least enable us to compile a list of the technological developments that were not a success over the last decade, and also of those that, although they were a part of a daily life for a considerable amount of time, are now experiencing market erosion processes. A short list could include, as far as market erosion is concerned: CDs; DVDs; and paid daily newspapers. The list of innovations that weren't a success would include: DAB (Digital Audio Broadcasting); Interactive Television; WebTV (which is not the same as the now successful IPTV); and the Sony MiniDisc, amongst others. For an example that will still be in the memory of most of the present generations we can go back to the video recorder era and recall the war between the better-quality Beta system and the lower-quality VHS system. Both provided the same services – reading and recording video signals – but Beta, which was preferred by the 'techies', was passed over by most consumers in favour of the lower-quality VHS system.

What list could one compile today of technologies associated with lower mediation quality than their predecessors but which seem to be successful nevertheless? Most IP sound and image transmissions today are lower quality. Despite this fact, never before have we listened to so much music in the mp3 format (the quality of which is lower than a CD or vinyl); never before have we listened to so many radio podcasts through IP with lower quality than via the airwaves; never before have we watched so many films on P2P networks (which also offer lower-quality image); and never before have we seen so many low definition home-made films posted, for example, on YouTube. The circulation and readership figures for the free dailies containing less news, shorter news articles and fewer pages are also approaching those for paid newspapers in many places around the world (Bakker, 2007b).

What conclusions can we draw from these lists and the theories presented here? Probably, that those 'new' media needed new content as well as production and distribution models but that those were not available historically at their launch. Furthermore, their failure is also due to the prior satisfaction of what Winston (1999) has referred to, in the media context, as a 'supervening social necessity'. Perhaps, just as the Wii seems to have taken the PlayStation and XBox by surprise, there is indeed some kind of law similar to Moore's law, but in this case applicable to the media supplying contents and not just the processing media. In other words, the media that have been a success in the markets have never totally disappeared but have always transformed themselves. They innovate incrementally but they normally do so by reducing the perceived 'quality' of their characteristics and targeting new customers looking for new 'qualities' in them. When the number of new customers exceeds the number of original customers, this innovation cycle comes to an end, but only to begin anew again. The last radical innovations in the field of the media, that is, those that broke with incremental innovation cycles, date back, in the best of cases, to the late 1960s. The Internet was born in 1969, and the satellite emerged in the context of the Cold War (Winston, 1999; Abbate, 2000).

Democracy and everyday life immersed in mediation

The centrality of the concept and practice of mediation is the third visible consequence of the emergence of the network communication model in our societies. Our societies are ones in which mediation is increasingly being used alongside face-to-face communication. Mediation is nowadays fundamental in giving meaning to the world that surrounds us and our daily lives. It gives us security, makes us feel part of something bigger than the family – which, despite the changes in our society and in our own concept of famillies, continues to be the prime element of identification and belonging for the majority of people (Castells, 2003; Cardoso *et al.*, 2005). Mediation is also a fundamental factor in our lives and in our search for order and meaning of life, just as it is also an element of our constant struggle for power and for control over the symbolic and the material, in space and in time (Silverstone, 2005; Giddens, 1999).

As Silverstone (2006) reminds us, each era has its own dominant genres and modes of representation (the news, talk shows, soap operas and series) and also has different forms of expressing the singular dimension of each individual (music, blogs, messages, file sharing, etc.). Given the central importance of mediation, it is fundamental to understand that it takes place in an environment which, itself, is the product of opposing forces that seek to dictate the directions things take in terms of representation models and the opportunities of individual expression. This is why gatekeeping today is much more complex than in other periods in the past (Cardoso, 2007; Barzilai-Nahon, 2008). It relates not only to journalists, but also goes beyond them and affects us all – in our choices in online search results, in the way we create ratings for best-selling books, the TV channels we watch and the newspapers we read, and so on. Mediation and the media are, at the same time, fundamental elements for the economic development of countries and for the exercise of democracy (Castells, 2007; Bennett, 2003). There is no point talking about just the Internet or just TV. All people in their day-to-day life deal with multiple media – from the newspapers to radio and from the Internet to mobile phones.

What is worth highlighting is that the future of development and democracy incorporates mediation and the way mediation is carried out. This is the same as saying that it depends on the way the media system is incorporated (the regulation, the players, the costs and the access barriers for individuals and companies) and also on who can access them. Mediation is, first and foremost, fundamental because the way in which the 'other' is portrayed in it – be it a close 'other' (a member of another party, a doctor, a minister, a teacher, an unemployed person, an immigrant/emigrant, a journalist, etc.) or a more distant 'other' (a Basque, a Catalan, a Chinese person, a Muslim, a Buddhist, a Coptic Christian, an American, etc.) – also influences the way we organize our reality, our experience of those realities, of those people, our values and, perhaps even our own actions, proposals and practices (Silverstone, 2002).

Hence, those who regulate themselves in the media, who are regulated in the media, who regulate the media and who allocate the instruments and practices of regulation are, for the simple choices they make, determining, in part, the world that we are building (Freedman 2008). In other words, they are determining whether or not we will be worthy heirs of the freedoms of initiative and market and of participation and democracy we have won in recent decades, and, one presumes, wish to maintain.

Furthermore, mediation requires us to be literate (Livingstone, 2004; Cardoso, 2007) – literate enough to understand the soap opera and the news. But it also requires us to use the phone, take part in SMS tele-voting, write emails, read and edit blogs, post in social networks, surf the net and fill out forms (Beyer *et al.*, 2007; Enli and Syvertsen, 2007). We need to have the literacies to work in the dissemination, innovation and application of knowledge.

The three cultural industry narratives

The fourth change perceptible in the context of communication, and also originating from the change of the communication model, focuses on the models of cultural industry development. We have moved from a model centred on cinema and, to a large extent, Hollywood (Hesmondhalgh, 2007; Taplin, 2006a; 2007), to one in which we share geographic spaces in different continents and in which there are three dominant possible narratives involving multiple combinations of cinema, television fiction and video games.

These strategies have had different driving forces behind them – sometimes the state and, in other cases, private enterprise. But it is also true that speaking the *lingua franca* of today (English) or having a considerable size in terms of population also clearly help. Also, as the World Trade Organization's GATT agreements in the 1990s showed, all countries in the audiovisual sectors have a 'glass house' weakness, given that none of them plays by the rules of free trade, either because they subsidize production or because they carry out dumping: making their national products available at below-cost prices outside their own domestic markets.

But why speak only of cinema, television fiction and games? Each of these entertainment industries combines a network of technical and technological skills and necessities that makes it possible to sustain another set of much diversified cultural entities and products. Cinema and television fiction, as well as computer and console games, need scripwriters, actors, actor direction, coordination and realization, programmers, composers, musicians, diffusion, distribution and promotion networks and the whole panoply of merchandizing that is built up around the end products when integrated promotion strategies are put in place. Hence, for one country to triumph in the audiovisual area, it has to opt for one of the three as a basis for sustaining the development of the cultural entities. The US has clearly opted for cinema (as has Nigeria) and then come television fiction and games. Japan has opted for computer games, India has chosen a mixture of cinema from Bollywood and games (outsourced by foreign companies); Brazil has gone with television fiction and its world renowned soap operas.

Identity is important and is an element of attractiveness for television contents, as demonstrated by *Os Grandes Portugueses* (a Portuguese version of the BBC programme *Great Britons*, shown on the public service RTP) or the preferences of viewers for fiction series in Portuguese, be they adaptations to Portugal of a foreign format, such as *Floribella*, or inspired by foreign models, such as *Morangos com Açúcar*, which is based on the Globo (Brazil) soap opera *New Wave*. Indeed, identity as a strategic weapon used by television is not only a feature of Portuguese television (see IP Network, 2005). Looking at the data, we see that not only Portugal has strongly committed to the production of soap operas in recent years; the same applies to Germany, Spain and Russia. In Europe *Floribella*, a soap opera from Argentina, is not the only example of the phenomenon of the adaptation of soap opera formats to the specific context of each country. The adaptation of *Betty la Fea* (Colombia) arrived in Europe via Spain, was a success in the German version and was also broadcast in the Netherlands in 2006 only to return to a world wide broadcast in its US adapted version *Ugly Betty*. As far as films shown on television and in cinema theatres are concerned, the US continues to dominate, but in terms of television series, national or, at times, European productions dominate. In countries such as France, Germany, Greece, UK, Belgium, Italy, Portugal, Spain, Finland, the Netherlands, Poland, Russia, Czech Republic and Turkey, seven of the ten most popular television series were of domestic origin in 2004–2005.

In a world that considers itself, and is perceived as, global; in a European political space; in a world in which they seek to impose the abstract, and incorrect, ideal of civilizational shock upon us (Huntington, 1996), people apparently seek out that which they think they are and relate it to their language and their territory and to the stories that are close and familiar to them. This would seem to be the power of identity and the media, which has the obligation of not losing the notion of the world of which they are a part. The power of identity is likewise the power that communication and mediation confer upon it.

Users as distributors

Cinema and music illustrate the fifth change we will look at, which is the multiplication of distribution channels and how we have come from *multimedia* in the late 1990s to user-based *multi-distribution* in the early twenty-first century, with the user playing a role in the exhibition of products and also a distribution node (Limonard and Esmeijer, 2007). Throughout the decades in which film productions were essentially viewed in cinema theatres, distribution channels for European cinema were always limited – if we compare them to the channels available today for English-speaking 'entertainment' cinema or, even more so, US cinema in Europe.

In a certain way for cinema today's world is still one of bipolar forces in which we have, on one side, films coming from the US and, on the other, national film productions, which are ever growing in numbers and more dispersed globally. So let us speak of a certain type of film production that is not considered 'blockbuster', is not distributed by the large multinational film distributors, does not have a gigantic marketing campaign and an avalanche of merchandizing accompanying its theatre premiere: the type of films produced in the rest of the world. How does this cinema differ from the 'other'? It differs on many levels, evidently. But here we shall deal only with distribution, with access. It is distribution that allows the user/cinemagoer effectively to see a film. In the cinema theatres or in our living rooms (on television or via a bought or rented DVD) it is easy for us to see any widely-distributed US film production. It is not so easy to watch films from other countries, of which only a limited few are shown in our theatres and, normally, for shorter periods of time. Also, they often never make it to the direct DVD market (and not even to the pirate DVD market, which normally closely follows the consumption patterns of the official market).

So what changes has networked communication brought for distribution? Cinema consumption and distribution are changing. New technologies are being integrated into people's habits, such as movie file-sharing, but intellectual property rights have not yet adapted to those new realities. Subsequently, most file-sharing activity is either free from such rights or poses a threat to them, in the shape of an alternative distribution circle to the market. The Internet has some distinct characteristics that make it very different from the other distribution technologies. It can be thought of as a meta-medium, a set of layered services that make it easy to construct new media with almost any properties one likes (Agre, 1998). Furthermore, it is a channel for multidirectional communication that is insensitive to geographical distances (Noam and Pupillo, 2008). These features allow reconfigurations in the distribution of cultural production. Cinema is no exception; its distribution was based on commercial channels that would, in a mostly unidirectional way, sell the movies to consumers, who paid for it. Nowadays, Internet operating networks are the support for a new kind of distribution, in a context of user empowerment. In fact, not only are users acting as producers (by uploading for example videos on YouTube), but they are also taking on roles of opinion leaders (by rating books, movies on the web), of gatekeepers, of innovators and of distributors, operating as channels for the diffusion of movies, music and so on. Furthermore, P2P in general, and video file sharing in particular, emerge as the reflection of the idea defended by Slot (2007) of users also taking on distribution roles in P2P.

Now, although it is very natural that we think of a new kind of protective strategy related to the cinema industry we can also argue that for certain cinematographies, like European cinema, P2P creates a possible link between the effects of new file-sharing networks and the survival and/ or potential growth of European cinema. Such an analysis departs from the idea that, given the steady decline in the distribution channels for European movies both in cinema theatres and for direct sale or renting, new distribution channels emerge among the people who like that kind of cinema. The combination of content and viewers in the same environment bolsters the presence of European cinema on P2P networks when compared with the world outside the Internet. Given the funding procedure of European cinema based on public funding, as opposed to the US tradition of private-led financing, there might be a very good argument to consider this a first step in terms of changing the business rationale of worldwide movies distribution.

Music has also been affected by the transformation of its distribution mechanisms. Listening to music in mp3 format is one of the forces that changed the world in the last ten years. The ten forces in action in the last twenty years, as suggested by Jonathan Taplin (2006b), to a large extent inspired by the work of Thomas Friedman (2005), are: the fall of the Berlin Wall; the public dissemination of the Netscape browser; the WorkFlow software; the Open Source movement; outsourcing; offshoring; the online research technology provided by Google and Yahoo!; the combination of digital, mobile, personal and virtual; the Wal-mart physical commerce model; and the online commerce or e-commerce model.

Open creativity or Open Source of life

The sixth change in the context of networked communication is the value given to the opening of creativity. In effect, creativity has never been valued as much as it is nowadays. Thanks to the segmentation of markets and products made possible by the information technologies, creativity, when transformed into innovation or product spin-offs, is today the main source of the creation of wealth for enterprises and, consequently, for the state (Benkler, 2006; Castells, 2005). For the citizens in general, too, thanks to a change of ethics in our societies – from work as an obligation or the Protestant work ethics of Weber (Castells, 2000; Himanen *et al.*, 2001) to work as pleasure or the hacker ethics (Himanen *et al.*, 2001) – creativity has taken on new value.

Creativity for the worker is his free pass to happiness at work – doing what he likes to do (Himanen *et al.*, 2001). Although not all of us can achieve the goal of turning what we are passionate about into a job, adherence to the hacker ethics is an option in our schools through the choice of the career path one wishes to follow. One can likewise argue that the hacker ethics (Himanen *et al.*, 2001) is not widespread amongst the population but is present in all professions connected with the various powers in our societies – from economic to cultural power, from technology to education, from politics to security and defence. Creativity has also gained the value it has today because of the democratization of digital publishing in our societies.

However, there are different degrees of this creativity for different people. Jo Pierson (2008) suggests that the reading of the role of users as content producers and/or innovators means that we must understand what is known as the '90-9-1' rule. An example: Wikipedia offers a universe of new contributions made by only 0.5 per cent of its total users and the editing of already existing entries by 2.5 per cent of its total visitors. Another example, from the Open Source field: we find the beginnings of new projects triggered by charismatic leaders, which make up 0.5 per cent of the total number of participants. Also in the field of Open Source, only 5 per cent of the total users edit the source codes of the applications (Pierson, 2008). The '90-9-1' rule reflects the existence of different innovation functions attributed to the users, or defined by them through their practices and appropriation of technologies and products. The users that make up 1 per cent of the total, and which Jo

Pierson refers to as 'using producers', are those that have both the technical qualifications and the motivation to make significant contributions and they are active mainly in the industrial and consumer markets (e.g., sports articles markets: think of skating and surfing, from boards to kites). This group can be defined as a co-design group. In other words, they collaborate with industry in the design of new products. It is work where the user does not act autonomously but in cooperation with enterprises.

The second group, the 'producing users', comprises the 9 per cent of users that participate actively in the creation and sharing of contents (collaborative contents). This is the group that is responsible for the new areas of active innovation such as Web 2.0, the participative Web and 'user-generated content', or in more practical terms: wiki, social tagging, blogging, podcasting, SMS, etc. Finally, Jo Pierson (2008) suggests that we refer to the remaining 90 per cent of innovators as 'everyday users': those who manage the technologies placed at their disposal in their daily relations with the others. Before reaching the monetary valuation by the market stage, the creator has to go along a path of creation of that which we currently call the 'Name'. This process is traditionally a lengthy one, with many intermediaries along the way. What the new forms of publishing bring is that they make it possible to accelerate the public visibility processes and, at the same time, eliminate some of the intermediaries.

Creative Commons is not the only example of this. Open Access academic publications are also a good example. In the context of the communication businesses, book and magazine publishers are not a market to be scoffed at. When something is 'open' this does not mean that it does not involve the exchange of money or that it is not valued in monetary terms. It merely means, as Wikipedia suggests (Benkler, 2002; Quiggin, 2006; Auray *et al.*, 2007; Halavais and Lackaff, 2008), that it is open to diverse people and that, in its diverse contexts, can be used freely and can be transformed. Openness merely means that, provided that credit is given to the person who created it or made the raw material available, the information, process or product can be used by third parties. In a way, we encounter here again the two business models we have already identified in the mass media field – paid contents and free contents, the latter relying on advertising or another form of sponsorship.

iLife with your iPhone

This pithy heading could serve as a summary for all that will be said about the role of the telephone in our lives and the reason why mobility and portability are the seventh trend towards change in the context of networked communication. The mobility and portability introduced by the mobile phone have changed our society (Castells *et al.*, 2006; Colombo and Scifo, 2006; Katz and Aakhus, 2002; Caron and Caronia, 2007), making it more mobile and flexible. But they themselves were changed by the practices of networked communication, for the mobile phone is the bridge between the two central nodes (Cardoso, 2008) of that communicational model: television and the Internet. Culturally and technologically, we seem to have come a long way since the days in which the telephone emerged with the purpose of transmitting theatre plays and concerts directly from the concert halls and theatres to people's houses (Winston, 1999): from the fixed object only available in the houses of the cultural and financial élites of the nineteenth century to the mobile object used in the streets.

If we had to choose an object that has accompanied us and, simultaneously, changed our everyday life – from love to work, from the home to the street – over the last three centuries, that object would be the telephone, and its most direct descendant: the mobile phone (Castells *et al.*, 2006; Colombo and Scifo, 2006; Katz and Aakhus, 2002; Caron and Caronia, 2007). The mobile phone has changed, and continues to change, our relationship with time, space and social practices and values (Castells *et al.*, 2006; Cardoso *et al.*, 2007). The mobile phone is a nomadic object – light and small – that involves sight, touch and hearing (Colombo and Scifo, 2006). The mobile phone is a repository of our memories, feelings and professional lives. It contains infinite traces of our lifestyle, our history and our attitudes. Just the idea of losing our mobile phone is enough to send chills down our spines, not for the cost of the device itself, but for all that it means in emotional and professional terms. Although the device, already referred to as the Smartphone, does not effect a process analogous to human thought, it does carry in it characteristics of our thought.

As the mobile phone plays an increasingly important part in our lives, the desktop computer – thanks to the development in processors, the growth in data storage capacity and the laws on the reduction of costs in the computer and Wi-Fi industry – has been disappearing from our homes and offices to be replaced by the portable version of the PC and Mac.

What the two aforementioned technological trends show is that, on the one hand, companies are more and more committed to the consumer's and citizen's appreciation of mobility and, on the other, that the mobile phone is developing into something that is more than a mere support for voice and text communication. We are thus, for the first time, after more than a decade of rapid growth in the use of the Internet and the adoption of mobile phones, faced with markets where the replacement of equipment seems to be the driving force behind growth in the mobile phone manufacturing sector and where the Internet access providers are beginning to see their growth potential stagnate. But what is really interesting in this process is that, albeit for different reasons, both the market and the state have the same goal – the need to involve more people in actively defining the informational society: more people capable of having the literacies necessary for operating the mediation tools that give them access to information, be it in the traditional media or in all those that emerge (Livingstone, 2004; Cardoso, 2006). Corporations and government ministries alike have understood that it will not be desktop or portable computers that will be, for now, in the hands of the majority of citizens, for whoever uses them either will be young or will have completed, in normal circumstances, at least secondary education (Cardoso *et al.*, 2008; Drotner and Livingstone, 2008). The other thing they have understood is that although mobile phones can be a solution, they also have their limits. These limits are: financial resources for the use of services; the existence of the acquired knowledge for using the interfaces; and the discovery of the interest in using them. In the coming years we will most likely witness a necessity to lower prices, not only for access terminals but also for services, in order to include more people in the utilization circuit. But this will prove useless if, on the other hand, we do not have more people with more educational training and informal experimentation in the technologies. Networked communication is, thus, also a combination of the rigidity – in physical and marketing strategy terms – of the interfaces of portable computer, mobile phone and access networks with their portability.

Media is still quite young

The influence of the networked communication model is also visible in the media that have been around in our lives over the greater part of the last century. Although the image we have of them may have been created in the twentieth century, they are undergoing change. Radio has a third life and television is no longer a technology and is only identifiable by the differentiated type of contents. Newspapers, too, are increasingly becoming news agencies.

There can be no doubt that the Web of today is different from the Web that Tim Berners-Lee and his students created back in the 1990s (Abbate, 2000). But, although the Web has not been social so far, the Internet has always been social (Castells, 2000; Cardoso, 1998). There was always more communication than there was publication of information and entertainment. If email was the tool of choice for the over-25 age group, chat with MSN, Yahoo! and Google Talk (and, before these, IRC, newsgroups and mailing lists) were the tools most used and most frequently utilized by those who logged on and log on to the Internet (Castells *et al.*, 2003, Cardoso *et al.*, 2005).

What changed was not the social aspect of the Internet, it was the arrival of that attribute on the Web through platforms such as MySpace, Facebook, hi5, Friendster or even Second Life, to name just a few. But, beyond these considerations, it is also important to distinguish between the cloud and Juno, or the trees and the forest. The questions that the expansion of the social Web raises have much more to do with information than with the much talked-of dangers of speaking to 'strangers' (the 'strangers' are the same ones that were always there outside the virtual world; now they are in the virtual world as well). What Web 2.0 brings is the change of paradigm of the relationship with information and that brings greater problems with it, because it not only impacts us individually; it impacts us individually and collectively at all levels of our life.

It is obvious that the new dimensions of accessibility of information, in terms of quantity and mobility, are a fundamental change for our societies and this is a positive change. This change brings, in theory, more freedom of thought, more reflexivity and more democraticity (Silverstone, 2006) amongst the communicating subjets: we the citizens. However, one must ask the question whether this change is not also changing the rules of the game without us realizing this and, thus, it is able to put us out of the game. Not because of a mistake on our part, but because we don't know that the rules have changed some time after the game began.

In the era of mass communication, the 'truth' (always something subjective, one should bear in mind) was frequently associated with what was said by the journalists (and also by professors and authors published and bound in paper – but what they had to tell us normally had less direct impact on our daily lives). What, in the end analysis, differentiates the journalist from the storyteller is the ethical dimension (Paulussen *et al.*, 2007; Franklin *et al.*, 2005; Heinonen, 1999). It is not their capacity to choose and select, for these are merely tools in the service of ethics.

At some stage in the early years of the twenty-first century we witnessed a fundamentally important development: the emergence of Wikipedia. Why Wikipedia? Because it changed our relationship with sources traditionally seen as of both lower social credibility and lower degree of updatedness, that is, sources that were not news (Benkler, 2002; Quiggin, 2006; Auray *et al.*, 2007; Halavais *et al.*, 2008). The logic went from 'what is written there is what is valid' (the encyclopedia model) to 'what is left unchanged by most people is what is valid'. So far, nothing to worry about – validation by more people normally means fewer errors. But the problem that Wikipedia, the wikis and their relatives the blogs brought with them is that although we now deal with different categories of information, generally speaking, just as they trusted television information, people also trust in the information they find on the Web (WIP, 2006). What this implicates is the need to adapt the teaching of the dimensions of the validation of information in the context of the new literacies: that texts written and published may or not be valid, may or not give us certainties, and that we should always treat all information as questionable until the opposite is proved.

Let us go on to the second question that the emergence of the social Web or Web 2.0 raises; it has to do with the diffusion of moving pictures or films and still images (photography). 'A picture is worth a thousand words' is a much-used adage. This may have been true in the past, but it is questionable whether it is nowadays. The manipulated photograph may be as old as photography itself (Reynolds, 2007), but the emergence of digital technologies has led to an exponential increase in the number of people capable of manipulating photos and film material (Lessig, 2004). The question is no longer whether or not this is possible, but one of the quality of the work and how many people are able to tell the difference between what is real and what has been 'doctored'. The popularization of image manipulation technologies has meant that we have to accustom ourselves to the fact that we cannot believe what we see, again questioning the old maxim of 'seeing is believing'. Nevertheless, this tells us something more. It tells us that the journalist is slowly going through a professional upgrading process as someone who, thanks to journalistic ethics, can be considered trustworthy – because what he writes, says or films will have a value different to much of what else is published. And if we cannot rely on this professional ethics our problems will be much greater.

Nevertheless, this new appraisal (or return of the perception) of the role of the journalist also means that the journalist will once again be different from the Internet user. In other words, he will have to see with his own eyes in order to believe and stop relying on the eyes of others, he will have to leave his desk and essentially become a field reporter. Generally speaking, what this change means is positive for communication and societies. It is also clear that, as with all changes, there are risks – but also many opportunities. We have to be conscious of this fact, and, above all, move from intuition to awareness of the fact. Because perhaps the majority of us have not verbalized this change in communicational paradigms (even if we have an inkling that it is there). And, as Silverstone (2006) argued, if one hasn't communicated publicly in the media then one doesn't exist.

Wikis, blogs, YouTube, social networks – what next? That is a question only future research and development can answer. As we have no facts on the future, it is impossible for the social scientist to make predictions. However, we can put forward one certainty, because historical regularity would seem to indicate it – that a given communicational model will always be joined by a new model. Hence, networked communication will, at some time in the future, be substituted by another model, that will again be a product of how we communicate between ourselves.

Note

1   One can, of course, identify misperceptions in Bakker's arguments. One of those misperceptions might be the fact that he merely explains what happens to mediation technologies that already have a consolidated market presence and have already reached very close to 100 per cent of the population.

References

Abbate, J. (2000) *Inventing the Internet*, Cambridge, Massachusetts: The MIT Press.
Agre, P. (1998) *The Internet and public discourse*, First Monda, 3. Available: <http://firstmonday.org/htbin/cgiwrap/bin/ojs/index.php/fm/article/view/581/502>.
Aroldi, P. and Colombo, F. (2003). *Le Età della TV*, Milan: VP Università.
Auray, N., Poudat, C. and Pons, P. (2007) 'Democratizing scientific vulgarization; The balance between cooperation and conflict in French Wikipedia', *Observatorio (OBS*)* 1 (3). Available: <http://obs.obercom.pt/index.php/obs/article/view/152>

Bakker, P. (2002) 'Reinventing newspapers; Free dailies – readers and markets', in Picard, R. (ed.) *Media Firms*, New York: Lawrence Erlbaum.

Bakker, P. (2007a) 'Free daily journalism – Anything new?', *Journalistica*, 4: 22–32.

Bakker, P. (2007b) 'Free Daily Readership', in *Worldwide Readership Research Symposia*, Vienna: 63–74.

Bakker, P. and Van Duijvenbode, M. (2007) 'Measuring Newspaper Innovations', *Ideas*, May/June: 10–13.

Barzilai-Nahon, K. (2008) 'Toward a Theory of Network Gatekeeping: A Framework for Exploring Information Control', *Journal of the American Information Science and Technology*, 59(9): 1493–1512.

Benkler, Y. (2006) *The Wealth of Networks*, New Haven: Yale University Press.

Benkler, Y. (2002) 'Coase's penguin, or, Linux and The Nature of the Firm', *The Yale Law Journal*, 112 (3): 369–446. Available: <http://www.firstmonday.org/issues/issue7_6/stalder>.

Bennett, W.L. (2003) 'New Media Power: The Internet and Global Activism', in Couldry, N. and Curran, J. (eds) *Contesting Media Power: Alternative Media in a Networked World*, Oxford: Rowman & Littlefield.

Beyer, Y., Gunn, S., Enli, A.M. and Ytreberg, E. (2007) 'Small talk makes a big difference: recent developments in interactive, SMS-based television', *Television and New Media*, 8 (3): 213–234.

Cardoso, G. (2007) *The Media in the Network Society: Browsing, News, Filters and Citizenship*, Lisbon: lulu.com and CIES-ISCTE. Available: <http://www.obercom.pt/en/content/mPublications/35.np3>.

Cardoso, G. (2008) 'From Mass to Network Communication: Communicational Models and the Informational Society', *International Journal of Communication*, 2:0. Available: <http://ijoc.org/ojs/index.php/ijoc/article/view/19/178>.

Cardoso, G., Espanha, R. and Gomes, V.A.C. (2007) 'Portugal Móvel', *Comunicação & Cultura*, 3, Primavera_Verão, Lisbon: Quimera.

Cardoso, G. (2006) 'Societies in Transition to the Network Society', in Castells, M. and Cardoso, G., Costa, A., Conceição, C. and Gomes, G. (2005) *A Sociedade em Rede em Portugal*, Porto: Campo das Letras.

Cardoso, G. (1998) *Para uma Sociologia do Ciberespaço: comunidades virtuais em português*, Oeiras: Celta Editora.

Caron, A. and Caronia, L. (2007) *Moving Cultures: Mobile Communication in Everyday Life*, Montreal: MQUP.

Carpentier, N. (2007) 'The on-line community media database RadioSwap as a translocal tool to broaden the communicative rhizome', *Observatorio (OBS*)*, 1:1. Available: <http://obs.obercom.pt/index.php/obs/article/view/44>.

Castells, M. (2006) *Observatorio global: crónicas de principios de siglo*, Barcelona: La Vanguardia Ediciones.

Castells, M. (2005) 'Innovation, Information Technology and the Culture of Freedom', Communication presented at the World Social Forum. Available: <http://www.openflows.org/article.pl?sid=05/01/31/2028221>.

Castells, M. (2000) *The Rise of the Network Society*, Oxford: Blackwell.

Castells, M. *et al.* (2003) *La Societat Xarxa a Catalunya*, Barcelona: Editorial UOC.

Castells, M. (2007) 'Communication, Power and Counter-power in the Network Society', *International Journal of Communication*, 1: 238–266. Available: <http://ijoc.org/ojs/index.php/ijoc/article/view/46/35>.

Castells, M., Fernandez-Ardevol, M., Linchuan Qiu, J. and Sey, A. (2006) *Mobile Communication and Society; A Global Perspective*, Cambridge: MIT Press.

Colombo, F. (1993) *Le nuove tecnologie della comunicazione*, Milan: Bompiani.

Colombo, F. and Scifo, B. (2006) 'The Social Shaping of Mobile Devices by the Italian Youth', in Haddon, L. *et al.*, *Users as Innovators*, Dordecht: Springer.

Caseti, F. and Odin, R. (1990) 'De la paléo à la néo-télévision', *Communications*, 51.

Drotner, K., and Livingstone, S. (2008) *The International Handbook of Children, Media and Culture*, London: Sage.

Eco, U. (2001) 'Il Medium Precede Il Messaggio'. Available: <http://www.espressoonline.kataweb.it/ESW_articolo/0,2393,12424,00.html>.

Eco, U. (1985) *La Guerre du Faux*, Paris: Grasset.

Enli, G. and Syvertsen, T. (2007) 'Participation, Play and Socializing in New Media Environments', in Nightingale, V. and Dwyer, T. (eds) *New Media Worlds*, Oxford: Oxford University Press.

Franklin, B., Hamer, M., Hanna, M., Kinsey, M. and Richardson, J. (2005) *Key Concepts in Journalism Studies*, London: Sage.

Freedman, D. (2008) *The Politics of Media Policy*, Cambridge: Polity Press.

Friedman, T.L. (2005) *The World is Flat: A Brief History of the Twenty-first Century*, New York: Farrar, Straus & Giroux.

Giddens, A. (1999) 'DNW Interview met Anthony Giddens', Available: www.vpro.nl/ programma/dnw/download/Interview_Giddens.shtml>.

Halavais, A. and Lackaff, D. (2008) 'An Analysis of Topical Coverage of Wikipedia', *Journal of Computer-Mediated Communication*, 13 (2): 429–440. Available: <http://www.blackwell-synergy.com/doi/abs/10.1111/j.1083-6101.2008.00403.x>.

Heinonen, A. (1999) 'Journalism in the Age of the Net. Changing Society, Changing Profession', *Acta Universitatis Tamperensis*, 685.

Hesmondhalgh, D. (2007) *The Cultural Industries*, London: Sage.

Himanen, P., Torvalds, L. and Castells, M. (2001) *The Hacker Ethic and the Spirit of the Information Age*, London: Vintage.

Himanen, P. (2006) 'Challenges of the Global Information Society', in Castells, M. and Cardoso, G. (eds) *The Network Society: From Knowledge to Policy*, Washington DC: Johns Hopkins Center for Transatlantic Relations.

Huntington, S.P. (1996) *The Clash of Civilizations and the Remaking of World Order*, New York: Simon and Schuster.

IP Network (2005) *European TV Key Facts*, IP NETWORK GmbH.

Katz, J.E. and Aakhus, A. (eds) (2002) *Perpetual Contact. Mobile Communications, Private Talk, Public Performance*, Cambridge: Cambridge University Press.

Kim, P. and Sawhney, H. (2002) 'A Machine-Like New Medium – Theoretical Examination of Interactive TV', *Media, Culture and Society*, 24: 217–233.

Lessig, L. (2004) *Free Culture. How Big Media Uses Technology and the Law to Lock Down Culture and Control Creativity*, New York: The Penguin Press.

Limonard, S. and Jop Esmeijer (2007) 'Business requirements and potential bottlenecks for successful new Citizen Media applications'. Available: <http://www.tno. nl/downloads%5CD6.1.1_BusinessRequirementsAndPotentialBottlenecks1. pdf>.

Livingstone, S. (1999) 'New Media, New Audience?', *New Media and Society*, 1(1): 59–66.

Livingstone, S. (2004) 'Media Literacy and the Challenge of New Information and Communication Technologies', *Communication Review*, 7: 3–14.

McLuhan, M. (1997) *Understanding Media – the Extensions of Man*, London: Routledge.

Meyrovitz, J. (1985) *No Sense of Place; The Impact of Electronic Media on Social Behavior*, New York: Oxford University Press.

Noam, E.M. and Lorenzo, M.P. (2008) 'Introduction' in Noam, E.M. and Lorenzo, M.P. *Peer-to-Peer Video: The Economics, Policy, and Culture of Today's New Mass Medium*, New York: Springer.

Ortoleva, P. (2004) 'O Novo Sistema dos Media', in Paquete De Oliveira, J.M. and Giddens, A., Cardoso, G. and Barreiros, J.J *Comunicação , Cultura E Tecnologias De Informação*, Lisbon: Quimera.

Paulussen, S., Heinonen, A., Domingo, D. and Quandt, T. (2007) 'Doing it Together: Citizen Participation in the Professional News Making Process', *Observatorio (OBS*)*, 1 (3). Available: <http://obs.obercom.pt/>.

Perez, C. (2004) 'Technological revolutions, paradigm shifts and socio-institutional change', in Reinert, E. (ed.) *Globalization, Economic Development and Inequality, An Alternative Perspective*, Cheltenham: Edward Elgar.

Picard, J. (2006) 'Drivers and Implications of Change in Media Industries', Paper presented at ISCTE, Lisbon, November.

Pierson, J. (2008) 'Identifying users as innovators', Paper presented at the COST 298 Management Committee Meeting, Delft WG Users as Innovators 27–29 February.

Quiggin, J. (2006) 'Blogs, wikis and creative innovation', *International Journal of Cultural Studies*, 9 (4): 481–496.

Reynolds, C. (2007) 'Image Act Theory. Seventh International Conference of Computer Ethics: Philosophical Enquiry', July 12–14, San Diego, California. Available: http://www.k2.t.u-tokyo.ac.jp/members/carson/papers/reynolds_cepe2007.pdf.

Silverstone, R. (2002) 'Mediating Catastrophe: September 11 and the Crisis of the Other', *Dossiers de L'Audiovisuel*, 105 (September).

Silverstone, R. (2005) 'The Sociology of Mediation and Communication', in Calhoun, C., Rojek, C. and Turner, B.S. (eds) *The International Handbook of Sociology*, London: Sage.

Silverstone, R. (2006) *Media and Morality: on the Rise of Mediapolis*, Oxford: Polity.

Slot, M. (2007) 'Users in the golden age of the information society', paper presented at a Meeting of Cost 298. Available: <http://www.cost298.org/index.php?fl=2&lact=3&bid=9>.

Taplin, J. (2006a) 'The IP TV Revolution', in Castells, M. and Cardoso, G. (eds) *The Network Society: From Knowledge to Policy*, Washington, DC: Johns Hopkins Center for Transatlantic Relations.

Taplin, J. (2006b) 'The Politics of the Future; The American Crisis, Moore's Law and the Third Way', Speech delivered at the Annenberg School for Communication, University of Southern California, 7 May. Available: <http://www.rcf.usc.edu/~jtaplin/ThePoliticsofTheFuture.pdf>.

Taplin, J. (2007) '"Crouching Tigers": Emerging Challenges to U.S. Entertainment Supremacy in the Movie Business', *Observatorio (OBS*)*, 1 (2). Available: <http://obs.obercom.pt>.

Thompson, J.B. (1995) *The Media and Modernity*, Cambridge: Polity Press.

Rantanen, T. (2005) 'The message is the medium: An interview with Manuel Castells', *Global Media and Communication*, 1(2): 135–147.

Winston, B. (1999) *Media Technology and Society. A History from the Telegraph to the Internet*, London: Routledge.

WIP (2006) *The World Internet Project*. Available:<http://www.worldinternetproject.net>.

Wolton, D. (1999) *Internet et après? Une théorie critique des nouveaux médias*, Paris: Flammarion.

8 Media life

Mark Deuze

Life in today's liquid modern society is all about finding ways to deal with constant change, whether it is at home, at work, or at play. Over the last few decades, these key areas of human existence have converged in and through our concurrent and continuous exposure to, use of, and immersion in media, information and communication technologies. Research in countries as varied as the United States, Brazil, South Korea, the Netherlands and Finland consistently shows that more of our time gets spent using media, and that multi-tasking our media has become a regular feature of everyday life. It must be clear that media are not just types of technology and chunks of content we pick and choose from the world around us – a view that considers media as external agents affecting us in a myriad of ways. If anything, today we have to recognize how the uses and appropriations of media penetrate all aspects of contemporary life. This world is what Roger Silverstone (2007), Alex de Jong and Marc Schuilenburg (2006), and Sam Inkinen (1998) label a 'mediapolis': a comprehensively mediated public space where media underpin and overarch the experiences and expressions of everyday life. It is the point of this essay to argue that such a perspective on life lived in, rather than with, media can and perhaps should be the ontological benchmark for a twenty-first century media studies (Deuze, 2009).

As media become pervasive and ubiquitous, forming the building blocks for our constant remix of the categories of everyday life (the public and the private, the local and the global, the individual and the collective), they become invisible – in the sense, as Friedrich Kittler suggests, that we become blind to that which shapes our lives the most. I propose that the key challenge of communication and media studies in the twenty-first century is, or will be, the disappearance of media. This is not a renewed claim for the kind of soft techno-determinism as espoused in the work of Marshall McLuhan and Manuel Castells (Stalder, 2006: 153). The increasing invisibility of media is exemplified by their disappearing from consciousness when used intensely – by their logic of immediacy (Bolter and Grusin, 1996). In this process, the primary bias of media technologies – the fact that people can read, edit and write their codes, programs, protocols, and texts – comes to shape our sense of reality. This is a reality that seems malleable as well, that could be manipulated, fast-forwarded, panned, scanned and zoomed in on (Stephens, 1998). In this statement of purpose, I follow the lead of David Harvey (1990), who signalled a gradual change in the human experience of space–time relationships in the course of the twentieth century – as exemplified by the increasing speed of travel and telecommunications – as a benchmark for a global change in people's sense of reality itself. Media become the playground for a search for meaning and belonging – not just by consumption or what Harvey calls 'flexible accumulation' of artefacts and ideas that would make up and reconstitute one's sense of self-identity, but also by producing, co-creating, assembling, and remixing 'a whole series of simu- lacra as *milieux* of escape, fantasy, and distraction' (1990: 302). Castells in this context has argued for an emerging culture of 'real virtuality' (1996: 364ff.), where reality itself is entirely captured by mediated communica- tion. With Harvey and Castells, I think it is important for media studies not to see people as hapless victims of this seemingly fragmented world- view, nor to assume that this shift towards a media life inevitably makes people's experience of society somehow less 'real' or 'true.' The potential power of people to shape their lives and identities can be found in the assumption that people produce themselves (and therefore each other) in media. This perhaps may additionally explain why people do not recog- nize their media habits because media are invisible to them as they are a constitutive part of it.

Beyond the blurring of boundaries between people as producers and consumers of information that is disseminated and co-created across multiple media platforms – a process Henry Jenkins (2006) calls 'conver- gence culture' – the distinctions drawn all too easily between humans and machines, or, as Lev Manovich (2001) explains, between culture and computers, can also be seen as becoming less relevant to a twenty- first century media studies. Michael Hardt and Antonio Negri have argued how 'the anthropology of cyberspace is really a recognition of the new human condition' (2000: 291). The newness of the contempo- rary human condition can perhaps best be understood in an abstract sense as a socio-technical experience of reality – a reality that seems to submit itself (potentially) to the affordances (or, as Deleuze and Guattari have suggested, 'agencements') of media: it can be cut, pasted, edited, remixed, and forwarded. This argument builds on the earlier suggestion that media should not be seen as somehow located outside lived experi- ence, but rather should be seen as intrinsically part of it. Our life is lived in, rather than with, media – we are living a *media life* (Deuze, 2007: 242).

Media studies and media life

In a way, the media life point of view does not differ much from earlier points of view offered by noted theorists, such as Marshall McLuhan's perspective on media as extensions of man affecting how we perceive and understand the world around us. Similarly, authors coming from a variety of disciplines have developed comprehensive perspectives on media and social theory (Thompson, 1995; Luhmann, 1996; Rasmussen, 2000; Fuchs, 2007; Hesmondhalgh and Toynbee, 2008), media ecology (Strate, 2006), and mediatizaton (Lundby, 2009) that supersede the existence of media in a material sense – aiming to explore how changes and developments in society interact with trends in media (production, use and content). Yet such approaches, however eloquent and inspiring, tend to confirm the traditional biases and boundaries of (critical) communication and media studies – reproducing people and their media in terms of production, content and reception, and interrogating the presumed consequences omnipresent media may or may not have for (the communicative relationships between) people and society. I would argue that it is time to take the next step: using a media life as the ontological point of departure for theorizing and operationalizing the way we see ourselves and the role we (can) play in society.

The media life perspective offers a prediction and explanation of increasingly invisible media; it builds an ontological argument such as proposed by Friedrich Kittler (2009), aiming to resolve ontology's hostility to media. As Kittler argues, 'philosophy [...] has been necessarily unable to conceive of media as media', in that the relation between observer and the observed as for example expressed in writing, audio or video recordings is generally not considered to be of influence to the work of the philosopher. This blindness to the structuring role of media in lived experience not only considers but moves beyond technical media – however significant the medium may be to the message – to address the essential nature of media as the invisible interlocutor of people's lives. In today's media culture, where people increasingly move through the world assembling (more or less deliberately) a deeply individualized media system – in other words, living in their own *personal information space* – such a viewpoint can form the basis of (empirical) investigation and understanding of everyday life.

Beyond the theoretical and empirical consequences of a media life-based ontology, I would like to touch on the discussion by Denis McQuail on the future of mass communication theory in the 2010 edition of his seminal handbook of the field. McQuail suggests a shift towards a somewhat post-industrial view of mass media, where media are not crucial to everyday life or public communication because of their potential to reach an entire national or otherwise mass public with a restricted range of content and experiences, but rather where their impact is premised on 'the voluntary engagement of the public in its own immersion in a rich and varied world of mediated experience.'[1] Similarly, Manuel Castells articulates the rise of a new form of socialized communication: mass self-communication.

> We are indeed in a new communication realm, and ultimately in a new medium, whose backbone is made of computer networks, whose

language is digital, and whose senders are globally distributed and globally interactive. True, the medium, even a medium as revolutionary as this one, does not determine the content and effect of its messages. But it makes possible the unlimited diversity and the largely autonomous origin of most of the communication flows that construct, and reconstruct every second the global and local production of meaning in the public mind (2007: 248).

The media life perspective engages with these various challenges to media and communication studies by taking the premises as for example articulated by Castells and McQuail to their logical extreme: media are everywhere, and therefore nowhere. Quite literally, I would suggest an ontological turn in media studies that neither tries to make media all-powerful (in terms of their hegemonic potential to consolidate power structures in social institutions such as the state, the economy and the family), nor aims to 'decenter' media research in an attempt to focus more specifically on the question of how can we can live, ethically, *with* and *through* media (Couldry, 2006). With Sonia Livingstone, a twenty-first century media studies must be grounded the assumptions that '[f]irst, the media mediate, entering into and shaping the mundane but ubiquitous relations among individuals and between individuals and society; and second, as a result, the media mediate, for better or for worse, more than ever before' (2009: 7). This mediation of everything is premised on the increasing invisibility of media which in turn makes media indivisible from (all aspects of everyday) life. The moment media become invisible, our sense of identity and indeed our experience of reality itself becomes irreversibly modified, because mediated.

The Truman Show delusion

The media life perspective applied to the theory and empirical evidence of media studies raises (and perhaps confirms) the issue, that our lived reality cannot be experienced separately, or outside of media. Metaphorically speaking, we are now all living inside our very own *Truman Show* (referring to the 1998 movie by director Peter Weir): a world characterized by pervasive and ubiquitous media that we are constantly and concurrently deeply immersed in, that we are the stars of, and that dominate and shape all aspects of our everyday life. Importantly, in this world it is also up to each of us to navigate the largely unwritten rules and often hidden pathways of 'an ocean of media'[2] on our own. In the film, actor Jim Carrey portrays the life of a man – Truman Burbank – who does not know his entire life is one big reality television show, watched by millions all over the world. In the course of the movie it becomes clear that the only way out for Carrey's character will be his individual ability, as the only 'True Man', to figure out whether the people in his life are actors (and to what extent they act), and where the fine line between the studio (stage, decor) and the 'real' world can be drawn. We have argued that the solution to this vexing dilemma can only be found by the individual, using his/her skills while all the time aware of at least the possibility of being constantly monitored and recorded. The rather ominous *Truman Show* metaphor is perhaps only appropriate insofar as it addresses people's complex, interconnected yet often solipsistic engagement with reality through media. When asked how the show can be so successful in convincing Truman that his world is real even though it so clearly features a fake reality, the director of Truman's reality show (named Christof, a not-so-subtle reference to Slavoj Žižek's concept of the 'small other' embodying the authority of, in this case, God) states: '[w]e accept the reality of the world with which we are presented.'[3] It is important to note the implication of this narrative, as it does not seem to be premised on a notion that Truman's world is unreal. The *Truman Show* is just another version of the real, one that is carefully staged and completely mediated, much like Plato's Allegory of the Cave, as the people in the cave, watching the puppets, were unaware of any other lifestyle or world other than the one which they were shown. Using the *Truman Show* as a metaphor for living a media life, we must additionally note that the ending of the movie – Truman escapes the studio – might in fact be the only truly unrealistic aspect of the film's story, as in our fully mediated existence, escape is impossible.

During the summer of 2008 psychiatrists Joel and Ian Gold made headlines around the world with their diagnosis of a new condition found in five of their patients. The brothers suggested that the combination of pervasive media, classical syndromes such as narcissism and paranoia, and an emerging media culture where the boundaries between the physical and virtual world are blurring produces a new type of psychosis: a 'Truman Show delusion' (TSD). People who suffer from TSD are more or less convinced that everything around them is a décor, that the people in their lives are all actors, and that everything they do is monitored and recorded. In an interview with Canadian newspaper the *National Post*, McGill University's Ian Gold attributes TSD to 'unprecedented cultural triggers that might explain the phenomenon. ... New media is opening up vast social spaces that might be interacting with psychological processes' (19 July, 2008, p.A1).

In *Newsweek*, his brother (affiliated with the Bellevue Hospital Center in New York) suggests that TSD 'is the pathological product of our insatiable appetite for self-exposure' (August 11, 2008, p.10). Earlier that week in a special report on the *WebMD* site, he links TSD more generally to the role media play in people's lives: '[w]e've got the "perfect storm" of reality TV and the Internet. These are powerful influences in the culture we live in [...] The pressure of living in a large, connected community can bring out the unstable side of more vulnerable people.'[4] The TSD additionally contains a belief that one's life has ceased being spontaneous, as one is always aware of (the possibility of) the scripted and broadcasted nature of everything one does. In a special report about the TSD on the website of the American Psychological Association (on June 6, 2009), the brothers identify specific features of modern culture – 'warrantless wiretapping and video surveillance systems [...] widely accessible technology [...] reality TV shows and MySpace' – as squaring with the *Truman Show*'s basic premise.[5]

In the APA report and in an earlier background story in the *International Herald Tribune* several experts are quoted who confirm the possibility of the TSD and suggest that '[o]ne way of looking at the delusions and hallucinations of the mentally ill is that they represent extreme cases of what the general population, or the merely neurotic, are worried about' (August 30, 2008, p.7). Writing in the *British Journal of Psychiatry*, Paolo Fusar-Poli and colleagues confirm the diagnoses of their American colleagues, describing the common symptoms as follows:

> First, there is the sense that the ordinary is changed or different, and that there is particular significance in this. This is coupled with a searching for meaning, which, in this case, results in the 'Truman explanation'. The third feature is a profound alteration of subjective experience and of self-awareness, resulting in an unstable first-person perspective with varieties of depersonalization and derealization, disturbed sense of ownership, fluidity of the basic sense of identity, distortions of the stream of consciousness and experiences of disembodiment (2008: 168).

The significance of this analysis of the contemporary human condition for our argument is the realization that:

- the TSD is perhaps best understood an amplification of a distinct sense of uncertainty and unsettlement in the population at large;
- the TSD accelerates a sense of urgency about one's life project of self-identity;
- the TSD indirectly acknowledges an alternate ending to the movie on which it is based, namely a scenario where Truman does not (cannot) leave, but stays to tell his own story.

Media life and society

It must be clear, then, that in the relationship between media and the human condition contemporary technologies, the things people do with them, and how all of this fits (and gets fitted) into the social arrangements that govern people's lives are several elements which serve to amplify and accelerate broader trends in society, such as:

- a primacy of self-governance and self-reliance over the deference to authorities such as parents, professionals and politicians;
- an extension of community premised on simultaneous co-presence and telepresence as directed by the individual and her/his concerns (documented in 2002 and subsequent publications[6] by Barry Wellman

as a shift from 'little boxes' and 'glocalized' communities to those
based on 'networked individualism', linking individuals with little
regard to space);

• the emergence of mass self-communication next to mass communication signifying the shift in almost all industrial societies from
survival values toward increasing emphasis on self-expression values
as comprising the major area of concern to people in such societies
(Inglehart and Baker, 2000).

According to Bauman, people's current endemic and, perhaps more
importantly, undirected uncertainty breeds a particular kind of fear – a
fear that is based on 'our ignorance of the threat and of what is to be
done' (2006: 2). All the more interesting is the connection Bauman sees
between people's uncertainty about their prospects in a rapidly moving
'runaway world' (as Giddens calls it), and the structure and consequences
of a deeply individualized society. However, this society is at the same
time, as Bauman indirectly admits, irrevocably connected. 'The new
individualism, the fading of human bonds and the wilting of solidarity,
are all engraved on one side of a coin whose other side bears the stamp
of globalization' (ibid.: 146). Considering the pervasive and ubiquitous
nature of media and the signalled uncanny capacity of contemporary
media to connect and isolate at the same time – to make the world concurrently larger and smaller – it becomes crucial for a twenty-first century
media studies to engage directly with people's experience of reality as
lived in media. This experience is rooted in, as noted in our discussion of
the TSD, people's sense that reality is fundamentally changed or different
– and that reality has become particular to their own experience of it. In
other words, the key to considering what it means to live a media life must
be an understanding of the 'off' nature or, what Slavoj Žižek (2006) has
theorized as a mode of parallax reality as lived (and mediated) experience. In other words: people in media life inevitably engage with reality
on the basis of a constant moving in between idealism (what we perceive)
and materialism (what is apparent), using the tools and techniques of
contemporary digital and networked media to edit and remix both their
perceptions and the appearance of that reality. One therefore wonders
whether people in this context are inevitably reproducing the very reality
they seek to modify, or whether there is in fact human agency in the technological affordances of media. In short: can we be free and mediated at
the same time?

Discussion

A future media studies can perhaps benefit from a new, or additional
ontological turn – after and next to the cultural, linguistic, and the spatial
turn. I have argued in this essay that media cannot be conceived of as
separate to us, to the extent that we live in media, rather than with media.

144   *Mark Deuze*

There are extensive social and cultural repercussions occurring, primarily due to the way media are becoming invisible, as media are so pervasive and ubiquitous that people in general do not even register the presence of media in their lives. The networked individualist and personalized information space that digital natives have created for themselves which constitutes their everyday reality influences work, play, learning and interacting by unsettling and liquefying all boundaries. Considering the largely informational and symbolic nature of life's processes (and an increasing immateriality of one's experience of society), research must find its starting point in a dynamic, perhaps even mobile understanding of media and society (Urry, 2007). Such an understanding is further grounded in a recognition (not an explaining away) of the increasing invisibility of media. Research should therefore not only focus on the way people use media in the context of people's sense of reality, moving beyond the production-content-reception premise of media and society, but also challenge any taken for granted technological inferences with everyday life.

Situating media *in*, rather than *with*, everyday life opens up ontological opportunities for decentring media research and draws our attention to the wider social context of finding, producing, editing and distributing meaning (through 'mass self-communication', as Castells points out). The purpose of the media life perspective is not whether we can make reality more real, or whether more or less engagement with media helps or handicaps such noble efforts. The point is rather how we can interpret media life in terms of how we can change it.[7] Humberto Maturana (1997) has raised what are quite possibly the essential stakes in our discussion of the interconnected relationships between humans and technology: 'I think that the question that we human beings must face is that of what do we want to happen to us, not a question of knowledge or progress. The question that we must face is not about the relation of biology with technology [...] nor about the relation between knowledge and reality [...] I think that the question that we must face at this moment of our history is about our desires and about whether we want or not to be responsible of our desires.'[8]

Living a media life is not necessarily submitting to the confounding reality of participating tactically in an all-encompassing reality show, nor does it contribute to a potential strategy of avoidance and disconnecting from such a reality. Kathryn Montgomery offers a glimpse of the potential of a media life point of view, offering that

> '[t]he transition to the Digital Age provides us with a unique opportunity to rethink the position of [people] in media culture, and in society as a whole [as] there is still enough fluidity in the emerging media system for actions to help guide its future (2007: 221).

If we live our lives in media and we chose to take responsibility for it, what exactly are our options to constitute each other and ourselves in society, to be (as stated earlier) free and mediated at the same time?

I am struck by the ending of The Truman Show [...] All the film can offer us is a vision of media exploitation, and all its protagonist can imagine is walking away from the media and slamming the door. It never occurs to anyone that Truman might stay on the air, generating his own content and delivering his own message, exploiting the media for his own purposes (Jenkins, 2004: 36–7).

Henry Jenkins hints at the beginnings of a media life option to understand our role in the world today – precisely because he considers escape as a flawed option. The fallacy of the escape clause is that it is premised on an understanding of human beings as possessing a core essence, literally a 'true' self (as the name Truman suggests). Such a point of view can be considered problematic, if not (as Slavoj Žižek argues) impossible. Our essence, as human beings, is not immutable, locked in to our physical presence, our cognition, and behaviours. Considering the current opportunity a media life gives people to create multiple versions of themselves and others, and to endlessly redact oneself, we now have entered a time where, as Luigi Pirandello considered in his novel *One, No One and One Hundred Thousand* (1990 [1925–6]), we can in fact see ourselves live, become cognizant about how our lifeworld is 'a world of artifice, of bending, adapting, of fiction, vanity, a world that has meaning and value only for the man who is its deviser' (p. 39). But this does not have to be an atomized, fragmented and depressing world. Our experience of the world in a media life perhaps must be seen as a world where we truly have individual and collective control over reality if only we would be at peace with the endless mutability of that reality (and developed the necessary read/write multimedia literacies to change it). As Pirandello wonders:

[w]hy do you believe firmness of will is so highly touted, and constancy of feelings? The former has only to waver a little, and the latter has only to be altered by one degree or change ever so slightly, and it's goodbye to our reality! We realize immediately that it was only our delusion (p. 42).

This delusion that is our reality in media life – possibly a mild and collectively shared form of the Truman Show delusion – can also be seen as ultimately liberating, something we can explore and navigate freely if we accept, with the protagonist in Pirandello's novel, that always rushing to find out who we really are only produces 'futile constructions' (p. 160).

Friedrich Nietzsche in *The Antichrist* (1967 [1895]), postulated that '[m]an is by no means the crown of creation: every living being stands beside him on the same level of perfection' (p. 14). From this blank slate, Nietzsche argued in *The Gay Science* (1974 [1882]), we might 'become those we are – human beings who are new, unique, incomparable, who give themselves laws, who create themselves' (p. 335). This is not to say that a life lived in media is a life lived without 'the social forces constraining people's ability to make choices and take action' (Hesmondhalgh and Toynbee, 2008: 18). What I would like to suggest is that the media life perspective exposes us to endless alternatives to and versions of ourselves, and that much of the confusion and anxiety about these options is grounded in people's struggle to position themselves in media (as well as the social pressure on people to stick to a version that was generated for them, for example as 'citizens' for democracy, or 'consumers' for capitalism). Society governed by media life is one where reality is, like many if not most websites, permanently under construction – but not only by unseen yet all-powerful guardians in the panoptic fortresses of governments and corporations that seek to construct a relatively cohesive and thus controllable reality, but also by all of us.

Perhaps a wonderful metaphoric example for this kind of society is the so-called 'Silent Disco' phenomenon, where partygoers dance to music received directly into headphones. The music gets broadcast via FM transmitter with the signal being picked up by wireless headphone receivers worn by the silent party attendees – often listening to different, individualized streams of music while still dancing together. This suggestion of being together and generally having a great time, yet still being alone in one's experience, captures the notion of a life lived in media. Here people are more connected than ever before – whether through common boundary-less issues such as global warming, terrorism and worldwide migration, or via Internet and mobile communication – yet at the same time on their own; as people increasingly participate in voluntarist and self-interested forms of social cohesion that are all too often confounded by a real or perceived impotence of people in their identities as citizens, consumers and workers 'to shape their own social environment and [to] develop the capacity for action necessary for such interventions to succeed', as Jürgen Habermas suggests (2001 [1998]: 60).

The governing principle of media life is a completely mediated self-creation in the context of always-available global connectivity. I realize that a possible consequence of the argument in this essay is to advocate that we should not dwell too much on existential contemplations and just go with all affordances media provide us with and be satisfied with the privilege of our times to use such technologies to make art with life. As Michel Foucault asks: '[w]hy should the lamp or the house be an art object, but not our life?' (1984: 350). Indeed, suggests Bauman, 'we are all artists of our lives – knowingly or not, willingly or not, like it or not' (2009: 125). In this work of art, people are on their own – much like Nietzsche advocated – but never alone (if anything, we must have an audience!). We can disconnect on demand, but nothing in the data on how we live our lives in media suggests we truly do so. Critically and deliberately, I suggest people – scholars, politicians, marketers and citizens alike – should only connect, as in the words of E.M. Forster in *Howards End* (1910): '[o]nly connect the prose and the passion and both will be exalted, and human love will be seen at its height. Live in fragments no longer.'[9] Media are where our passion materializes in the prose of our life narrative.

Notes

1 Quoted from an unpaged document provided by the publisher in advance of publication.
2 Quote taken from a story on people's concurrent media exposure in the *Christian Science Monitor* of 28 September 2005; available at URL: http://www.csmonitor.com/2005/0928/p13s01-lihc.html.
3 See URL: http://www.reellifewisdom.com/reality_we_accept_the_reality_of_the_world_with_which_we_are_presented
4 Source URL: http://www.webmd.com/mental-health/features/truman-show-delusion-real-imagined?page=2.
5 Source URL: http://www.apa.org/monitor/2009/06/delusion.html.
6 See for a list of relevant works by Wellman URL: http://www.chass.utoronto.ca/~wellman/publications/publications.html#network_theory.
7 Here I am paraphrasing Karl Marx's 11th thesis on his gravestone at Highgate Cemetery (East) in London: 'The philosophers have only interpreted the world in various ways. The point, however, is to change it.'
8 Source URL: http://www.inteco.cl/articulos/006/texto_ing.htm.
9 Full text available at URL: http://www.gutenberg.org/etext/2891.

References

Bauman, Z. (2000) *Liquid modernity*, Cambridge: Polity Press.
Bauman, Z. (2006) *Liquid fear*, Cambridge: Polity Press.
Bauman, Z. (2009) *The art of life*, Cambridge: Polity Press.
Bolter, J.D. and Grusin, R. (1996) 'Remediation', *Configurations*, 4(3): 311–358.
Castells, M. (1996) *The rise of the network society, the information age: economy, society and culture*, Oxford: Oxford University Press.
Castells, M. (2007) 'Power and counter-power in the network society', *International Journal of Communication*, 1: 238–266.
Couldry, N. (2006) *Listening beyond the echoes: media, ethics, and agency in an uncertain world*, Boulder: Paradigm Publishers.
De Jong, A. and Schuilenburg, M. (2006) *Mediapolis: popular culture and the city*, Rotterdam: 010 Publishers.
Deleuze, G. and Guattari, F. (1987) *A thousand plateaus: capitalism and schizophrenia*, Minneapolis: University of Minnesota Press.
Deuze, M. (2007) *Media work*, Cambridge: Polity Press.
Deuze, M. (2009) 'Media industries, work and life', *European Journal of Communication*, 24(4): 1–14.
Foucault, M. (1984) 'On the genealogy of ethics', in Rabinow, P. (ed.) *The Foucault reader*, London: Penguin Books.
Fuchs, C. (2007) *Internet and society: social theory in the information age*, London: Routledge.
Fuchs, C. (2009) 'A contribution to theoretical foundations of critical media and communication studies', *Javnost/The Public*, 2(1): 5–24.
Fusar-Poli, P. with Howes, O., Valmaggia, L. and McGuire, P. (2008) '"Truman" signs and vulnerability to psychosis', *British Journal of Psychiatry*, 193(2): 168.
Habermas, J. (2001 [1998]) *The postnational constellation*, Cambridge: MIT Press.
Hardt, M. and Negri, A. (2000) *Empire*, Cambridge: Harvard University Press.
Harvey, D. (1990) *The condition of postmodernity*, Malden: Blackwell.
Hesmondhalgh, D. and Toynbee, J. (eds) (2008) *The media and social theory*, London: Routledge.

Inglehart, R. and Baker, W.E. (2000) 'Modernization, cultural change, and the persistence of traditional values', *American Sociological Review*, 65(1): 19–51.

Inkinen, S. (ed.) (1998) *Mediapolis: aspects of texts, hypertext and multimedial communication*, New York: Walter de Gruyter.

Jenkins, H. (2004) 'The cultural logic of media convergence', *International Journal of Cultural Studies*, 7(1): 33–43.

Jenkins, H. (2006) *Convergence culture: where old and new media collide*, New York: New York University Press.

Kittler, F. (2009) 'Towards an ontology of media', *Theory, Culture and Society*, 26(2–3): 23–31.

Livingstone, S. (2009) 'On the mediation of everything', *Journal of Communication*, 59(1): 1–18.

Luhmann, N. (2000 [1996]) *The reality of the mass media*, Cambridge: Polity Press.

Lundby, K. (ed.) (2009) *Mediatization*, New York: Peter Lang.

Manovich, L. (2001) *The language of new media*, Cambridge: MIT Press.

Maturana, H.R. (1997) *Metadesign*, Instituto de Terapia Cognitiva, INTECO essay. Available: <http://www.inteco.cl/articulos/006/texto_ing.htm>.

Montgomery, K. (2009) *Generation Digital*, Cambridge: MIT Press.

Rasmussen, T. (2000) *Social theory and communication technology*, Farnham: Ashgate.

Silverstone, R. (2007) *Media and morality: on the rise of the mediapolis*, Cambridge: Polity Press.

Stalder, F. (2006) *Manuel Castells*, Cambridge: Polity Press.

Stephens, M. (1998) *The rise of the image, the fall of the word*, Cambridge: Oxford University Press.

Strate, L. (2006) *Echoes and reflections: on media ecology as a field of study*, Cresskill: Hampton Press.

Thompson, J.B. (1995) *The media and modernity*, Cambridge: Polity Press.

Urry, J. (2007) *Mobilities*, Cambridge: Polity Press.

Žižek, S. (2006) *The parallax view*, Cambridge: MIT Press.

9 Consumer culture and new media: commodity fetishism in the digital era

Matthew P. McAllister

The millennial era is an extraordinary one for developments in consumer culture. Especially central to these developments is the use of new media and their commercial and consumerist manifestations. The multimedia, e-commerce and interactive characteristics of the Internet, the mobile commercial (or 'm-commerce') possibilities of smart phones, the creative power of digital video production, and digital video recorders/on-demand media are just a few of the media developments that radically change the way that brands are bought, sold, marketed and understood. These changes influence such factors as the diversity and vibrancy of media systems, the relationship of consumption to definitions of prosperity and happiness in our lives, the role of surveillance and privacy, environmental impact and issues of personal agency.

Critical-cultural media studies scholarship contributes significantly to understanding how digital media technologies influence modern consumer culture and twenty-first century societies, including developing new critical concepts. Alternatively, established critical concepts may be re-applied to new consumerist contexts, either in totality or in modified forms. Older concepts can still offer analytical depth for understanding new consumerist phenomena. Applying older critical perspectives to new media may also encourage modification and improvement of these perspectives. Schor (2007), for example, argues that perspectives such as Veblen's 'conspicuous consumption' and the Frankfurt School still have much to offer about modern directions in consumer culture. Scholars have also critiqued new promotional contexts using analytical lenses such as Williams' television 'flow' (Brooker, 2001; Budd *et al.*, 1999; Gray, 2008) and Debordian 'spectacle' (Watts and Orbe, 2002).

In this spirit, this essay will explore how the Marxian term of 'commodity fetish', especially as applied in critical media studies, may offer insights about recent developments in new mediated forms of consumer culture. The goal here is not to undertake a philosophical deconstruction of the term (see Miklitsch, 1996). Rather, the concept is applied largely as an organizational schema to review certain key themes highlighted by the growing critical scholarship about digitally mediated consumer culture and trends in new media consumerism. However, such themes and trends also encourage a rethinking of the concept for modern commercial phenomena.

Commodity fetishism in commercial media studies

Commodity fetishism, despite its nineteenth-century origins in Marx's *Capital*, is not a forgotten or non-influential concept in modern media studies. It is arguably a foundational concept for many critical approaches to advertising and promotional culture. Although in this literature perhaps the most extensive discussion is Jhally (1987), it is also explicitly discussed in reviews of critical media studies and consumer culture scholarship (Budd *et al.*, 1999; Leiss *et al.*, 2005; Mosco, 1996; Paterson, 2006), and applied to trends in media licensing (Waetjen and Gibson, 2007). The concept is also the basis – either explicitly or implied – in much work critiquing the semiotics of advertising, as will be discussed.

Jhally (1987) explains that Marx's original delineation of commodity fetishism was developed before modern consumer and image culture. Appropriating the term 'fetishism' – reminiscent of anthropological studies of mystical elements in religion – for Marx it was the capitalist-created commodity itself (rather than promotional discourse about the product) that fetishized the commodity. In mass production capitalism, it is difficult to 'read' the true nature of commodities since the object's origins in a particular production context are masked or hidden, unlike systems in which an individual craftsperson's skill is evident in the product. In the modern commodity, labour's commodification and separation from the means of production are 'mystified' (Jhally, 1987: 26–7). The commodity, when separated from its production process, is reified, appearing as a natural, autonomous object, created as if by magic, and not by a very particularized – and exploitative – means of production.

As an object without an obvious production origin, the modern commodity was further exploitable by other meaning systems. In what Mosco calls a 'double mystification' (1996: 143), the gap between the commodity and its production context was eventually filled by the image-based orientation of later capitalism, especially in advertising and other promotional discourse (see also Jhally, 1987; Ewen, 1976). Such commercial symbols as store displays, packaging and especially advertising, linked commodities to a new set of social relations, relations established in consumption contexts rather than production.

As commodity discourses, advertisements and other promotional forms rarely discuss issues of production with the commodity. But the promotion discourse of consumer culture does much more than further mask production. It is in the additional meanings that advertising attempts to impose upon commodities (or, now, 'brands') – and even upon consumers themselves – that semioticians and/or rhetoricians of advertising contribute to the concept of commodity fetishism. Although the specific term 'commodity fetishism' is not predominantly engaged by important scholars such as Williamson (1978) and Goldman (1992), both recognize that the production context is further removed from brand advertising and examine the reintegration of brands into modern social relations. Goldman explores how advertising constructs 'commodity-signs' by linking specific commodities to what Williamson calls 'referent systems'. When done successfully, advertising creates 'sign value' to enhance the use and exchange value of commodities. Goldman notes that advertising extends the mystification process inherent in modern capitalist commodities by equating social values with commodities: skin cream equals peer acceptance and diamonds equal eternal love. Such semiotic manoeuvres further reify the commodity with its linkages to these values. As Williamson argues, advertising can construct several different relationships between brands and social referent systems. In fact, brands can be so established as commodity-signs that they can become meaning signifiers themselves in culture. As Goldman explains: 'Not only are commodities joined to signs commodities get produced as signs, and signs become produced as commodities' (1992: 37). It is no wonder, then, that in discussing this semiotic process in advertising, Raymond Williams argues, using similar metaphors to Marx, that advertising is a 'magic' system, imputing commodities with special social and psychological powers (Williams, 1980).

It is not only in the commodity where meaning is created in advertising. Consumers are also commercially 'constructed' as persons who have desires and lifestyles consistent with or even requiring the product, as the phrase 'lifestyle marketing' signals (Leiss *et al.*, 2005). Williamson (1978) labels this 'appellation' – how advertising symbolically creates consumer subjectivity. In some cases, the association with a targeted lifestyle is so strong that brands can reject other potentially desirable referent systems, such as the trope in beer commercials that a brand of beer should be valued in male lifestyles over sex or economic success (Messner and Montez de Oca, 2005). In such ways, a company like Nike can construct commodity-signs of brands and consumers around a neo-liberal ideology of 'just do it' while at the same time producing these commodities in dehumanizing factory conditions (Andersen, 1995; Goldman and Papson, 1998; Stabile, 2000).

How might commodity fetishism offer insights about new media and consumer culture? The next section will apply the two main components of commodity fetishism to such trends, but in reverse order to that discussed above. First, the creation of commodity-signs and sign value in new-media contexts is explored, including speculation about likely future trends in the digitally enhanced, fetishized commodity-sign. A review of the role of production discourse and activity in interactive promotional activity and commodity-signs then follows, prompting a rethinking of commodity fetishism in its application to twenty-first century promotional trends.

New media and the commodity-sign

Four converging trends in digital consumer discourse refine the ability of marketers to construct commodity-signs. The four trends that then potentially add symbolic 'magic' to the commodity are the Internet as a multimediated channel for commodity-sign construction; the emphasis on interactivity, data mining, and target marketing; the ever-evolving power of digital production techniques; and the blurring of the commercial into other mediated texts.

Scholars from both a cultural perspective (Spurgeon, 2008) and a more administrative/practitioner perspective (Schumann and Thorson, 2007) have discussed the Internet as an advertising vehicle. Such work notes that the Internet facilitated the creation of thousands (if not more) of commercially defined virtual spaces: websites for branded products designed to advance the construction of commodity-signs. The multimodal and interactive nature of the Internet greatly increases mechanisms for creating coherent symbol sets around brand in a malleable and enduring promotional environment. Sound, images, graphics, video, text are integrated in ways that were unheard of before. The Internet, in fact, has facilitated Integrated Marketing Communications (IMC): the coordination of different promotional forms to create and reinforce a consistent brand meaning. Branded websites are venues for traditional promotional forms – the standard-length commercial; brand logos, mascots, jingles; and press releases – all coordinated to construct brands. In addition, the stability and accessibility of web locations means that the normally time-constrained nature of traditional media can be circumvented. The life of a particular ad is extended as print and television commercials can be archived on a commercial website to be accessed by visitors at any time.

The Internet also has facilitated the creation of new, hybrid promotional forms for commodity-sign construction. One example is branded games ('advergaming'), based upon the commodity-sign assumptions or icons of a brand. A site like postopia.com offers games and activities featuring licensed breakfast cereal characters. Similarly hybrid is the long-form ad – audiovisual commercials five minutes or longer: normally too expensive to place on television but no more expensive to distribute on the Internet than shorter forms, and providing more symbolic depth. Much publicity was generated for early examples of such forms, such as BMW's 2001 'webisodes', titled *The Hire*, starring actor Clive Owen, directed by such talents as Ang Lee, and prominently featuring BMW in the 'plots' (Lehu, 2007: 213–15). The entire series was available for DVD purchase on Amazon.com long after the campaign ended. American Express used a similar tactic in 2004 long-form web ads with comedian Jerry Seinfeld and an animated Superman. Such hybridity increases the symbolic capital in commodity-signs by integrating them into traditionally non-advertising forms (games and long-form entertainment).

Other strategies are adopted from the entertainment industry. Several scholars have argued that film and television are radically changing, given promotional and monetizing possibilities offered via digitization. The website of a television programme like *Lost*, for example, can sell not just *Lost* merchandise, but can also extend the programme's fan loyalties through additional web-only information about characters' backstory and motivations (Gray, 2008; see also Brooker, 2001; Proffitt *et al.*, 2007). The Internet allows a similar kind of 'overflow' of branded and/or trademarked characters found in commercials. Instead of a website devoted to Jack from *Lost*, the purely advertising version is a website for Bergwood, the excessive (and accident-prone) US college football fan featured in Allstate Insurance commercials (see www.bergwood.net). The site offers Bergwood and Bergwood/Allstate-branded merchandise (or 'bergchandise') and advergames. The goofy, but likeable Bergwood advertising character – or, following Williamson, 'referent system' – that Allstate features in its TV commercials is further developed and reified in this web-enhanced manner.

Branded websites often mix promotion with e-commerce, offering the ability to purchase commodities, with this function literally placed next to commodity-signs. E-commerce sites such as Amazon.com also routinely carry web ads for the products they sell, blurring the distinction between e-commerce and promotional websites. Spurgeon (2008: 44) speculates that sites like Amazon will eventually morph into giant web shopping 'channels', with the selling function becoming a form of digital point-of-purchase advertising. Even with sites not explicitly e-commerce or promotional, such as news or entertainment sites, the fact that user 'click-through' behaviour has become an important measure of advertising effectiveness is likely to continue to commercialize the Internet (Spurgeon, 2008). Unlike older media such as television that measure the potential exposure to advertising through viewer ratings, the click-through measure indicates the users' attraction to an ad, and willingness to move into a commercial space because of the ad. Such measurements increase the incentives of non-commercial sites to create an ad-friendly environment and ensure visitors notice the ads, an incentive that has implications for traditional media, as discussed below.

Changes in data mining and niche marketing also impact the influence of the commodity-sign. Given the ability to combine different consumer and financial databases, and the data 'footprint' of interactive media such as digital video recorders (DVRs) and digital shopping and purchasing, marketers are increasingly using consumer databases to enhance target marketing (Andrejevic, 2007; Fernback, 2007; Turow, 2006, 2009). With database marketing – the 'holy grail of leverage' over buying behaviour (Turow, 2009) – interactive media and e-commerce have facilitated the creation of large consumer databases; new labels offered by critics for the resulting consumer profiles include the 'data self', and 'digital data gaze' (Fernback, 2007: 325; Andrejevic, 2007: 107). These data profiles facilitate targeted advertising to specific consumers based upon the preferences and profiles extrapolated from these databases, cultivating what marketers benignly term 'Customer Relationship Marketing'.

Critical scholars who discuss the manipulation and privacy implications of data mining focus on opportunistic reach: the use of target marketing announces the availability of a particular product when specific consumers are most vulnerable to a selling message or purchasing opportunity. For example, if a marketer knows that someone tends to purchase a product (say, vegetarian pizza), and a new, similarly demographically targeted product is developed (a brand of whole-wheat crust pizza), that marketer will target that specific consumer with that specific announcement. In a digital version of 'pseudo-individuality' (Horkheimer and Adorno, 2006: 63), marketing software generates personalized targeting automatically as it correlates consumer databases in a technique paradoxically called 'mass customization'. Marketers may also create special offers for particular consumer 'niches', creating a 'niche envy' when people outside of a group become aware of offers not available to them (Turow, 2006). Andrejevic (2007) speculates that with 'm-commerce' – sales messages distributed through mobile technologies such as smart phones and even 'smart clothes' equipped with radio frequency ID (RFID) technology – retail stores could literally hail consumers about specific purchases as they near retail outlets.

Such trends are trumpeted as consumer advantages given the promise of eliminating unwanted advertising such as mass-distributed junk mail (Spurgeon, 2008). However, these techniques are potentially manipulative as consumers become especially vulnerable to certain kinds of commodity purchases over others (even for those not affordable), or certain times over others (when hungry). As Andrejevic (2007: 103) argues, 'It's one thing to remember a customer's preferences in order to serve them up "the usual", and quite another to use information about the fact that their clothing size might have changed recently to market them diet pills....' Other implications include the further erosion of privacy and the delineation of consumers into smaller, and ultimately divisive, marketer-defined niche groups (Turow, 2006).

The confluence of interactivity, data mining, 'mass customization', and target/relationship marketing enhances the construction of commodity-signs. As mentioned above, much work about personalized ads focus on the *timing* of an ad announcement – ads sent to a consumer based on perceived interests; on contextually based need (smart clothes sensing that a wearer is hungry); or on purchasing opportunity. But advertisements do more than announce a product's existence or availability. They also construct meanings by symbolically linking a product with desirable referent systems, referent systems that can vary from person to person. An interactive media future could mean more information about what referent systems, and what particular symbols, match up with a particular consumer's dreams and desires. As digital production technology becomes more advanced and combines with database information, could the advertising future mean that smart ads will also shape the referent systems in a persuasive appeal for what they know about a consumer's past interests and current mood?

So, with digital production techniques, an even more fetishized future would combine different sales voices, faces, linguistic styles and appeals for the same products for different people. It may not be a generic digital salesperson who greets you and knows your purchasing patterns, but a particularized set of referents based on what marketers know about your past referent system patterns, including your media use. If a marketer knows that you watch Brad Pitt movies, then the salesperson could be shaped to resemble (or be a digital facsimile of) the actor. If they know you like hip-hop, then the language of the message can be adjusted. And in a future where media are becoming more on-demand and interactive, the information to be used to create customized referent systems grows.

The target marketing future can be extended even further, given IMC and modern media incentives. As advertising becomes accustomed to the flexibility of online advertising, and targeted technologies such as DVRs allow audiences to more easily avoid the 30-second commercial, advertisers are exploring ways to market on traditional media in addition to the classic advertisement. Media companies in turn seek to maintain advertising revenue in the midst of advertiser spending shifts and to monetize and promote their own branded products (DVDs, on-demand, and merchandizing). Combing these, the traditional media are increasingly receptive to intrusive and hybrid commercial forms that facilitate their goals. Products displayed in media content (product placement) is one such form, labelled by Gray as 'the advertising of the future' (2008: 88). More intense versions include product integration (the folding of branded products into narratives and character identities) and branded entertainment (where the very premise of a programme, song, film, book or game centres on a branded product) (Lehu, 2007).

In the near commercial future, these incentives may be coupled with the digitization of television, delivered on demand through an Internet or IP television system (Bar and Taplin, 2007). In this system, the interactivity of the Internet could be brought to both televisual commercials and programmes. The mere potential exposure to a promotional message, as is currently measured by Nielsen ratings, will be inadequate. Click-through advertising measurement, a standard indicator of ad effectiveness on the Internet, may become the standard to judge advertising success in television. With this, every television programme could become its own home shopping environment. This does not just involve the commercials interrupting the programmes and the commodity-signs in the commercials, but commercial iconography integrated in programmes themselves. With the hyperlinked and hybrid Internet as a model, it is possible that click-through technology could also be applied to TV programmes and movies, where the ability to purchase products placed or integrated into texts will be built into the experience. Certain commodities could be 'hyperlinked' in television texts, where just a point and click will create a buying opportunity. Do you like the shirt a character is wearing on *Grey's Anatomy*? Pause, click and purchase it through your interactive TV.

This can be taken further. If niched and database advertising creates unique commodity-signs based upon 'data selves', with advanced digital production and interactive capability, the creation of targeted and unique product placements in programmes is possible, at least in certain circumstances. Particular brands or variations of brands (colours, flavours, varieties) could be placed in particular programmes that maximize their appeal based upon a consumer/viewer's particular data profile. The technology and the economic incentives encourage not just that every programme be a home shopping programme, but also that personalized entertainment-shopping complexes use your favourite Hollywood stars, hawk your personalized products, all (seemingly) just for you: a semiotic dance between individualized, data-driven commodity-signs results, including the signs offered by our audiovisual entertainment systems. And, if such a system is implemented, the more we participate, the more data is collected, the more refined is the individualized data profile, and the more fetishized is the brand.

New media, consumer labour, and the production-commodity-sign

The commodity-sign is the main way that commodity fetishism tends to be discussed in advertising criticism, and the potential for extending the commodity-sign is significant with new media. But what of Marx's original focus with commodity fetishism: the distraction from labour and the production context of modern capitalist commodities? This aspect of commodity fetishism is also complicated with digital media. As will be argued, consumption discourse in new media often highlights, rather than hides, symbols of production and the role of labour. Does this aspect of commodity fetishism – its mystification of production – no longer apply to the digitally promoted commodity? The masking of production is still relevant for digital commercial forms with qualification, as two sections below argue. First, digital promotion offers a particular kind of production discourse, specifically about the advertising process, often folded back as, ironically, a new symbolic tool for the commodity-sign. Second, we also find a particular presentation and use of consumer labour in this discourse – typically framed as empowering but still with exploitative elements and often also integrated as a referent system in the promoted brand. In both cases, production becomes symbolic capital for digital branding.

'Behind the scenes' of promotional discourse

To argue that 'production' is highlighted in digital promotion is to broaden the idea of production in commodity fetishism, as argued by Miklitsch (1996). The production of the physical commodity – mass manufacturing and spaces of material production – is still mostly hidden in digital commercial forms. But aspects of the service economy, specifically advertising and marketing activity, are often a key part of the new discourse of brands, via a celebratory meta-discourse about advertising. This is different from ironic, self-reflexive postmodern advertising (Goldman, 1992; Goldman and Papson, 1996). Rather, it is an earnest discourse in which the advertising process is explicitly trumpeted in promotional discourse around branded goods.

Influenced by 'the making of' extras found on movie DVDs, advertisers are increasingly creating their own 'behind the scenes' features about advertising campaigns and making them available online. Here the production of the commodity-sign, not the physical commodity, is highlighted. And it should come as no surprise that this production-oriented discourse is self-interested and celebratory. Issues of persuasion (let alone potential manipulation of audiences and media systems) are very rarely discussed in such video features. Rather, similar to the Hollywood version, the theme of such features is the creation of art and spectacle, and the obstacles faced in this goal.

For example, one four-and-a-half-minute feature profiles the making of a 2006 TV commercial for Johnnie Walker whisky. Part of the 'Keep Walking' campaign, the futuristic commercial is about an android who wishes to be human and, it is presumed, to be able to truly enjoy Johnnie Walker (Iezzi, 2006: 18). Opening with sombre music and shots of the crew, a voiceover from an ad agency executive states:

> I think the idea of 'Keep Walking', like any great idea, is trying to live beyond a piece of advertising, it's trying to elevate itself into a place where it is inspirational to people. So 'Keep Walking' is about reminding people that life is the journey, not just the destination.

Following this high-minded declaration, the mini-documentary focuses on the artistic legacy of Johnnie Walker ads and this particular commercial's elaborate special effects and transcendent themes. Such features are now common for high-profile campaigns – American Express commercials featuring Jerry Seinfeld and Ellen DeGeneres have similar offerings – and are widely distributed on the brands' websites and video distribution sites like YouTube (where 'Keep Walking' may be found).

Such extra-textual discourses highlight the production of the commodity-sign in a way that did not commonly exist before digital media. And it could be argued that there is potential 'demystification' of the commodity-sign that occurs given the peek behind the advertising curtain that such features allow. Yet the promotional nature of these 'behind-the-scenes' videos encourages viewers to assume the perspective of the advertiser, and to understand the ad as a creative, not a persuasive, endeavour. In addition, the features do not just reflect the existing commodity-sign, but add to it: the campaign's goal is to associate this brand of scotch whisky to the awe-inspiring essence of humanity. The feature's focus on this goal reinforces the commodity-sign image established by the ad itself.

Complementing these features is the increased attention to advertising campaigns paid by news outlets, including local and national broadcast and cable television news (Wood *et al.*, 2004). Sparked by 'event' advertising such as the US Super Bowl (Watts and Orbe, 2002), news organizations also have economic reasons to create sympathetic or at least non-fundamentally critical pieces about the creation and success of advertising campaigns. News stories allow media outlets to provide 'value-added' promotion to current or potential advertisers; entice business-oriented viewers attractive to advertisers; and create a more 'ad-friendly' environment. Although given that news stories do involve a third-party construction of the discourse (unlike the self-promotional 'making of' features) and therefore may have some critical distance, such stories still tend to use advertising-industry sources, and to be framed from an advertising perspective, asking questions such as, is the ad effective at selling or not? After the Super Bowl, for example, the US network TV morning news programmes air stories about the 'winner and loser' ads. Super Bowl ad stories also appear during the week before the game, 'handicapping' the potential for an ad's success. In this case, then, even if the production of the commodity-sign is highlighted in such stories, the questions the story asks are from the perspective of the advertising industry, rather than from a larger social perspective. With YouTube and network television websites, such stories have a long shelf life.

The integration and promotion of consumer labour

In addition to increased advertising-production discourse on the Internet, promotion in the digital era also has a relationship with labour that complicates the mystification effect of commodity fetishism. Scholars argue that digital labour generally, given its outsourcing potential, is especially exploitative and bifurcating (Rodino-Colocino, 2006). With promotional media, there is a blurring of production and consumption that is certainly complicated, but an aspect of this complication is that unpaid labour is integral to, and even celebrated by, digital commercialism. Such unpaid labour may additionally feed back into a campaign to become part of the commodity-sign.

Scholars have asserted that, even in pre-digital forms, consumers serve as labour in advertising. Consumers must provide 'interpretative labour' of commodity-signs for such signs to have meaning (Goldman, 1992: 9).

Arvidsson (2005) similarly posits that consumers' public display and use of brands – an 'enacting' of brands – creates and enhances the brands' social value. Scholars like Jhally (1987) contend that consumer labour is also built into the political economy of advertising-driven media such as television. Watching advertising is a form of labour, with 'payment' being the more-desired content accompanying the ads. Andrejevic (2002) extends this metaphor to surveillance-oriented digital media, where users tolerate data-gathering as their labour value, or their 'work of being watched'. This 'being-watched' labour grants them the full interactivity that surveillance technologies such as Internet cookies and DVRs offer. Cohen (2008) argues that Web 2.0 interactive sites like YouTube and Facebook, unlike traditional media, depend upon users to create their content – it is the business model for such sites (see also van Dijck, 2009).

The involvement of consumers as a form of productive labour, or at least the 'best practices' of such involvement, is valued by other scholars who see digital media as enhancing the emancipatory potential of what Schor calls the 'agentic' consumer (2007: 24). This perspective is most notably associated with media fandom on the Internet (such as Jenkins, 2006), but also applied to traditional brand advertising contexts (Spurgeon, 2008). Such scholarship argues that the blurring of production and consumption empowers consumers, with new digital technologies allowing for more democratic production and distribution, as implied by hybrid terms such as 'prosumer' and 'produser' (Spurgeon, 2008: 16–7). Spurgeon offers consumer-created and distributed videos of consumers mixing Mentos and Coca-Cola, and the volcano effect that results, as 'proof positive' that audiences are actively involved in the 'management of media culture' (Spurgeon, 2008: 2).

The blurring of production and consumption allowed by digital media, although often creative, can be exploited as unpaid labour. Zwick *et al.* (2008) posit that the use of unpaid consumer labour may be doubly exploitative, in that it does not compensate for the productive time, effort and skills of consumers, yet these consumer-provided resources enhance the brand's symbolic value and thus the price to these same consumers. Consumer labour also encourages a 'producerly' mindset in these active consumers (Andrejevic, 2007) or, to use a Foucauldian term, an enacting of governmentality in new consumerism (Zwick *et al.*, 2008).

Despite the implications for economic and social control, the integration of unpaid consumer labour is not hidden in digital media discourse – unlike traditional commodity fetishism – but instead often foregrounded and publicized. Digital consumers assume at least four different producerly roles as unpaid labour, roles that may be also used as materials to enhance the sign value of digital commodity-signs. These four roles are consumers as unpaid focus group members, consumers as unpaid publicity and distribution channels, consumers as unpaid ad creators, and consumers as referent system in the commodity-sign.

Consumers as unpaid focus group members

As mentioned earlier, new media has built into its very logic the valorization of consumer data. Sites such as YouTube collect information about user behaviours such that 'the user's role as a data provider is infinitely more important than his role as a content provider' (van Dijck, 2009: 49). Given also that much of YouTube's content is explicitly commercial, this provides a level of feedback about commercial symbols that traditional media cannot match.

In addition, many websites that feature brands – both media brands and non-media commodity brands – include discussion boards where users post opinions and reply to topic threads about the brands. These public forums can serve as sources of marketing research, leading to 'web farming', where marketers lurk on such sites for ideas and information (Fernback, 2007: 317). Fan sites such as televisionwithoutpity. com (TVWoP) can 'serve as an impromptu focus group, providing instant feedback to plot twists and the introduction of new characters', as industry personnel check for fan opinions (Andrejevic, 2007: 139). Even if production companies do not use online feedback to influence the direction of programmes, the belief that they do encourages online contributors to take producer-oriented perspectives on how to make the show more appealing and marketable (Andrejevic, 2007). This adds to a feeling of online agency and that the producers do care about fans, thus enhancing the programme as 'fan friendly'. In some cases, fan sites increase the consumption of television programmes, as posts will enhance the entertainment value of even badly scripted shows. Here, Andrejevic argues, fan posters serve as unpaid 'punch-up' scriptwriters. TVWoP is owned by NBC Universal, illustrating the use of fan sites for corporations; a similar site, tv.com, is owned by CBS.

Fernback (2007) notes that the privacy policy statements of e-commerce and branded websites declare the companies' rights to use such sites for marketing research and even sell results to third parties. Other interactive features, such as clicking on surveys or 'voting' for favourites, can also serve as valuable feedback about consumer preferences. In the case of call-in television programmes like *Big Brother*, such feedback also is a form of consumption, given the cell minutes or text messages that will be charged against the users' allocation, the feedback about entertainment preferences provided, and spin-off apps such as programme updates that can be purchased (Nightingale and Dwyer, 2006).

Consumers as unpaid publicity and distribution channels

'Viral' or 'stealth' marketing takes many forms, but one form is the distribution of a sponsored video, image or electronic postcard by email from fans. In such cases, the sender adds to the commodity-sign's source credibility since the promotional message comes from a friend, not a company.

Viral marketing in this way enacts the spirit of commodity fetishism by separating messages from their original promotional contexts and ultimately contributing to our 'age of deceit' (Schejter, 2007).

Social networking sites like Facebook encourage such fan distribution of branded messages. Users can 'share' a brand's Facebook page with others, but even if they do not, one's Facebook friends can still be notified, via the 'News Feed' function, when one 'fans' such a site (Cohen, 2008). 'Fanning' a branded site makes information available about the fan to the creator of that site, and it becomes a part of the Facebook fan's profile available for their Facebook friends to see at any time. In some cases, though, and previewing the below point, promotional discourses are created by fans via social networking. Facebook users create their own brand-based sites or apps (Hearn, 2008), such as 'I Love Chapstick'. Grimes (2008) points out that children's branded sites like nick.com offer restricted chat rooms where young users may only chat by choosing a limited range of options of phrases from pull-down menus. Many of the pull-down phrases contain the names of licensed characters, which literally puts branded words in the mouths (or chats) of participating kids.

Consumers as unpaid ad creators

Perhaps the ultimate blurring of consumer and producer is user generated content (UGC). While a site like YouTube facilitates distribution of content, digital cameras and editing software allow content creation. UGCs are often touted as an especially empowering new media trend. But marketers co-opt this form with a special version: user generated *commercials* (Turow, 2009). Scores of brands, including Doritos and Dove skin care, hold contests for the best 'amateur' commercial for their brand. Winners can earn significant revenue, but submissions for high-profile contests may number thousands. UGC submissions are really a 'lottery', given the long odds of collecting the big money (Clifford, 2008).

UGC contests serve several functions. They attract younger demographics. They force participants – at least those who want to win – to adopt the brand's perspective in their creation. They generate ideas for advertisers. They generate publicity as creators post their entries to YouTube or Yahoo! Video. Companies encourage additional identification, viewing and news coverage through a voting process to determine the winner. The contest rhetoric, UGCs' 'rough around the edges' quality, and resulting news publicity all construct authenticity by highlighting their 'prosumer' nature, which in turn adds to the commodity-sign of the brand. In these ways, the idea of a 'fan-friendly' brand is reinforced by a UGC and the accompanying promotional discourses.

Consumer as referent system in the commodity-sign

As the above notes, consumer labour in new media contributes to the brand equity of commodity-signs. Viral marketing and UGCs are about adding to the ethos of brand by highlighting brand loyalty; loyal fans love us so much that they volunteer to create and distribute our ads, marketers brag. As new media develops, marketers will continue to integrate the 'prosumer' as symbolic capital in different ways.

For example, it was mentioned earlier that the humour of certain beer ads is the degree of sacrifice that male beer drinkers are willing to endure for their beer (Messner and Montez de Oca, 2005). In such instances, the symbolic capital of the commodity sign transcends traditional referent systems such as material success and romantic conquests. A similar message, but one with a digital twist, is Burger King's 2009 'Whopper Sacrifice' campaign, in which Facebook users earned a free hamburger if they dropped 10 'friends' from their Facebook network (Quenqua, 2009). In this case, a Whopper does not get you friends; it is more important than friends. Unlike beer ads, it is the consumer invoking this commodity-sign, not an advertising character. Highlighting the use of this campaign to build the commodity-sign, Burger King stopped the campaign because its desire to publicize 'unfriending' violated Facebook's policy. Normally when someone is 'unfriended' on Facebook they are not notified, but Burger King did in fact notify Facebook users when their friend status was sacrificed to a free Whopper. That notification, in fact, was the whole point: Burger King wanted Facebook users to be told, this person likes Whoppers more than you.

Conclusion

The concept of commodity fetishism helps explain digitally driven consumer culture, albeit with a couple of twists. The dynamics of production and the role of labour are not completely hidden, but it is not the means of production of the physical good that is highlighted. Rather, the digital discourse focuses on the means of symbolic production, or production of the commodity-sign in promotional digital media. Such discourse includes both a cooptation of consumer labour in this production, and the selective celebration of this production in the commodity-sign. In this case, then, the basic premise of commodity fetishism still holds: the constitutive power of the commodity-sign trumps a multi-perspectival engagement with the realities of labour and global capitalist production. At the same time, the semiotic power of the digital commodity-sign is significantly enhanced, given the productive and distributive power of new media, and its integration of databases, different promotional forms, and media texts.

The above discussion is admittedly pessimistic about the anti-fetish potential in digital commercial outlets. But other venues offer significant resistance to large-scale advertising and commodity-signs (Harold, 2007; Klein, 1999). The Internet of course is not entirely corporate controlled, and is used by activists and other groups to critique the exploitative potential of consumer culture and defetishize the commodity-sign. This characteristic of the Internet is especially important given traditional media's desperation for, and potential deference to, advertising. Non-advertising funded organizations such as Commercial Alert (commercialalert.org) and Adbusters (adbusters.org) focus on the commercialization of the public sphere and particularly egregious commodity-sign practices. Other websites index and critique exploitative production practices, such as wiserearth.org, often in more graphic detail than advertising-based or government-licensed media could tolerate.

The increasing selective exposure tendencies in new media – especially as smart media learn our preferences and automatically direct us to certain media venues – could perhaps limit the reach of such sites. But in an era of the digital commodity fetish, the power of the commodity-sign and the symbolic uses of labour, such sites and practices are more important than ever.

References

Andersen, R. (1995) *Consumer Culture and TV Programming*, Boulder, CO: Westview.

Andrejevic, M. (2002) 'The work of being watched: Interactive media and the exploitation of self-disclosure', *Critical Studies in Media Communication*, 19(2): 230–248.

Andrejevic, M. (2007) *iSpy: Surveillance and Power in the Interactive Era*, Lawrence, KS: University Press of Kansas.

Arvidsson, A. (2005) 'Brands: A critical perspective', *Journal of Consumer Culture*, 5(2): 235–258.

Bar, F. and Taplin, J. (2007) 'Cable's digital future', in Banet-Weiser, S., Chris, C. and Feitas, A. (eds) *Cable Visions: Television Beyond Broadcasting*, New York: New York University Press.

Brooker, W. (2001) 'Living on Dawson's Creek: Teen viewers, cultural convergence, and television overflow', *International Journal of Cultural Studies*, 4(4): 456–472.

Budd, M., Craig, S. and Steinman, C. (1999) *Consuming Environments: Television and Commercial Culture*, New Brunswick, NJ: Rutgers University Press.

Clifford, S. (2008) 'Decades after the jingle lady, a gold mine in digital ditties', *New York Times*: 28 October, A1, A20.

Cohen, N.S. (2008) 'The valorization of surveillance; towards a political economy of Facebook', *Democratic Communiqué*, 22(1): 5–22.

van Dijck, J. (2009) 'Users like you? Theorizing agency in user-generated content', *Media, Culture, and Society*, 31(1): 41–58.

Ewen, S. (1976) *Captains of Consciousness: Advertising and the Social Roots of Consumer Culture*, New York: McGraw-Hill.

Fernback, J. (2007) 'Selling ourselves: Profitable surveillance and online communities', *Critical Discourse Studies*, 4(3): 311–312.

Goldman, R. (1992) *Reading Ads Socially*, NY: Routledge.

Goldman, R. and Papson, S. (1996) *Sign Wars: The Cluttered Landscape of Advertising*, New York: Guilford.

Goldman, R. and Papson, S. (1998) *Nike Culture*, Thousand Oaks, CA: Sage.

Gray, J. (2008) *Television Entertainment*, New York: Routledge.

Grimes, S.M. (2008b) 'Saturday morning cartoons go MMOG', *Media International Australia*, 126: 120–131.

Harold, C. (2007) *OurSpace: Resisting the Corporate Control of Culture*, Minneapolis: University of Minnesota Press.

Hearn, A. (2008) 'Meat, mask, burden: Probing the contours of the branded "self"', *Journal of Consumer Culture*, 8(2): 196–217.

Horkheimer, M. and Adorno, T.W. (2006) 'The culture industry: Enlightenment as mass deception', in Durham, M.G. and Kellner, D.M. (eds) *Media and Cultural Studies: Keyworks*, Malden, MA: Blackwell.

Iezzi, T. (2006) 'Johnnie Walker campaign keeps walking toward higher ground', *Advertising Age*, 23 October: 18.

Jenkins, H. (2006) *Convergence Culture: Where Old and New Media Collide*, New York: New York University Press.

Jhally, S. (1987) *The Codes of Advertising: Fetishism and the Political Economy of Meaning in the Consumer Society*, New York: Routledge and Kegan Paul.

Klein, N. (1999) *No Logo: Taking Aim at the Brand Bullies*, New York: Picador.

Lehu, J. (2007) *Product Placement and Brand Strategy in the Entertainment Business*, London: Kogan Page.

Leiss, W., Kline, S., Jhally, S. and Botterill, J. (2005) *Social Communication in Advertising: Consumption in the Mediated Marketplace*, 3rd edn, New York: Routledge.

Messner, M.A., and Montez de Oca, J. (2005) 'The male consumer as loser: Beer and liquor ads in mega sports media events', *Signs: Journal of Women in Culture and Society*, 30(3): 1879–1909.

Miklitsch, R. (1996) 'The commodity-body-sign: Toward a general economy of "commodity fetishism"', *Cultural Critique*, 33: 5–40.

Mosco, V. (1996) *The Political Economy of Communication,* Thousand Oaks, CA: Sage.

Nightingale, V. and Dwyer, T. (2006) 'The audience politics of "enhanced" television formats', *International Journal of Media and Cultural Politics*, 2(1): 25–42.

Paterson, M. (2006) *Consumption and Everyday Life*, London: Routledge.

Proffitt, J.M., Tchoi, D.Y. and McAllister, M.P. (2007) 'Plugging back into The Matrix: The intertextual flow of corporate media commodities', *Journal of Communication Inquiry*, 31(3): 239–254.

Quenqua, D. (2009) 'Friends, until I delete you', *New York Times*, 29 January: E1.

Rodino-Colocino, M. (2006) 'Laboring under the digital divide', *New Media and Society*, 8(3): 487–511.

Schejter, A. (2007) '"Jacob's Voice, Esau's Hands": Transparency as a First Amendment right in an age of deceit and impersonation', *Hofstra Law Review*, 35: 1489–1518.

Schor, J.B. (2007) 'In defense of consumer critique: Revisiting the consumption debates of the twentieth century', *Annals of the American Academy of Political and Social Science*, 611: 16–30.

Schumann, D.W. and Thorson, E. (eds) (2007) *Internet Advertising: Theory and Research*, Mahwah, NJ: Lawrence Erlbaum.

Spurgeon, C. (2008) *Advertising and New Media*, London: Routledge.

Stabile, C.A. (2000) 'Nike, social responsibility, and the hidden mode of production', *Critical Studies in Media Communication*, 17(2): 186–204.

Turow, J. (2006) *Niche Envy: Marketing Discrimination in the Digital Age*, Cambridge, MA: The MIT Press.

Turow, J. (2009) 'Advertisers and audience autonomy at the end of television', in Turow, J. and McAllister, M.P. (eds) *The Advertising and Consumer Culture Reader*, New York: Routledge.

Waetjen, J. and Gibson, T.A. (2007) 'Harry Potter and the commodity fetish: Activating corporate readings in the journey from text to commercial intertext', *Communication and Critical/Cultural Studies*, 4(1): 3–26.

Watts, E.K. and Orbe, M.P. (2002) 'The spectacular consumption of "true" African American culture: "Whassup" with the Budweiser guys?', *Critical Studies in Media Communication*, 19(1): 1–20.

Williams, R. (1980) *Problems in Materialism and Culture: Selected Essays*, London: Verso.

Williamson, J. (1978) *Decoding Advertisements*, London: Marion Boyars.

Wood, M.L., Nelson, M.R., Cho, J. and Yaros, R.A. (2004) 'Tonight's top story: Commercial content in television news', *Journalism and Mass Communication Quarterly*, 81(4): 807–822.

Zwick, D., Bonsu, S.K. and Darmody, A. (2008) 'Putting consumers to work: "Co-creation" and new marketing governmentality', *Journal of Consumer Culture*, 8(2): 163–196.

10 How does the Internet change journalistic investigation and how should communication science deal with this issue?

A multimethod approach for researching journalists' investigative work in TV, radio, printed press and online media

Marcel Machill and Markus Beiler

Introduction

The Internet has developed within a few years into an important source of information for many people. But at the same time the network not only has effects on recipients, but also on the producers of media offerings. In particular, research – as a fundamental part of the daily work of journalists and as a decisive prerequisite for the guarantee of the quality of journalistic contents – is addressed.

The Internet has quite a few apparent advantages in this connection: it can facilitate preliminary research, simple facts can be easily controlled, and information is temporally and spatially available on an unlimited basis. But online research also involves risks, particularly if researchers largely refrain from using methods beyond the Internet (Meier, 2004: 252).

There is a particular risk of a distorted reality. This goes against the function of journalism and the self-image of journalists, which is to portray reality as it is. For instance, three-quarters of German journalists feel committed to this 'objective reporting' (Weischenberg *et al.*, 2006b: 356). The manner in which the reality to be depicted and investigated by journalists has radically changed through the Internet. For one thing, the problem consists in the credibility and reliability of sources on the Internet, which on account of the low access barriers are easily manipulated and are not subject to any professional quality standards.

A distortion of reality can occur during the use of search engines in particular because their ranking and updating algorithms are highly selective: certain websites – and, as a result, the information and opinions contained there – have no chance of being listed in perceptible ranking positions. In addition, numerous sites are only irregularly updated by search engines (Lewandowski *et al.*, 2006). A further factor is search engines' susceptibility to manipulation.

These problems of search engines will be intensified through the risk of dependency on a single search engine. Also associated with 'Google-ization' is the question as to whether the result is 'a journalistic self-referentiality of an entirely new dimension' (Machill and Beiler, 2005: 232), because only already published information will be adopted.

The studies in this field of research conducted up to now are particularly quantitative interviews which have measured the utilization of the Internet or specific online offerings with regard to journalistic work in general, and have also ascertained attitudes towards the Internet, but do not provide any deeper insight into the research process. Therefore these studies can also only be cited to a limited degree as the basis for a discussion about the influence of the Internet in research. However, journalistic research is a very complex process which consists of various partial research steps which adopt varying functions. Here it is to be assessed if one would like to investigate the relative importance of the Internet in journalistic research. Moreover, intensive knowledge of the competence of journalists to research online and especially by means of search engines is lacking.

This aspect has to take into consideration a methodical investigative approach. In the following, it will be shown by way of example how this has been implemented during the investigation of the research work of German journalists. The methodical design can also be applied in other countries, and also lends itself to international comparative studies which seem to be urgently called for in view of the worldwide, fundamental changes in journalistic work through the convergence and digitalization of media as well as under the framework conditions of the globalization of media systems. Insofar as that is concerned, the results of the sample study of German journalists can also provide suggestions for research projects in other countries.

Methodology in the area of researching journalists' research work

In order to be able to adequately investigate the previously described research subject matter on an empirical basis, a multi-methodical design with quantitative and qualitative approaches – which reciprocally support and complement each other – is required, because every method has its specific fields of application for certain questions, but is also largely limited to them. This is why complex, multidimensional research subjects must utilize several methods if they intend to examine the respective partial aspects on a valid basis and linked together.

On the one hand, the concrete research work of journalists is addressed with the research subject at hand. Observation is always the method of

choice if it concerns the action of people. Secondly, evaluations and attitudes of journalists towards the Internet and search engines as a means
of research shall be investigated. The interview is to be applied as the
preferred method with regard to cognitions. Thirdly, competencies with
regard to the search engine research of journalists shall be tested. An
experimental approach lends itself to this purpose. In the following, the
advantages of the three utilized methods will be presented and it will be
shown how they have been linked with one another in order to illuminate
the research field in a multidimensional capacity. Moreover, their respective implementation in the multi-method study at hand will be described.
However, due to space limits of this volume, we will concentrate on the
observation when it comes to the presentation of the empirical results
(cf. p. 170).

In contrast to quantitative surveys, an observation permits a comprehensive description of the journalistic research process through analysis of
the integration of a variety of research tools for various research actions.
The significance of the Internet for the research can therefore also be
analysed in detail. Compared to observation, surveys have the further
disadvantage that human behaviour can only be verbalized with difficulty.
Only observation permits intensive, qualitative and direct insights into
'natural' research work. It was performed on an open and non-partici-
pating basis at the journalists' normal workplace.

The systematic nature of the observation phase was ensured by using
a detailed observation code book. Various research actions and, in a
general manner, all actions without relevance for the research have been
recorded. The research actions are subdivided into three research sub-
processes. On the basis of theoretical considerations (e.g. Haller, 2004:
84), a distinction was made between:

1   finding topics and assessing their relevance;
2   cross-checking research;
3   scope-extension research,

which are subdivided into various research steps.

Within the framework of finding topics and assessing their relevance,
all of the research actions which serve in the finding of news and topics
as well the assessment of their relevance for a publication or the public
were encoded. The partial process is subdivided into the steps: news
and topics monitoring, processing the material that has been received
and assessing the topic. Cross-checking research consists of the research
steps of performing a source check and checking the facts. It encompasses activities performed by a journalist to validate the credibility of a
source or the correctness of the information available to him or her. The
scope-extension research involves activities by means of which a journalist
attempts to supplement and extend the starting information for the creation of a contribution. Distinctions are made between the steps identifying

additional sources, acquiring additional information and searching for and sifting through additional material.

The research tool used in each particular case was recorded in connection with each observed research action. This dimension is subdivided into thirteen computer-aided and nine non-computer-aided research tools as well as a 'special category', news agencies (due to their special significance). The category computer-aided research tools covers all of the activities in which a journalist resorts to the Internet or the computer during his or her research, for example for emails, search engines, various web offerings or computer-aided databases and archives such as Wikipedia. The non-computer-aided research tools represent the 'classic' instruments of research such as phone calls, letter post and faxes, on-site appointments and interviews, printed reference works or internal editorial discussions. The design of the investigation enables the research steps and tools to be evaluated in combination.

In conclusion, the practical applicability and intercoder reliability of the observation code book was tested in a simulated editorial office on the basis of predetermined activities performed by a journalist. The mean level of agreement between the eleven encoders and the predetermined encodings amounted to a very satisfactory 72 per cent in the case of the research steps and to an excellent 87 per cent (or rather to 99 per cent for correctly encoded research steps) in connection with the research tools. The observers were at the end of a four-and-a-half-year course of journalism studies having successfully concluded a period of on-the-job training.

In addition to the results of the observation phase, the survey provides further insights into journalistic research on the Internet. It is only possible to obtain opinions and attitudes of journalists towards the Internet and search engines as a research instrument by conducting a survey. Furthermore, the survey provides insights from a wider group of persons than is possible using a time-consuming observation procedure. The survey was standardized quantitatively and carried out in written form.

The first dimension of the questionnaire was the integration of the Internet into everyday research work. The share of online research, the frequency of online use in connection with various research actions and the importance of particular Internet pages, the use of new forms of online communication and the attitude towards the influence of the Internet on journalistic work were determined. The second dimension included questions on the utilization of search engines. Information was gathered on the frequency of the use of search engines and certain search functions, the importance of search engines for different research tasks and the attitude towards the importance of search engines for journalistic work.

Of course, the importance of search engines in research can be investigated by means of interview and observation. But they cannot specifically analyse search engine utilization and competence in a comparative manner. A qualitative experiment, with which the research behaviour can be systematically investigated and which – unlike an interview – is not dependent on a self-assessment, permits such insights. The experiment was performed in a controlled field situation at the workplace and computer belonging to each of the journalists. The test persons were requested to perform three search tasks with the aid of the most utilized search engine, Google. During this process, their research behaviour was systematically observed and encoded. The success of the search was determined by getting the test persons to answer in writing various half-closed questions before and after a search task in each case. Using a code book, the answers were then evaluated content-analytically for accuracy.

The population of the multi-method study consists of journalists that work in Germany on a permanent or freelance basis for daily newspapers, for radio and television companies belonging to the public-service or private sector and online media which are (also) involved in reporting current, national political events. In 2005 this amounted to 34,169 journalists (Weischenberg *et al.*, 2006a).

Empirical results

A total of 235 journalists involved in 34 media companies (some with several editorial offices) were observed. Thirteen daily newspapers (two national, eleven local), eight radio stations (five public-service, three private), seven television stations (three public-service, four private) and six online offerings (one a purely Internet newspaper, five offshoots of other media) participated. During the process of sample selection, in an initial stage involving a quota plan, various media or editorial offices were asked to participate in the observation phase. For reasons of research pragmatism and access to the field, the selection of specific journalists that were to be observed was performed ad hoc on site in editorial offices by the editor-in-chief, the head of the editorial office or directly by the observer. Attention was paid to achieving the greatest possible variance. In order to obtain a comprehensive picture of everyday research work, each journalist was observed for a complete working day.

Of the observed journalists, 43 per cent worked for the daily newspaper, 37 per cent for television, 23 per cent for radio and 11 per cent for online media. Men constituted 60 per cent, 40 per cent were women. The participating journalists were on average 37.2 years old. About three-quarters (74 per cent) were permanent members of staff, approximately one-quarter (26 per cent) being freelancers; 81 per cent worked as editors, 12 per cent in a leading capacity and 6 per cent as on-the-job trainees. On average, the observed persons had 13.3 years of professional journalistic experience and had used the Internet for professional purposes for 7.1 years. A course of on-the-job training had been successfully completed by 70 per cent; 43 per cent worked in politics/current affairs departments, one-quarter being employed in the department for local affairs.

Consequently, it was possible to achieve a sample of journalists which, in terms of the fundamental tendencies, corresponds to the population of the four areas of the media that were included (cf. Weischenberg *et al.*, 2006a). This permits generalizing statements to be made.

Overall, 30,057 activities were encoded, 21,145 of them being relevant to research. The total observation period was calculated as 1959 hours, 34 minutes (8:20 hours per journalist). As a result, from an international perspective, this investigation can be regarded as the most extensive observation study on journalistic research.

On average, the 235 observed journalists spent 43.0 per cent of their working time or 3:55 hours per day on research. Online journalists and journalists working for private radio spent the least time on research (38.7 or 38.9 per cent), editors at public-service television the most (49.9 per cent). Daily newspaper journalists (42.1 per cent), those working for public-service radio (42.5 per cent) and private television (44.5 per cent) made up the middle ground. The reason for the low research share among online journalists is presumably due to the fact that they have to perform a number of activities that are not originally journalistic in nature. The situation is similar with radio. By contrast, there is considerable division of labour at television companies.

In order to be able to assess the significance of the sub-processes or steps in the research as well as the research tools, in the following they are evaluated on the basis of the share of the frequencies with which certain activities are performed and, secondly, on the basis of the share of the duration which is taken up by the relevant action. The frequency and duration shares were aggregated at the person-related level so that each observed journalist is included in the analysis with equal weighting in spite of differences in the number of observed activities.

Frequency and duration of the sub-processes and steps in research

The research sub-process 'finding topics and assessing their relevance' accounts for an average frequency share of the research performed per journalist of 40.8 per cent (Table 10.1). The corresponding share of the duration amounts to 47.8 per cent. Consequently, the journalists spend on average just over one-and-three-quarter hours (1:46 hours) per day searching for news items and topics and assessing their relevance. This research sub-process consists in detail of the research steps 'news and topics monitoring' (frequency and duration share of 16.9 and 18.4 per cent respectively), 'processing received material' (13.2 and 11.9 per cent respectively) and 'assessing a topic' (10.5 and 17.2 per cent respectively).

Cross-checking research only accounts for a frequency share of 7.9 per cent and a duration share of 5.5 per cent. Consequently, journalists only spend about eleven minutes per day checking sources and information in terms of plausibility or correctness. Of the 90.0 research actions per

Table 10.1 Research sub-processes and steps: frequency and durations

	Percentage share per journalist		Number of actions per journalist	Duration per journalist in hours	Duration per action in minutes
	Frequency	Duration			
Finding topics and assessing their relevance	40.8	47.8	38.4	1:46:14	2:46
News and topics monitoring	16.9	18.4	16.5	0:41:09	2:29
Processing received material	13.2	11.9	12.3	0:24:52	2:01
Assessing a topic	10.5	17.2	9.3	0:39:25	4:14
Other	0.2	0.2	0.2	0:00:48	3:46
Cross-checking research	7.9	5.5	6.6	0:11:22	1:43
Source check	0.9	0.6	0.8	0:01:21	1:45
Facts check	6.9	4.7	5.8	0:09:11	1:35
Other	0.1	0.3	0.1	0:00:50	10:22
Scope-extension research	51.3	46.7	45.0	1:37:09	2:10
Identifying additional sources	14.9	8.6	14.0	0:19:31	1:23
Acquiring additional information	28.4	29.3	24.0	0:60:04	2:29
Searching for and sifting-through additional material	7.7	7.9	6.6	0:15:42	2:21
Other	0.3	0.8	0.3	0:01:52	6:44
Total	*100.0*	*100.0*	*90.0*	*3:34:45*	*2:23*

n = 235 journalists

journalist that are observed per day, only 6.6 serve this activity. It is even the case that a source check hardly occurs at all (frequency and duration share of 0.9 and 0.6 respectively). Therefore, on average, a journalist examines the validity of his or her source less than once per day (0.8 times). The frequency and duration share of the research step 'facts check' amounts to 6.9 and 4.7 per cent respectively. With an average of 1:43 minutes compared to the average length of all research actions of 2:23 minutes, actions that serve in the checking of sources or information are also very short.

The low share accounted for by cross-checking research can be explained, on the one hand, by the lack of any necessity to do so since journalists know the majority of the sources and consider the material provided by news agencies to be trustworthy. The second explanation may be due to the lack of the necessary financial and time-related resources at many editorial offices.

The scope-extension research accounts for a frequency share of 51.3 per cent and a duration share of 46.7 per cent. With regard to frequency, it is therefore the most important research sub-process. In terms of the duration, it is almost on a par with finding topics and assessing their relevance. The scope-extension research comprises the steps 'identifying additional sources' (frequency and duration share of 14.9 and 8.6 respectively), 'acquiring additional information' (28.4 or 29.3 per cent) and 'searching for and sifting-through additional material', for example, infographics or photos (7.7 or 7.9 per cent). The core journalistic research activity is therefore acquiring additional information for a journalistic contribution.

The older the journalists are, the larger the frequency and duration share relating to 'finding topics and assessing their relevance' and the lower the corresponding shares relating to cross-checking and scope-extension research. They are therefore more involved in the selection of news and setting the topics and less preoccupied with content production. It is in fact the case that journalists with a leading role are much more involved in 'finding topics and assessing their relevance' and much less concerned with scope-extension research than editors or on-the-job trainees. The lower share for checking research among older journalists can be ascribed to their greater professional experience.

With a frequency share of 53.5 and 50.9 per cent respectively, the main focus of the activity of online and radio journalists (Table 10.2) is on finding topics and assessing their relevance. Scope-extension research only accounts for a share of 39.9 or 43.5 per cent. By contrast, in the case of television and the daily newspaper, the process of finding topics and assessing their relevance is of low prominence (33.0 and 38.0 per cent). Conversely, scope-extension research achieves the greatest frequency share in these two areas of the media (55.5 and 55.0 per cent respectively). The shares for duration in the media comparison reveal the same trends as the frequency shares. For this reason, a presentation is dispensed with.

The findings can be explained with the varying production frequency: radio features the news at least hourly. Online journalists must even ensure permanent up-to-date status. Consequently, these media are occupied to a greater extent with the monitoring of the news situation and the selection of topics. At the same time, they lack the capacity to extend comprehensively all of the news topics. By contrast, there is only one editorial deadline per day at daily newspapers. It is therefore possible to concentrate on the scope-extension of research there. A mixture of both production frequencies is to be found with regard to television. On the one hand, editorial offices for news with several daily programmes providing the latest news of the day have been observed along with magazine programmes that are transmitted only once per day or week.

The strikingly high share relating to cross-checking research at the public-service television stations (13.8 per cent) is probably attributable to their good level of funding and high-quality journalistic standards. In addition, they produce investigative magazines for which the validation of sources and facts is an essential prerequisite.

Table 10.2 Research sub-processes and steps: frequency shares according to types of media (in %)

	Daily newspapers	Radio (public-service/private)	Television (public-service/private)	Online	Total
Finding topics and assessing their relevance	38.0	50.9 (53.2/48.0)	33.0 (28.6/39.4)	53.5	40.8
News and topics monitoring	11.5	27.0 (31.7/20.9)	12.4 (11.4/13.8)	31.7	16.9
Processing received material	16.1	13.9 (11.0/17.7)	8.2 (7.0/10.1)	13.4	13.2
Assessing a topic	10.3	9.7 (10.0/9.3)	12.1 (9.7/15.6)	8.3	10.5
Other	0.1	0.3 (0.5/0.1)	0.3 (0.5/0.0)	0.0	0.2
Cross-checking research	7.0	5.5 (4.8/6.5)	11.5 (13.8/8.0)	6.6	7.9
Source check	0.3	0.7 (1.1/0.3)	2.1 (2.6/1.4)	0.1	0.9
Facts check	6.5	4.8 (3.7/6.2)	9.3 (11.0/6.7)	6.5	6.9
Other	0.1	0.0 (0.0/0.0)	0.1 (0.1/0.0)	0.0	0.1
Scope-extension research	55.0	43.5 (42.0/45.5)	55.5 (57.6/52.6)	39.9	51.3
Identifying additional sources	17.4	13.7 (13.7/13.7)	14.6 (13.3/16.5)	7.5	14.9
Acquiring additional information	30.0	25.4 (24.0/27.3)	31.7 (33.6/28.9)	19.1	28.4
Searching for and sifting-through additional material	7.1	4.4 (4.3/4.5)	9.0 (10.2/7.2)	13.2	7.7
Other	0.5	0.0 (0.0/0.1)	0.3 (0.5/0.0)	0.0	0.3
Total	*100.0*	*100.0 (100.0/100.0)*	*100.0 (100.0/100.0)*	*100.0*	*100.0*
Basis (number of journalists)	100	46 (26/20)	64 (38/26)	25	235

Frequency and duration of the research tools

The utilized research tool was recorded for each research action (Table 10.3). Computer-aided research tools have established themselves across the board. The share of their frequency in relation to the entire research process amounts to almost half (47.0 per cent). The 'classic' non-computer-aided research tools possess a frequency share of 40.6 and the news agencies 11.5 per cent. In the case of the share of the duration, the proportion of computer-aided and non-computer-aided research tools is inverted (37.2 and 51.3 per cent respectively; new agencies 11.5 per cent). Computer-aided research tools are therefore used more frequently but for shorter periods than classic research tools. Time-wise they are therefore highly efficient. Accordingly, at 1:48 minutes, a computer-aided research action lasts almost only half as long as a non-computer-aided one (3:12 minutes). Overall, the journalists conduct research for an average of 1:18 hours per working day by computer, for almost two hours without (1:53 hours) and 24 minutes by means of news agencies.

The most important computer-aided research tool is email. In relation to all of the research tools it has a frequency share of 12.1 per cent and a duration share of 10.7 per cent. Overall, in terms of both frequency and duration, it is the third most important research tool. With regard to frequency, search engines are the second most important computer-aided research tool and the fourth most important one overall (8.3 per cent). Its duration share (4.1 per cent) is only half as great as the frequency share. They therefore represent highly effective research tools which are frequently used and only require a small amount of time. A research action involving search engines is by far the shortest (1:11 minutes) of all of the research tools. Journalists look to search engines during research almost eight times per day and nine minutes long. Google accounts for 90.4 per cent of the frequency of the search-engine research. Google alone is the fifth most frequently observed research tool (7.6 per cent).

If one adds to this the use of websites of various primary sources that are, as a rule, interest-driven, with a frequency share of 8.0 per cent, they are the third most important computer-aided research tool. Each of the web offerings summarized here is, by contrast, insignificant if considered in isolation. For example, websites belonging to companies or ministries and authorities only have a frequency share of 2.2 and 2.1 per cent respectively. In terms of frequency, the web offerings of editorial media (7.5 per cent) are of almost the same importance as the various summarized online pages. From the point of view of duration, editorial media web offerings are even somewhat more important (6.7 as against 5.9 per cent). They are followed by computer-aided in-house archives (frequency and duration share of 7.1 and 6.6 per cent respectively) and computer-aided databases and archives (3.3 and 2.6 per cent respectively). Interactive forms such as, for example, weblogs or chats are hardly used at all (frequency and duration share of 0.5 per cent each).

Table 10.3 Research tools: frequency and duration

	Percentage share per journalist		Number of actions per journalist	Duration per journalist in hours	Duration per action in minutes
	Frequency	Duration			
Computer-aided	47.0	37.2	43.3	1:18:15	1:48
Email	12.1	10.7	11.0	0:22:09	2:01
Search engines and web catalogues	8.3	4.1	7.8	0:09:16	1:11
Google	7.6	3.7	6.9	0:08:07	1:10
Various online offerings	8.0	5.9	7.1	0:12:49	1:48
Companies	2.2	1.7	2.4	0:03:51	1:38
Ministries, authorities and cities	2.1	1.5	1.7	0:03:05	1:46
Clubs, associations and NGOs	2.1	1.6	1.7	0:03:29	2:05
Scientific establishments	0.9	0.6	0.7	0:01:15	1:46
Private persons	0.3	0.2	0.3	0:00:30	1:28
Parties and politicians	0.3	0.3	0.3	0:00:40	2:19
Online offerings from editorial media	7.5	6.7	7.1	0:14:19	2:01
In-house archives	7.1	6.6	6.6	0:12:44	1:55
Databases and archives	3.3	2.6	3.1	0:05:50	1:51
Interactive forms	0.5	0.5	0.5	0:00:55	1:41
Other	0.1	0.1	0.1	0:00:13	1:57
Non-computer-aided	40.6	51.3	35.2	1:52:33	3:12
Phone calls	15.0	13.9	13.3	0:30:22	2:16
Internal editorial discussions	12.9	19.3	11.5	0:43:10	3:45
Personal filing system, in-house archives and reference works	3.8	2.8	3.0	0:05:24	1:49
Print media, radio and television	3.4	5.0	3.2	0:11:52	3:41
Raw material	1.5	2.1	1.1	0:03:48	3:34
On-site appointments and interviews	1.4	5.9	0.9	0:12:51	14:22
Letter post and faxes	1.3	1.1	1.1	0:02:20	2:03
Documents and writings	1.1	1.1	1.0	0:02:29	2:33
Other	0.2	0.1	0.1	0:00:17	2:26
Agencies	11.5	11.5	11.5	0:23:57	2:04
Total	*100.0*	*100.0*	*90.0*	*3:34:45*	*2:23*

n = 235 journalists

In the case of the non-computer-aided research tools as well as overall, with regard to their frequency share of 15.0 per cent, phone calls are the most important, followed by internal editorial discussions (12.9 per cent). In terms of the duration share, the internal editorial discussions are even the most important (19.3 per cent; phone calls 13.9 per cent). Almost one-fifth of the research time is therefore taken up by editorial conferences or short questions put to colleagues. Other classical research tools are of lesser significance overall: personal filing system, in-house archives and reference works (frequency and duration shares of 3.8 and 2.8 per cent respectively), print media, radio and television (3.4 and 5.0 per cent respectively), raw material (1.4 and 5.9 per cent respectively), on-site appointments and face-to-face interviews (1.4 and 5.9 per cent respectively), letter post and faxes (1.3 and 1.1 per cent respectively) as well as documents and writings (1.1 per cent each).

The computer-aided research tools are therefore a permanent feature of everyday research and have supplemented the classic research instruments. Although it no longer appears possible to imagine a situation without email, the telephone continues to assume a key role in research. Internal editorial discussions also have a significant role to play. Search engines appear to be highly specialized, efficient research tools. If the online and offline use of journalistic offerings for research is added together, the result is a frequency and duration share of 10.9 and 11.7 per cent respectively, an indication of the strongly self-referential tendencies in journalism.

With increasing age, the frequency and duration share of computer-aided research decreases whereas the use of non-computer-aided research tools remains roughly constant and the use of the news agencies increases. An exception here is the emails which are used to an equal extent by all age groups. This may be due to the fact that no journalist can refuse to participate in this form of communication. The increase in the share of news agencies with age can be explained on the basis that older journalists are more involved in finding topics and assessing their relevance. Key to understanding this finding is the professional position assumed by this group. Leading journalists fall back on news agencies almost twice as frequently as normal editors. The frequency and, even more clearly, the duration of the use of computer-aided research tools also increase with the duration of professional online use.

The highest share in terms of the frequency and duration of computer-aided research tools was observable in the area of entertainment and tabloid journalism. The shares are slightly lower in the culture or feature sections as well as in the sphere of business. Heavy utilization of news agencies is to be found in the areas politics and/or current affairs, business, and sport. Very low usage of agencies occurs in connection with entertainment and/or tabloid journalism and, in particular, with local news since news agencies do not focus on these two areas.

Online journalists differ greatly from their colleagues (Table 10.4). They are characterized by the second heaviest use of computer-aided research tools (frequency share of 50.9 per cent), by far the lowest use of non-computer-aided research tools (19.0 per cent) and make by far the greatest use of agencies (30.1 per cent). This is attributable to considerable significance being placed on finding topics and assessing their relevance. In a comparison of the media, the duration shares exhibit the same trends as the frequency shares. Consequently, a presentation is dispensed with.

Daily newspaper journalists exhibit a comparatively low use of computer-aided research tools and a high use of non-computer-aided ones (44.9 and 46.1 per cent respectively). They are therefore somewhat more conservative. In addition, computer-aided research tools do not always make sense in the case of local reporting, which represents a key part of the fare offered by daily newspapers in Germany. The use of news agencies here is slightly below the total average (9.0 per cent) due to their lack of coverage of local affairs.

Similar to online editors, radio journalists mainly conduct computer-aided research (50.6 per cent). In private radio the use of news agencies is extremely low (1.4 per cent) since many stations have not subscribed to any agencies. Instead, the news is selected and processed by central editorial offices or service providers and made available in the in-house archive. By contrast, agency use of the public-service providers is the second highest of all of the media (22.5 per cent). The role and the updating rhythm that finds expression here is similar to that found in the online media. Television journalists are to be found between the extremes of daily-newspaper journalists on the one hand and online and radio journalists on the other.

The share of the research tools within the individual steps in research

In the following, the research steps and tools are considered in combination. For this purpose, the frequency shares of the research tools are broken down according to the eight individual research tools and subdivided on the basis of the particular media sector. This permits statements to be made about the specialization of individual research tools and about certain patterns of research. In the corresponding tables, only those research tools which can still be regarded as relevant at all in terms of their frequency share are listed for each research step. The remaining research tools are summarized in the category 'other'. For reasons of clarity, an analysis of the duration shares is dispensed with because they tend to permit the same interpretations.

In the case of news and topics monitoring, only three research tools are relatively significant (Table 10.5). The most important are news agencies, with a frequency share of more than one-third (34.8 per cent). The computer-aided research tools just about achieve a slightly higher share

Table 10.4 Research tools: frequency shares according to types of media (in %)

	Daily newspapers	Radio (public-service/private)	Television (public-service/private)	Online	Total
Computer-aided	44.9	50.6 (47.3/55.0)	46.1 (48.5/42.7)	50.9	47.0
Email	14.6	10.6 (7.7/14.3)	9.2 (9.0/9.6)	12.7	12.1
Search engines and web catalogues	7.5	7.5 (8.1/6.6)	11.4 (11.9/10.6)	5.7	8.3
Various online offerings	8.8	6.3 (7.6/4.6)	10.1 (11.8/7.6)	2.7	8.0
Online offerings of editorial media	4.4	9.2 (9.1/9.3)	8.3 (7.3/9.6)	14.4	7.5
In-house archives	5.0	13.3 (11.0/16.3)	4.6 (5.3/3.5)	10.6	7.1
Databases and archives	4.0	3.4 (3.8/3.0)	2.3 (2.9/1.3)	3.1	3.3
Interactive forms	0.4	0.4 (0.0/0.8)	0.2 (0.1/0.4)	1.5	0.5
Other	0.2	0.0 (0.0/0.0)	0.1 (0.1/0.1)	0.2	0.1
Non-computer-aided	46.1	36.0 (30.2/43.7)	43.6 (40.3/48.5)	19.0	40.6
Phone calls	19.4	11.5 (7.7/16.5)	14.9 (14.0/16.0)	3.7	15.0
Internal editorial discussions	11.7	15.5 (14.6/16.6)	13.5 (12.5/14.9)	11.3	12.9
Personal filing system, in-house archives and reference works	5.4	2.1 (2.1/2.1)	3.8 (3.3/4.5)	0.6	3.8
Print media, radio and television	2.7	4.3 (4.2/4.3)	4.2 (4.1/4.4)	2.5	3.4
Raw material	0.3	0.5 (0.2/0.9)	4.8 (3.8/6.3)	0.1	1.5
On-site appointments and interviews	2.6	0.8 (0.1/1.7)	0.5 (0.4/0.7)	0.0	1.4
Letter post and faxes	1.8	0.8 (0.5/1.2)	1.1 (1.6/0.5)	0.6	1.3
Documents and writings	2.0	0.3 (0.2/0.5)	0.7 (0.5/1.1)	0.0	1.1
Other	0.2	0.3 (0.5/0.0)	0.1 (0.2/0.0)	0.2	0.2
Agencies	9.0	13.3 (22.5/1.4)	10.3 (11.2 8.8)	30.1	12.5
Total	100.0	100.0 (100.0/100.0)	100.0 (100.0/100.0)	100.0	100.0
Basis (number of journalists)	100	46 (26/20)	64 (38/26)	25	235

Table 10.5 News and topics monitoring: frequency shares of the research tools according to types of media (in %)

	Daily newspapers	Radio (public-service /private)	Television (public-service /private)	Online	Total
Computer-aided	35.8	48.1 (35.2 /66.7)	39.1 (33.3 /47.1)	40.2	39.8
Search engines and web catalogues	1.1	0.9 (0.1 /2.1)	3.5 (2.5 /4.9)	3.3	1.9
Various online offerings	4.4	2.7 (4.3 /0.3)	0.5 (0.9 /0.0)	0.4	2.5
Online offerings of editorial media	19.9	21.2 (14.3 /31.1)	26.7 (18.0 /38.6)	28.0	22.9
In-house archives	4.0	17.6 (11.7 /26.2)	6.3 (8.5 /3.2)	3.7	7.4
Other	6.5	5.6 (4.8 /6.9)	2.1 (3.3 /0.4)	4.9	4.9
Non-computer-aided	29.9	21.5 (17.1 /27.9)	28.2 (25.0 /32.5)	10.8	25.5
Phone calls	3.4	0.6 (0.7 /0.6)	0.1 (0.0 /0.2)	0.7	1.6
Internal editorial discussions	1.3	4.1 (3.7 /4.7)	2.2 (3.7 /0.1)	5.0	2.5
Print media, radio and television	20.0	14.8 (10.2 /21.3)	22.7 (19.9 /26.6)	5.1	17.9
Other	5.2	2.0 (2.5 /1.3)	3.2 (1.5 /5.7)	0.0	3.4
Agencies	34.3	30.4 (47.7 /5.4)	32.7 (41.6 /20.4)	49.0	34.8
Total	*100.0*	*100.0 (100.0 /100.0)*	*100.0 (100.0 /100.0)*	*100.0*	*100.0*
Basis (number of journalists)	86	44 (26 /18)	57 (32 /24)	25	212

(39.9 per cent). Among the computer-aided research tools, journalistic web offerings are the most important here and are the second most important (22.9 per cent) in this research step overall. All of the non-computer-aided research tools only reach a frequency share of a quarter (25.5 per cent). The greatest share here belongs to the print media, radio and television (17.9 per cent of all research tools).

In a comparison of the media, the highest share of news agencies is to be found among journalists working for online media and public-service radio (49.0 and 47.7 per cent respectively). About half of news and topics monitoring is performed by selecting news agency announcements. In particular, the private television and radio journalists (38.6 and 31.1 per cent respectively) as well as the online editors (28.0 per cent) fall back on the online offerings of editorial media.

Self-referentiality has a special quality in online journalism because online journalists mainly search within their own sector of the media. By contrast, online journalists make extremely little use of offline media (5.1 per cent). Expressed in a positive light, one could say that online journalists observe their competitors in order to differentiate themselves from them when setting topics. Overall, the greatest self-referentiality is discernible in private television. Online and offline media arrive at a share of two-thirds. Setting one's own topics appears to be hardly possible here.

The heavy use of online media in private radio seems to be a substitute for the lack of news agencies (5.4 per cent). The high share of computer-aided in-house archives in radio (17.6 per cent) among the private stations (26.2 per cent) can be explained by the feeding of pre-selected and trans-mission-ready announcements by external service providers or central editorial offices. In public-service radio, announcements and contribu-tions are exchanged between the stations.

With a frequency share of 76.6 per cent (Table 10.6), the only research tool to feature significantly during the processing of received material that is made available to journalists is email. For example, subscription-based newsletters, received press releases or announcements from reporters on site are involved here. Overall, phone calls also still have a certain impor-tance (7.4 per cent).

The dominance of email is discernible across all of the media sectors, in particular in the case of television (91.7 per cent) and online media (91.1 per cent). The level drops slightly for radio (64.4 per cent) and daily newspapers (69.5 per cent). At daily newspapers, phone calls are more important than at all the other media (12.2 per cent). Importance is still attached to letter post and faxes, too (7.3 per cent). Both appear plausible given the locality of the reporting. Computer-aided in-house archives are important in radio (9.0 per cent). In this system, the 'obliga-tory announcements' that are to be adopted are indicated. The greatest share of letter post and faxes occurs in private radio (10.0 per cent). As with the daily newspaper, this can be explained by the locality as well as by the inclusion of the listeners.

Table 10.6 Processing received material: frequency shares of the research tools according to type of media (in %)

	Daily newspapers	Radio (public-service / private)	Television (public-service / private)	Online	Total
Computer-aided	71.4	78.3 (73.7/84.5)	91.7 (92.8/90.2)	91.1	80.2
Email	69.5	68.2 (64.4/73.3)	91.4 (92.8/ 89.5)	83.2	76.6
In-house archives	0.4	9.0 (8.5/9.8)	0.3 (0.0/0.7)	2.3	2.2
Interactive forms	0.2	0.0 (0.0/0.1)	0.0 (0.0/0.0)	4.4	0.6
Other	1.2	1.1 (0.8/1.2)	0.0 (0.0/0.0)	1.2	0.8
Non-computer-aided	24.7	18.0 (19.9/15.4)	7.7 (6.6/9.3)	8.5	17.2
Phone calls	12.2	7.4 (10.8/2.9)	0.7 (0.7/0.6)	4.1	7.4
Internal editorial discussions	1.0	3.1 (4.1/1.6)	0.9 (1.6/0.0)	0.3	1.3
Raw material	0.6	0.0 (0.0/0.0)	2.5 (0.0/4.5)	0.1	0.8
Letter post and faxes	7.3	5.2 (1.6/10.0)	2.1 (2.4/1.8)	3.9	5.1
Other	3.7	2.3 (3.3/1.0)	2.3 (2.0/2.5)	0.1	2.6
Agencies	3.9	3.7 (6.4/0.2)	0.6 (0.6/0.5)	0.4	2.6
Total	100.0	100.0 (100.0/100.0)	100.0 (100.0/100.0)	100.0	100.0
Basis (number of journalists)	100	42 (24/18)	60 (35/25)	25	227

The assessment of a topic with regard to its relevance for the public and its suitability for the medium mainly occurs within the framework of internal editorial discussions (frequency share of 80.9 per cent; Table 10.7), whether in the form of a large editorial conference or shorter discussions with colleagues. The editorial conferences also explain why, with an average of 4:14 minutes, activities relating to this research step are by far the longest of all of the observed activities. Phone calls are also of importance (11.8 per cent). Overall, non-computer-aided research tools arrive at a share of 94.8 per cent. Computer-aided research tools do not play a significant part (4.3 per cent).

The greatest share of internal editorial discussions is revealed for online journalists (90.8 per cent). The reason for this lies in the fact that they must not only achieve agreement within their editorial office but also with the parent medium.

Only 53 of the 235 observed journalists performed a source check at least once during the working day under observation. This low case number prevents a more detailed interpretation of the utilized research tools, especially one involving a comparison of the media. The tendency is for journalists to verify sources by means of phone calls (32.8 per cent) at various websites (26.7 per cent) and in internal editorial discussions (17.8 per cent). All the same, 202 of the 235 journalists performed a facts check at least once. However, this research step only accounts for a frequency share of 6.9 per cent of all of the research actions. Consequently, it is difficult to make statements here, too. Similar to the source check, it can be basically stated that the accuracy of information is validated by phone calls (30.8 per cent), internal editorial discussions (23.3 per cent) and various online offerings. The personal filing system, in-house archives and reference works also still play an important role (5.6 per cent), in particular in the case of the daily newspaper (9.8 per cent). Taking the entire research sub-process of cross-checking research, it is possible to additionally conclude that, with a frequency share of 61.8 per cent, non-computer-aided research tools are the most important (computer-aided research tools 34.5 per cent, news agencies 3.7 per cent).

During the identification of additional sources (Table 10.8) computer-aided research accounts for two-thirds (66.1 per cent) and non-computer-aided research for one-third (33.4 per cent). Search engines are by far the most important research tools. Almost half of the research actions (43.7 per cent) relating to searches for additional sources by journalists are influenced by search engines. Consequently, search engines in general and Google in particular have a decisive effect on the entire course of research, at least within the area relating to scope-extension research. It is namely the case that the subsequent steps involving the acquisition of additional information and supplementary material depend in part on the previously selected sources.

The dominance of the search engines also explains why, at 1:23 minutes, activities within this research step are on average the shortest.

Table 10.7 Assessing a topic: frequency shares of the research tools according to types of media (in %)

	Daily newspapers	Radio (public-service/private)	Television (public-service/private)	Online	Total
Computer-aided	5.4	7.2 (8.6/5.3)	1.3 (1.7/0.6)	3.0	4.3
Email	4.1	3.7 (4.2/3.1)	0.8 (1.0/0.6)	0.8	2.8
Other	1.2	3.5 (4.5/2.2)	0.5 (0.7/0.0)	2.2	1.5
Non-computer-aided	93.5	92.1 (90.2/94.7)	98.4 (98.3/98.6)	95.9	94.8
Phone calls	14.0	6.7 (8.6/4.1)	14.4 (8.5/22.9)	4.8	11.8
Internal editorial discussions	76.3	84.4 (81.0/89.1)	82.1 (87.1/75.0)	90.8	80.9
Other	3.1	0.9 (0.6/1.5)	1.9 (2.6/0.8)	0.2	2.1
Agencies	1.1	0.7 (1.2/0.0)	0.3 (0.0/0.8)	1.1	0.8
Total	*100.0*	*100.0 (100.0/100.0)*	*100.0 (100.0/100.0)*	*100.0*	*100.0*
Basis (number of journalists)	98	41 (24/17)	63 (37/26)	24	226

Table 10.8 Identifying additional sources: frequency shares of the research tools according to types of media (in %)

	Daily newspapers	Radio (public-service/private)	Television (public-service/private)	Online	Total
Computer-aided	60.8	65.3 (71.7/57.4)	69.7 (73.0/65.4)	80.9	66.1
Email	2.6	0.6 (0.9/0.3)	4.4 (3.3/5.8)	3.9	2.8
Search engines and web catalogues	39.8	49.4 (52.1/46.1)	41.6 (38.0/46.3)	53.8	43.7
Various online offerings	7.7	4.7 (5.9/3.3)	18.9 (26.1/9.4)	6.3	9.9
Online offerings of editorial media	0.6	3.8 (6.9/0.0)	1.1 (1.8/0.1)	5.9	2.0
In-house archives	6.6	6.3 (5.5/7.2)	1.9 (2.8/0.6)	6.6	5.3
Databases and archives	2.9	0.4 (0.3/0.5)	1.8 (1.0/3.0)	4.3	2.3
Other	0.6	0.0 (0.0/0.0)	0.1 (0.0/0.2)	0.0	0.3
Non-computer-aided	38.6	33.6 (26.3/42.6)	30.3 (27.0/34.6)	19.1	33.4
Phone calls	20.5	17.2 (10.7/25.4)	20.4 (19.0/22.3)	9.8	18.7
Internal editorial discussions	2.8	12.4 (13.3/11.2)	5.3 (3.6/7.5)	8.0	5.9
Personal filing system, in-house archives and reference works	13.8	3.9 (2.4/5.8)	4.2 (4.5/3.8)	1.0	7.9
Other	1.5	0.1 (0.0/0.2)	0.4 (0.0/1.0)	0.3	0.8
Agencies	0.6	1.1 (2.0/0.0)	0.0 (0.0/0.0)	0.0	0.5
Total	100.0	100.0 (100.0/100.0)	100.0 (100.0/100.0)	100.0	100.0
Basis (number of journalists)	95	45 (25/20)	58 (33/25)	23	221

Search engines are namely extremely efficient. With their domain in the identification of additional sources, search engines are therefore a highly specialized research instrument with consequences for the entire search process. The thesis regarding the Google-ization of research can therefore be regarded as confirmed. The risk of a distortion of reality exists.

Phone calls are also important (18.7 per cent). Various websites relating to primary sources (9.9 per cent) at which contact persons can be identified also have certain significance. Now and again colleagues are also asked about an additional source in internal editorial discussions (5.9 per cent).

Online journalists identify additional sources in a computer-aided manner by far the most frequently (80.9 per cent), particularly using search engines (53.8 per cent). At the same time, they resort much less to the telephone (9.8 per cent). Daily-newspaper journalists utilize computer-aided research tools comparatively little (60.8 per cent). They make more than average use of non-computer-aided research tools (38.6 per cent). One particularly striking feature is their use of a personal filing system, in-house archives and reference works with a much greater than average frequency share of 13.8 per cent. This can be explained particularly in terms of the locality of daily newspapers. Their journalists possess a number of short-term contacts and the editorial offices have exclusive archive material at their disposal. The fear here, though, is the creation of an internal self-referentiality in which the same contacts are repeatedly called upon.

In the case of acquiring additional information, a significant role is played by a wider range of research tools than in the other research steps (Table 10.9). In spite of the fairly one-sided selection of the sources, the journalists therefore use a variety of contents in order to enrich the core of a journalistic contribution with further information.

In comparison with other media, online journalists use news agencies (40.2 per cent) and journalistic online offerings (19.8 per cent) by far the most frequently. Online journalists therefore tend to be 'copiers' who hardly perform any genuine research, inter alia, because they have less time overall for research. In the case of the daily-newspaper journalists, the non-computer-aided research tools slightly outweigh the computer-aided research tools (49.5 compared to 42.7 per cent). Once again, they use relatively few news agencies (7.7 per cent). Instead, they resort disproportionately to the telephone (27.5 per cent).

In accordance with the character of this research step as indicated at the outset and after consideration of the differences between the media, it is possible to state that the process of searching and sifting through supplementary material is determined to a considerable degree by the various prevailing technical conditions and the demands imposed by production.

Table 10.9 Acquiring additional information: frequency shares of the research tools according to types of media (in %)

	Daily newspapers	Radio (public-service/private)	Television (public-service/private)	Online	Total
Computer-aided	42.7	51.8 (52.2/51.2)	50.6 (53.8/45.9)	49.7	47.4
Email	5.5	3.4 (0.6/6.8)	3.7 (5.0/1.8)	4.6	4.5
Search engines and web catalogues	2.2	1.7 (0.9/2.8)	7.3 (10.1/3.1)	2.4	3.6
Various online offerings	17.4	16.5 (18.3/14.1)	16.1 (15.8/16.4)	6.0	15.7
Online offerings of editorial media	5.1	13.9 (16.3/10.9)	15.1 (12.2/19.3)	19.8	11.1
In-house archives	4.2	8.9 (10.3/7.1)	4.2 (5.4/2.5)	9.3	5.7
Databases and archives	7.6	6.6 (5.8/7.5)	3.8 (5.1/1.8)	7.4	6.3
Other	0.7	0.8 (0.0/1.9)	0.5 (0.2/1.0)	0.2	0.6
Non-computer-aided	49.5	36.7 (27.8/47.9)	31.8 (29.3/35.5)	10.1	38.0
Phone calls	27.5	17.8 (12.5/24.4)	15.4 (15.3/15.6)	3.1	19.7
Internal editorial discussions	3.6	7.6 (5.4/10.3)	3.6 (2.2/5.5)	3.3	4.3
Print media, radio and television	1.9	4.9 (5.0/4.7)	2.6 (2.5/2.8)	2.7	2.8
Personal filing system, in-house archives and reference works	5.6	1.9 (1.7/2.1)	4.1 (3.2/5.4)	0.5	3.9
On-site appointments and interviews	4.9	2.0 (0.4/3.9)	1.1 (1.1/1.1)	0.1	2.8
Documents and writings	4.7	1.0 (0.6/1.5)	1.6 (0.6/3.1)	0.0	2.6
Other	1.4	1.7 (2.1/1.0)	3.4 (4.4/2.1)	0.4	1.8
Agencies	7.7	11.5 (19.9/0.9)	17.5 (16.9/18.6)	40.2	14.6
Total	*100.0*	*100.0 (100.0/100.0)*	*100.0 (100.0/100.0)*	*100.0*	*100.0*
Basis (number of journalists)	98	45 (25/20)	64 (38/26)	24	231

Discussion

Journalists have permanently integrated computer-aided research tools into their daily research work. They rank alongside the classic research instruments. This at the same time means that, in spite of all the fears to the contrary, non-computer-aided research has not (yet) been displaced by the Internet. The observation phase has revealed that, in relation to use frequency, computer-aided research enjoys a greater share than the non-computer-aided variety. Conversely, the classic research tools dominate in terms of the duration of use.

It is not possible to talk about a wholesale use of computer-aided research. Instead, the journalists integrate computer-aided research tools into their research process in a highly differentiated manner. Depending on the particular research aim, the journalists therefore make use of the research tools that appear the most suitable. However, person-related factors also influence this process. For example, younger journalists tend to use more computer-aided research tools than their older colleagues. Indications of media-related influences on the research behaviour were also apparent. In this context, it is necessary to mention, for example, the particularities of the given media sector with regard to production technology, the frequency of updating or the target group.

The results indicate that, compared to the classic research tools, the Internet plays an important role, above all in cases where it helps to perform tasks more efficiently and opens up new research possibilities. This is supported by the quite different shares of the computer-aided and non-computer-aided research tools as well as the shares of the news agencies that were determined for the individual steps in the research (see Figure 10.1).

The model identifies, true to scale, the mean frequency shares of the research steps in relation to the entire research process (vertical axis) and the mean frequency shares of the categories of research tools (white = computer-aided, light grey = non-computer-aided, dark grey = news agencies) within a research step (horizontal axis). Per research step, the research tools with the highest mean frequency share within the computer-aided and non-computer-aided research tools are entered in each case.

The telephone continues to be the most important research tool. Search engines, and in particular Google, dominate in connection with the identification of additional sources. This can be determined for all of the journalists and media. Search engines are a highly specialized and efficient research tool. In many cases there appears to be no alternative. Consequently, search engines have a crucial influence on the entire (further) course of the research. Google-ization is therefore already a reality. This situation requires careful reflection, since the danger of a distortion of reality or of one-sided reporting exists if trust is placed unhesitatingly in the logic of a single search engine. In addition, the

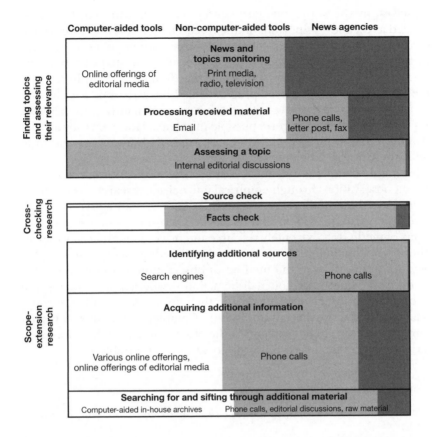

Figure 10.1 Model of the research process: mean frequency shares of the research steps and tools

exploratory process points to only a moderate level of search-engine competence on the part of journalists.

Further cause for concern is provided by the self-referentiality of the media, for example, in the case of news and topics monitoring as well as, however, in the acquisition of new information. Against the background of the importance of the Internet for research, food for thought is provided by the finding that a cross-check on research hardly occurs and that, essentially, the validation of sources does not take place at all. And yet it is the reliability of the sources and the accuracy of the information that represent the necessary foundation for the quality of journalistic reporting. An exception to this is only to be found in the well-funded and high-quality public-service television stations. Good journalism therefore clearly comes at a price.

The Internet has not only assumed an important position in research work in terms of real activity, but also in the estimation of the journalists themselves, as the supplementary survey has demonstrated. Google is regarded as the most important online research tool. It is not the case that journalists lack an awareness of the attendant problems here. Indeed, they themselves draw attention to the problems associated with both the Internet and search engines. However, the dominant attitude towards these research tools is one of pragmatism. Likely reasons for this are production pressures and economic factors. Journalists are therefore competent enough to recognize possible problems. However, they are not consistent enough in their behaviour or are not always in a position to modify their research behaviour.

This highly complex, dynamic research field also continues to call for constant observation through empirical journalistic research. As has been shown, a multi-methodical investigative design in a quantitative and qualitative process can provide useful results in this connection. Nevertheless, the mix of methods is extremely resource-intensive. This especially applies to the observation of journalists in their natural editorial office setting. Yet a broader application of the method of observation would be desirable in the future, since such journalistic action – whether it is during the procurement of information or during the exploitation of information – can be recorded more directly and validly. Complementary methods such as survey and experiment can enrich the observational results. Moreover, internationally related research projects would be desirable.

References

Haller, M. (2004) *Recherchieren. Ein Handbuch für Journalisten*, 6th edn, Konstanz: UVK.

Lewandowski, D., Wahlig, H. and Meyer-Bautor, G. (2006) 'The Freshness of Web Search Engine Databases', *Journal of Information Science*, 32(2): 133–150.

Machill, M. and Beiler, M. (2005) 'Qualität und Perspektiven der online-journalistischen Ausbildung an Hochschulen', in Fasel, C. (ed.), *Qualität und Erfolg im Journalismus*, Konstanz: UVK.

Machill, M., Neuberger, Chr., Schweiger, W. and Wirth, W. (2004) 'Navigating the Internet: A Study of German-Language Search Engines', *European Journal of Communication*, 19(3): 321–347.

Meier, K. (2004) 'Qualität im Online-Journalismus', in H.-J. Bucher und K.-D. Altmeppen (ed.) *Qualität im Journalismus. Grundlagen – Dimensionen – Praxismodelle*, Wiesbaden: Westdeutscher Verlag.

Wegner, J. (2002) 'Der neue Google-Faktor', *message werkstatt* 1: 2–3.

Weischenberg, S., Malik, M. and Scholl, A. (2006a) *Die Souffleure der Mediengesellschaft. Report über die Journalisten in Deutschland*, Konstanz: UVK.

Weischenberg, S., Malik, M. and Scholl, A. (2006b) 'Journalismus in Deutschland 2005. Zentrale Befunde der aktuellen Repräsentativbefragung deutscher Journalisten', *Media Perspektiven*, 7: 346–361.

Wyss, V. and Keel, G. (2007) 'Google als Trojanisches Pferd? Konsequenzen der Internet-Recherche von Journalisten für die journalistische Qualität', in Machill, M. and Beiler, M. (eds), *Die Macht der Suchmaschinen / The Power of Search Engines*, Köln: Halem.

11 Philosophical linkages between public journalism and citizen journalism[1]

Linda Steiner and Jessica Roberts

Controversy over public journalism wracked journalism scholars and practising journalists in the early 1990s, when it was advocated as solving two widening gaps: between political figures and citizens, and between news organizations and their readers. Declines in voter participation in elections, and more importantly in civic participation in public affairs, seemed to indicate that citizens were increasingly disengaged and were withdrawing from political processes. The public's disaffection with political discourse and cynicism about government were at least partly blamed on journalism's horse-race approach to campaigns and its treatment of politics as pivoting on self-interested tactics. That is, democracy was suffering. Journalists could help democracy by listening to people and trying to enhance civic commitment and participation in democratic processes.

For almost twenty years, public journalism was hotly debated, albeit using very different grounds. Some people said it simply represented good journalism, that it was not significantly different from conventional journalism, or at least those forms that required journalists to immerse themselves in community problems. Some critics claimed that reversing these disjunctures between citizens and public officials and especially between citizens and journalists would compromise journalists' standing as detached professionals. Some scholars accepted public journalism's philosophical commitment to enhancing civic participation but doubted that, in practice, it could overcome commercial media's profit constraints. It was called a cynical marketing ploy involving catering to attractive 'demographics'. Appealing to the civic conscience of individual journalists would neither demand nor inspire fundamental changes to news organizations' commercial logic (e.g., Schudson, 1999). Others worried that public journalism naïvely forgot that 'likable' newspapers will not be feared and respected, therefore are left ineffective. Journalists mocked public journalism as evangelism promulgated by preachers and then consultants and business executives.

With the help of several Knight-Ridder newspaper executives as well as Knight Foundation leaders, Professor Jay Rosen and Davis Merritt, editor of the *Witchita Eagle*, assiduously advocated and defended public journalism. By 1998 more than 60 per cent of daily newspapers had experimented with public journalism (Arant and Meyer, 1998). Although many news organizations remained opposed to and unchanged by the movement, a few of its key features were adapted, if not adopted, by conventional journalists. But public journalism never mustered commitment from newsroom ranks or journalism educators, so students graduated with little receptivity to public journalism.

The 2003 demise of the Pew Center for Civic Journalism, with its seed money, awards and encouragement, signalled the end of the movement. *Editor & Publisher*'s Allan Wolper (2003) celebrated the end of Pew's support, which he regarded as inherently unethical, for 'reach-out-and-touch-someone' projects. Leonard Witt's (2003) column titled 'This Movement Won't Be Buried: Reports of Public Journalism's Death are Greatly Exaggerated', insisted that public journalism would survive. But a year later Witt, president of the Public Journalism Network, switched to 'Sustainable Journalism' or 'Representative Journalism', saying consumers should pay for high quality journalism 'just like they pay for a haircut or cable TV' (Witt, 2008). PJNet describes itself as interested in public and citizen journalism, but its foci have become social media and networking.

In any case, mentions of public journalism significantly tailed off after 2003. But both disjunctures remain acute, particularly the cognitive and intellectual distance between citizens and professional journalists. This chapter, therefore, analyses the major challenges posed by and to public journalism, with an eye to assessing public journalism's relevance to structures, technologies, or journalistic forms that promote collaborations between professional journalists and citizen journalists. After examining emerging trends, especially in the US, that potentially build on public journalism's strengths, in theory and practice, we analyse whether citizen journalism can succeed where public journalism failed. We consider the claims and criticisms of public (or civic) journalism and citizen (or crowd-sourced or open source) journalism, as the bases for enhancing the viability of a civic-minded journalism. We assess the extent to which its theorization supports its claims and goals. As with public journalism, citizen journalism's philosophy is somewhat unclear; its definition is still emerging. Nonetheless, citizen journalism understands people as having political roles, interests and relationships, and as actively interested in sharing news they deem relevant. It understands, or perhaps intuits, that a knee-jerk definition of all forms of journalism as acquiring and distributing information misses the point.

Defining public journalism

From the freelance and unpaid 'correspondents' of colonial newspapers, as well as letters to the editor, to broadcast media 'tip lines', US journalism has invited citizens' efforts; individuals have often used new technologies to share news with others and with news organizations. More importantly, journalists, citizens and political figures have long agreed that good journalism was necessary to an informed citizenry and thus at the heart of democracy. In 1793, in the inaugural issue of his *American Minerva*, Noah Webster described newspapers as 'the common instruments of social intercourse, by which the Citizens of this vast Republic constantly discourse and debate with each other on subjects of public concern' (in Glasser, 2000: 683). Public journalism's philosophical antecedents, however, are most directly Jürgen Habermas' theory of the public sphere, but also the Walter Lippmann–John Dewey debate about journalism's democratic responsibilities, and the 1947 Hutchins Commission on Freedom of the Press. Public journalism thereby drew on ongoing legacies of doing and thinking about journalism as promoting civic commitment and participation in democratic processes. As such public journalism emphasized listening to citizens rather than politicians, experts, or other élites, and highlighting how citizens could help solve the issues they deemed significant. Instead of conceiving of readers as merely receiving news, public journalists addressed citizens as members of deliberative publics, concerned with issues that transcend their immediate self-interests.

The claim that journalists should help create and sustain a public sphere was stated only in general terms and it was never clear whether public journalism projects could be undertaken alongside more conventional reporting. Early on, this vagueness was probably strategic, given the criticism that the movement originated in the academy, not newsrooms, and was then imposed by publishers and editors. This lack of distinct philosophical and operational definitions left unclear how public journalism should be conducted or assessed. One idea was to adopt a communitarian democratic framework. Communitarianism, however, underestimates the problem of conflicting visions of the common good, both within and beyond the local community. On the other hand, in regarding citizens as individuals sharing little more than their interest in free choice and residence in a given nation-state, a liberal democratic framework minimizes the strong sense of shared purpose needed to undergird participation in joint deliberation and action (Haas and Steiner, 2006).

Including the reasoning public and sharing authority

Public journalism celebrated the 'reasoning public', comprising citizens sharing a commitment to 'common reasoning', activated through dialogue and deliberation. In nearly half of some 650 public journalism projects, news organizations sponsored public discussion formats, such as focus groups, roundtable discussions, and town-hall meetings (Friedland and Nichols, 2002). For example, news organizations convened citizen groups to identify issues that they wanted covered and developed stories based on those discussions. By reporting citizens' interactions during subsequent meetings, the judgements formed during face-to-face dialogues could be rechannelled into mass-mediated deliberations and thereby considered by a wider audience.

In any case, while public journalists were criticized for retaining the notion that professionals know better than citizens what citizens need (Schudson, 1999), more often public journalists were accused of abdicating their professional authority and responsibility for setting the news agenda. Public journalists always retained the authority to articulate their own agenda, that is, to retain professional autonomy even while they worked to preserve commitment to public service and respect for citizens. But conventional journalists complained that letting citizens set the news agenda substituted community judgement for journalists' judgement and this compromised their critical stance and ability to remain detached. In *Editor & Publisher*, consistently the most hostile to public journalism, Nat Hentoff dismissed the notion of finding out what readers want to know, saying '[w]e owe it to our readers – and our own self-respect – also to tell them what they need to know, and in a way that will impel them to want to read it' (2002). This notion of public journalists' double stance lingers on in a central tenet of the PJNet: 'We believe journalists should stand apart in making sound professional judgments about how to cover communities, but cannot stand apart in learning about and understanding these communities.'

Arguably, even the model of neutral information that dominates journalism, while it is a thin and inadequate version of news, implies a role for journalism in democracy and expresses the values of openness, fairness, diversity and transparency. Conventional journalists not only expose problems but also try to show how they can be solved effectively. Engagement is merely another way to address the problems of democracy. Nonetheless, the idea that journalists should help solve problems sparked the most heated attacks by scholarly and journalistic critics, who attacked public journalism as manipulative, if not propagandistic. Trying to facilitate community engagement and action or recommend solutions outside the editorial pages was political advocacy, or worse, collaboration with the government. According to the *American Journalism Review*'s editor: 'If a newspaper or television station is the driving force behind a community project ... who is going to believe that it will cover that project with balance and objectivity' (in Rosen, 1999: 180). Terry Anderson, the journalist who unsuccessfully ran for office after his release as a hostage in Lebanon, was typical: 'The function of the press is not to solve problems, but to report on problems' (in St. John, 2007: 257).

What worked

Public journalism had some impact, especially in terms of rhetorically connecting journalism and democracy, and reconceptualizing journalists' definitions of and relationships to their audiences (as citizens, not consumers). Compared to conventional news organizations' coverage of politics, public journalism practices produced more election-related reporting, with mobilizing information and more focus on substantive issues and policy; they de-emphasized polls, campaign strategies, and image-management. They relied more on non-élite sources, including women and minorities, than on élite sources (Kurpius, 2002). Research (albeit fragmentary) showed that such features increased knowledge of community issues and people's stands; and increased citizens' participation in problem-solving; inclination to contact public officials; and voting (Meyer and Potter, 2000).[2]

Public journalism produced at best modest increases in readership. No wonder: public journalism projects were expensive and did not treat citizens as individuated consumers obsessed with fashion and private lives. Marginalized groups and the poor are hardly the markets coveted by advertisers. Ignoring market imperatives, they focused on – but of course without permanently solving – deeply embedded but potentially off-putting and commercially unpopular community issues: race relations and poverty, alcohol and drug abuse, child care, domestic violence, health care, homelessness, immigration, public housing, racial profiling, unemployment and welfare (Friedland and Nichols, 2002).

Nor did public journalism transform news organizations. The goal was never to change every journalistic routine, however, but to reinvigorate a larger democratic mission. Its best practices, albeit not its ideas, were incorporated by mainstream news organizations, including those exploiting the easy, affordable accessibility of online interactivity; nearly every news organization now maintains a web 'presence' that invites audience participation, for example, encouraging readers to post critiques, respond to readers' threads in reader-directed forums, and contribute news and photos, or at least news tips. News organizations are even sharing information technologies with citizens.[3] Some of this is indirect, such as 'professional' journalists who post confessional sidebars about their work to encourage a more intimate relationship with readers.

The death of public journalism

Public journalism died, but probably not because of philosophic weaknesses (such as its failure to recognize differences and conflicts among publics) or the market-vulnerable notion of consensus inherent in its 'civic' projects. Nor did it result from journalists' criticisms or opposition. Meanwhile, journalists' insistence on professional autonomy is at best moot, given a dramatic shift to information produced, shared and controlled by citizens, and a continuing scepticism about conventional news organizations' credibility. In 2009, 8–10 per cent of US poll respondents said they had a great deal of confidence in 'mass media' reporting and 35 per cent had a fair amount; the majority reported little to no confidence (Morales, 2009; PEJ, 2009). Moreover, nearly all news organizations are now suffering significantly reduced budgets. Of 351 editors and publishers surveyed, 65 per cent had laid off workers since January 2008; 71 per cent said reductions in personnel and wages 'somewhat' or 'greatly affected' the quality of coverage (Liedtke, 2009). Ironically, 28 per cent of the APME respondents planned to charge for online content.[4] That is, the economy and a host of Web 2.0 technologies (but their inability to monetize their online news) fundamentally challenged all news organizations. Ironically, perhaps, citizen journalism, which perhaps inherits public journalism's philosophy, dealt the fatal blow to public journalism.

Crowdsourcing models

James Surowiecki (2004) reasoned that aggregating people's solutions under the right circumstances (which includes diversity and independence) produces the 'wisdom of crowds'. That is, a crowd's 'collective intelligence' can be harnessed for government and nonprofit projects as well as entrepreneurial crowdsourcing projects. Crowdsourcing means inviting unknown people to engage in problem-solving and even in sorting through proposed solutions; by outsourcing to amateurs and/or volunteers the work traditionally performed by employees, it potentially puts professionals out of paid work.[5] Celebrating 'the age of the crowd', Jeff Howe (2006) wrote, 'The open source software movement proved that a network of passionate, geeky volunteers could write code just as well as the highly paid developers at Microsoft'. Indeed, although he didn't coin the term until 2008, Howe first referred to crowdsourcing in a 2006 Wired article about iStockphoto, whose 22,000 'iStockers' charge $1 to $5 per stock photograph, not the $100 to $150 professional freelancers charge. 'Amateur' content was also disseminated on cable television (Bravo's *Outrageous and Contagious*: Viral Videos); film (50 fans filmed a Beastie Boys concert), and news. The notion of mass collaboration is probabilistic; indeed, the argument is that the more people are involved, the better the quality of information and the better for democracy. Moreover, 'the best collective decisions are the product of disagreement and contest, not consensus and compromise' (Surowiecki, 2004: xix).

Notably, sites such as Wikipedia and other forms of technology-intensive 'informational' crowdsourcing projects may be wholly, or at least partly, motivated by the satisfaction of participation and collaboration and producing cultural capital. For example, citizen science projects – scientific research accomplished by volunteers not credentialled as scientists, such as the Audubon Society's annual bird count – aim as much to promote engagement with science and scientific method as to collect and analyse data. Crowdsourcing contributors are paid little or nothing; usually the reward is recognition, thanks or intellectual satisfaction. Cost-savings do not drive crowdsourcing; or, at a minimum, profit is combined with self-efficacy and intrinsic motivations: the joy of solving technical problems, finding friends and community, developing skills, and sheer fun. Monetary profit was the strongest motivator for iStockers' participation, but peer recognition, developing individual skills, and having fun were also important (Brabham, 2008). Likewise, Wikipedia editors told Johnson (2008) that they enjoyed developing skills (in both writing and collaborating), got personal satisfaction from editing, and identified with the online encyclopedia's values and its community. For example, one respondent said,

> I like the ideals of the project. Human knowledge should be available to everyone, regardless of ability to pay or location in the world. Similarly, the ability to contribute to that base of knowledge should be open to everyone that wants to do so constructively.

Creating 'user-generated content' (UGC) helps minimize self-doubts, helps people feel important, and connects users with others (Daugherty *et al.*, 2008).

Jimmy Wales, Wikipedia's co-founder, rejects the term crowdsourcing as 'incredibly irritating' and as entirely different from building collaborative structures with proactive, transparent processes for settling disputes (McNichol, 2007). Wales' objections notwithstanding, Wikipedia is the contemporary paradigm for collective action, providing a public good through creative, democratic, massively crowdsourced collaboration. Indeed, Wikipedia defies expectations about free-riding, the central problem of the commons, when individuals over-consume, fail to contribute, or otherwise abuse a resource and damage the commons (Johnson, 2008). Citizendium, a rival encyclopedia (a 'citizens' compendium of everything') launched in 2007 by Wikipedia co-founder Larry Sanger, similarly demonstrates citizens' desire to contribute to a public informational good (Citizendium, 2009), this time, with contributors identifying themselves and submitting to experts' 'gentle' oversight.

> [W]e will be organized as a genuine republic of letters governed by a rule of law. There will be no 'dictators', but a regularly changing group of people tasked to manage a public trust in conformity with a relatively stable code of rules.... [W]e will have very little tolerance for the sort of immature disruption and abuse that plagues so many other Internet communities.

Citizendium's doubters complain that, when Wikipedia had several million articles, Citizendium had 12,491. On the other hand, critics have not challenged Citizendium's philosophy for global collaboration.

Digital video, blogging, podcasting, mobile phone photography, wikis, and user-forum posts are thus shifting the balance of power between message producers and audiences, who now can make their own content choices, bypassing traditional gatekeepers. Granted, marketing, advertising and design experts know how to exploit citizens' interest in using Web 2.0 technologies. "'User Generated Content" means free cultural product for monetization and cross-licensing, "participation" means free user data to mine and sell to advertisers, and all user activity is subject to surveillance and censorship' (Costanza-Chock, 2008: 857). However, users seem aware of this problem, and smart about how their work is used. Moreover, we should not exaggerate what percentage of the population knows how to use new technologies. Half of the 2009 US respondents said they used search engines to hunt for news at least once a week; 22 per cent have customized webpages that include news. This includes 12 per cent of the least involved news consumers, the so-called 'disengaged'. But only 4 per cent have ever posted their own news content, including videos or photos; only 7 per cent even occasionally post comments about news stories (Smith *et al.*, 2009).

Although we mention crowdsourcing to illustrate the intrinsic satisfaction of producing information, news organizations are recognizing its informational place. WNYC, the public radio station in New York City, has initiated several crowdsourcing experiments. The *Washington Post*'s Story Lab will experiment with crowdsourcing, for example, regarding story ideas; readers may help with data collection, and comment on stories. While it does not satisfy Glasser's (2000) call for journalists to explain their processes, much less their politics, Story Lab will explain why stories are reported or omitted. ProPublica recruited volunteer citizen reporters to monitor progress on 510 projects approved for federal stimulus money. Yahoo! News' YouWitnessNews allows users to submit photos and videos to be used in Yahoo! News articles and features. The *Guardian* of London invited readers to help investigate claims about misused public monies. In 80 hours some 20,000 volunteers coded 170,000 documents (Andersen, 2009). Talking Points Memo's Muckraker site invited readers to parse the 3,000 Justice Department emails about federal prosecutors apparently unjustly fired; within hours, Muckraker readers found compromising passages that led to further journalistic investigation (Howe, 2008).

NowPublic.com brokers citizens' stories, photos and videos, offering them to legacy organizations; its 'Crowd Power' tool locates photos and video from the web when citizens cannot supply them. Many stories feature strong opinions and partisan accusations, but its most recommended stories offer more balanced reporting. While predicting that crowdsourcing ultimately will revolutionize journalism, *OJR*'s (*Online Journalism Review*) editor treats crowdsourcing as 'another way of reporting, one that will stand along the traditional "big three" of interviews, observation and examining documents', essentially a descendant of establishing a telephone 'tip line' (Niles, 2007). Unlike more traditional notions of citizen journalism, crowdsourcing does not require readers to learn advanced reporting skills or ethics, said Niles, who charges for his crowdsourcing training, for example, in how to avoid bogus data. 'Nor does it allow any one reader's work to stand on its own, without the context of many additional points of view' (Niles, 2007).

The shift to citizen partnerships

Around 2000, attention shifted from professionals listening to citizens, to publics and professionals sharing control. Citizen-shared news acts 'as a corrective and a supplement to the output of commercial, industrial journalism' (Bruns, 2008: 69). Sometimes more dramatic claims are legitimate: The demonstrations against military rulers in Burma in 2007 and the Iranian election protests in 2009 were critical issues that legacy journalists literally could not cover. Citizens could, and did. In 2006 *CyberJournalist.net* said experiments were emerging too quickly to keep count. Jan Schaffer (2007) studied almost 500 citizen media sites in 2007. The Knight Citizen News Network lists nearly 800 citizen media sites. And if legacy journalists first responded with open suspicion, they quickly recognized potential, so looked to co-opt it; the appeal to citizens precluded the direct hostility directed at the top-down public journalism. The *Washington Post* admitted, 'With the media landscape in turmoil and readers empowered to construct their own windows onto the world, the role of traditional news organizations is ever more in question.'[6] Describing the blogosphere and legacy journalism as increasingly symbiotic, a former *Washington Post* editor (Downie and Schudson, 2009) called on journalists, nonprofit organizations and government to facilitate citizens' dissemination of public information.[7]

Bruns (2008) dates citizen journalism to activists' proactive and highly networked organizing of Indymedia before the 1999 World Trade Organization meeting in Seattle. The pioneering South Korean site OhmyNews launched in 2000; by 2009, some 70,000 citizens had written stories that were edited by volunteer editors (Woyke, 2009). OhmyNews later launched citizen journalism sites in English and Japanese. All its citizen reporters must abide by a strict Code of Ethics, whose first principle is that everyone must work in the spirit that 'all citizens are reporters', and identify themselves as citizen reporters while covering stories. NewAssignment.net sought to show that 'open collaboration over the Internet among reporters, editors and large groups of users can produce high-quality work that serves the public interest, holds up under scrutiny, and builds trust' (Rosen, 2006).

The terminology of citizen journalism is problematic, perhaps reflecting both semantic quibbles and substantive philosophic debates. The terminological turmoil may also highlight a useful willingness to experiment; emerging through trial and error, citizen journalism refers to a huge range of structures and models, with very different practices and ambitions. Some of what goes by this term is sporadic and happenstance, and turned over to legacy media. This end of the spectrum includes both highly 'accidental journalism' (the 30 seconds of film capturing the assassination of President Kennedy sold to *Life Magazine* for $150,000) but also citizens' intentional undertaking of a 'watchdog' role by sharing pictures and video of police brutality at the 2006 May Day immigrant protests in

Los Angeles and the Bay Area police shooting in 2009 of an unarmed man. Within 24 hours of the 2005 London underground bombings, the BBC received 1,000 stills and videos, 3,000 texts and 20,000 emails. This outpouring convinced BBC management: '[W]e had to change. We would need to review our ability to ingest this kind of material and our editorial policies to take account of these new forms of output' (Boaden, 2008).

At the other end are ongoing, consistent, organized and systematic efforts to 'repurpose' news or to undertake original reporting (which we emphasize). Jan Schaffer (2007) includes as citizen journalism sites entirely run by volunteers; owned and controlled by legacy organizations; hybrids of citizens supervised and/or trained by paid staffers; totally independent yet professional journalists operating either for profit or nonprofit, sometimes with foundation support or investors, and also incorporating citizen-written material; profit and nonprofit sites begun by individuals; and community cooperatives where volunteers, share decision-making, sometimes at formal meetings. Although 78 per cent of respondents said they provide 'journalism', with 46 per cent saying they provided mainly news and information, apparently citizens do not consistently call themselves journalists (Schaffer, 2007: 23). Schaffer, who directed the Pew Center for Civic Journalism before launching J-Lab, therefore prefers 'hyperlocal citizen media', although many projects are community-oriented but not hyperlocal.

The pro-am term applies in both the sense of enthusiastic, knowledgeable, committed amateurs who work to professional standards, but outside hierarchical organizations with professionals at the top (Leadbeater and Miller, 2004) and also as partnerships of amateurs and professionals (Rosen, 2006). Yet, 'pro-am journalism' has significant downsides, including the two-part term's refusal to highlight convergence not merely across platforms and industries, but also across roles. Mainstream journalists long spurned any designation as 'professionals' – not because they aligned themselves with citizens, but because a trade orientation relieved them of professionalism's more onerous burdens. The current crisis suggests that this insistence may have backfired. Ironically, given their objection to public journalism as encouraging journalists to see themselves as citizens, some paid journalists now object that 'citizen journalism' implies that they are not citizens. Meanwhile, citizens probably find the term irrelevant. Note the comments of a Wikipedia editor who does not want to read *Encyclopedia Britannica* articles by paid writers: 'Today he's writing about model trains, tomorrow's he's going to be writing Model T's, you see what I mean? I'd rather read an article by a guy who's really crazy about model trains' (Johnson, 2008). Credibility has shifted from news professionals who are not subject matter experts to amateur journalists who became subject matter experts (Leadbeater and Miller, 2004).

Terms such as networked or distributed journalism, open or user-driven news, and even participant journalism, foreground the process, if not the product, which is indeed deliberative, collaborative, flexible, conversational, networked. But these problematically de-centre and depoliticize those doing the participating. Even Minnesota Public Radio's 'Public Insight Journalism' explicitly casts listeners as 'sources'. Lastly, because participants may not be legal residents, one analysis of the online immigrant rights movement rejected the term citizen journalism as 'dead on arrival as an organizing concept for participatory reporting by noncitizens' (Costanza-Chock, 2008: 856). In any case, citizen journalism includes both citizen–legacy collaborations and sites established by individual journalists, apart from their paid work. In order to highlight how participants in this new formation are political beings with political interests and responsibilities, we refer to them as citizens. Therefore, we retain the term citizen journalism, henceforth CJ, to refer to ongoing projects controlled and operated by citizens, where citizens define and report what is relevant to them.[8] The term is admittedly imperfect. Just as 'public journalism' and even 'the public's journalism' problematically suggested a single, unified public, so citizen journalism atomizes the individual, ignoring how larger and shared interests come into being through interaction. Nonetheless, we contrast this (on a range from least to most negative) to legacy, conventional, corporate, fortress, or industrial journalism, henceforth LJ.

This notion of CJ highlights experiments that are primarily citizen-based, even if professional journalists are involved. Next Door Media covers five Seattle neighbourhoods, with a professional serving as the editor and reporter for residents' photos, videos and written reports. One such sub-site won the 2009 Online News Association's award for community collaboration. In 2009 The *Seattle Times* began a year-long partnership with local blogs and invited Next Door Media editors to question mayoral candidates during a debate. Introduced in 2006, iReport likewise allows citizens to post news reports live-time. CNN, which now owns iReport, vets the stories and selects some for airing on CNN; of nearly 400,000 reports submitted to iReport by December 2009, more than 20,000 had been vetted. The red 'stamp' on stories used on CNN platforms indicates both citizen participation and a professional standard of reliability.

Launched by the *Huffington Post* project and NewAssignment.net in 2008, OffTheBus organized groups of citizens – ultimately 12,000 people participated – to cover twelve presidential hopefuls: 'Let a distributed, diverse crowd of amateur users with lots of different starting points have a go at campaign news and commentary, seeded by a few pros' (Huffington and Rosen, 2008). Citizens did the reporting; editors were gatekeepers. OffTheBus contributor Mayhill Fowler (2008) gained national fame after revealing that presidential candidate Barack Obama had told California supporters that embittered and ignored rural Pennsylvanians cling to 'guns or religion or antipathy for people who aren't like them'.[9]

Assignment Zero, a successor project of NewAssignment.net and Wired.com, applies crowdsourcing to reporting in the same way. The site takes advantage of what Rosen calls 'the people formerly known as the audience' and bets that 'openness has editorial advantages bigger than its well-known weak points. (Which include trolls, fools, spam, sabotage, edit wars and the inflow of "crap")' (Rosen, 2007). While acknowledging that people could use an open platform to post meaningless information or advertising, he noted that a professional newsroom 'only knows what its own people know or dig up' (Rosen, 2007). Howe (2007) called the project 'a highly satisfying failure': its seven essays fell far short of its original goal, yet matched the quality of insight of national magazines. He attributed the major problems to the nebulousness of crowdsourcing and technological problems that hindered collaboration. Nonetheless, he said, Assignment Zero worked better than traditional hierarchies. Assignment Zero participants articulated several reasons for participation, 'including the enhancement of one's status within the community, the opportunity to learn or perfect a skill, the chance for financial gain or simply the intangible rewards from working with others toward a shared goal' (Howe, 2007).

Twitter bringing more people to the table

The micro-blogging site Twitter has extended self-publication to a large population and made frequent updating easy. In 2008 as many people were using Twitter or status update services as blogging on online journals; the number has grown significantly since then (Lenhart and Fox, 2008). Critics allege that 140 characters cannot handle context; worse, errors steadily accumulate in tweeting (Morozov, 2009). Citizens are using Twitter to break news stories, from the California wildfires in 2008 to the 2009 Mumbai massacre. Again, new technologies have always been exploited by activists, and by individuals to share news on a one-time basis. Moreover, although Tweets by elected politicians often are prepared and posted by public relations staff, hypothetically they offer an alternative for political news, especially for following 'the real-time nuts and bolts of campaigns racing to the finish line' (Calderone and Libit, 2009).

Some sites are experimenting with Twitter to test whether it can strengthen community, in the way that conventional community news does. For example, Charlottesville citizens created a virtual community for Twitter users; through Cvilletwitter.com, they offer analysis, commentary and conversation. Many federal and municipal government agencies use Twitter to inform the public. But citizen-based sites like Twitter can be more effective than the traditional model of dissemination running from authority to news media to public. For example, Flu Wiki, a public health forum, promises to be 'A reliable source of information, as neutral as possible, about important facts...; A venue for anticipating the vast range of problems...; A venue for thinking about implementable solutions to foreseeable problems' (Palen, 2007: 56).

News organizations use Twitter to post updates on stories and search for leads, and now are mining their Twitter contacts for information.

Regarding the 2009 shootings at Fort Hood, Texas, the *New York Times* compiled a list of nearby Twitter users, including local citizens, news outlets, and military accounts (Kanalley, 2009). The *Times* online showed updates from Twitter users that the editors were following. And if these stories are not always reliable (such as the Tweet, widely picked up by LJ, that the Fort Hood shooter had been killed), so LJ clearly remains equally vulnerable to ethical and professional errors. Although Twitter cannot offer the consistent engagement encouraged in public journalism, it reverses the top-down information model and arguably promotes informal citizen partnerships.

The information model

Citizen journalism essentially challenges the long tradition and continuing dominance of 'information' in US history, democratic theory and journalism, including public journalism. Not surprisingly evidencing this belief in information, the Knight Commission on the Information Needs of Communities in a Democracy calls for 'aggressive action to ensure the information opportunities of America's people, the information health of its communities, and the information vitality of our democracy' (Knight Commission, 2009: 1). The Commission said people need information to participate in civic affairs: 'Access to news and information is critical to democracy…. News organizations also foster civic understanding, engagement, and cohesion. When they work well, they help make communities open, officials accountable and publics engaged' (Knight Commission, 2009: 3).

The Knight Commission equated access to information with participation, as seen in an early assertion: 'The inability of some to participate fully in community life through a loss of information harms not only those directly affected. It also harms the entire community. Democratic communities thrive when all sectors are active participants' (Knight Commission, 2009: 1). It called for informed communities, 'where the information ecology meets the personal and civic information needs of people' (p. 5). The Knight Commission (2009: 17) listed five values as paramount to an 'information system' in democracies, and relevant to assessing citizen journalism: openness (being maximally available to everyone as a producer and consumer); inclusion (reflecting the entire community's interests); participation (supporting people's engagement with information for personal and civic purposes); empowerment of individuals and communities; and common pursuit of truth and the public interest. This language presumes that information motivates engagement and drives self-governance, a logic also evident in the Commission's claim that newspapers' decreasing ability to inform readers was 'plainly reason to be concerned for local journalism, and, therefore, for local democratic governance'.

What CJ realizes, however, in contrast to public and legacy journalism, is that democratic processes do not necessarily derive from information. In short, what drives CJ is engagement in democracy, participation – 'being' in the commons. Turning the usual logic on its head, engagement motivates self-governance, and then information behaviours. Already in 1980, futurist Alvin Toffler coined the portmanteau 'prosumer' to refer to audiences as producers and consumers of content. Highlighting how the role of consumer and 'end user' have disappeared in the current context of fluid, flexible, heterarchical ad hoc communication processes, Axel Bruns (2008) coins the term 'produser' to refer to the hybridized communities that harness and share collected intelligence.[10] Brabham (2008) described web technologies as vehicles for pleasurable, distributed, mass production.[11] The 'you' named *TIME*'s 2006 'Person of the Year' specifically used Web 2.0 technologies to help others without pay, which 'will not only change the world, but also change the way the world changes' (Grossman, 2006). Taking up the public journalism philosophy discarded by public journalism (or, better, by those who discarded public journalism), CJ has thus promoted empowerment and participation. The question remains the degree to which it provides an open-ended, unbounded public sphere in which all citizens can participate. All participatory forms of journalism are not necessarily the public's journalism.

The problems and the future

Much more work is yet to be done to fulfil the promise of CJ, especially with respect to including people who otherwise are at best witnesses to public deliberation. While public journalism sought real deliberation, citizen journalism thus far has made little effort to facilitate deliberation or ensure participation by an entire community. Most citizen journalism sites grew from desires to make better use of audience resources, not to engage audiences in real conversation. They emerged from crowdsourcing strategies, rather than a coherent journalistic, political or moral philosophy. Citizen journalism thus appears to take a liberal 'free market' approach: the doors are open for all, but little regulation or guidance is provided. In this sense, as currently defined and practised, citizen journalism has adopted public journalism's concern with democracy, but not its experiments with deliberation; it has not achieved the ideal of public deliberation posited by Habermas and others. Moreover, public journalism was criticized for pushing consensual solutions to problems that were not suffered equally by all social groups (Pauly, 1999). Conceiving of the public sphere as comprising multiple discursive domains and foregrounding issues of subordinate social groups would have promoted public deliberation in ways that helped people understand their conflicting (or unequal) interests and ensured that subordinate groups enjoy the opportunities to articulate their distinct concerns. But the same lack of a thorough coherent public philosophy that undermined public journalism besets citizen journalism.

CJ has advanced, albeit minimally, opportunities for citizens to criticize news coverage in terms of explicit values and to hold journalists accountable. But, like public journalism, it has not yet designed adequate models for collective evaluation of citizen content. Public journalists never managed to nurture a public sphere 'about' journalism; it failed to ensure sustained, meaningful citizen participation or establish effective mechanisms for responding publicly to citizens' criticisms. Its top-down mandate hindered genuine newsroom support. Public journalism projects often presumed that any involvement of experts tainted the authentic expression of public opinion. CJ suffers both analogous and contrary problems, perhaps in this case, because it emerged haphazardly from the ground up. Most cheery accounts of citizen–professional collaborations overstate the case: citizens would be better positioned to redefine news and their role in journalism if they devoted less energy to demonizing 'media', 'media gatekeepers' and government, and concentrated on robust self-critique. Citizen journalism has done no better than public journalism in supporting formal (or even informal) accountability systems such as news councils, citizen review boards, or publicly elected gatekeepers. Citizendium's elected 'Citizens' are drafting a charter, including a Constabulary responsible for monitoring and enforcing appropriate behaviour. But such elections cannot generate commitment to site-wide, much less cross-platform, public critique. Furthermore, the singular grammar of 'citizen' renders participants as isolated individuals, potentially and perhaps even practically detached from one another, from communities, and especially from a public or the 'commons'.

Inequality in access to the Internet and Web 2.0 technologies does not bode well for citizen journalism. Stimulating citizens to debate and take action on issues that do not affect them directly or personally (i.e., that affect 'others') requires democratic, fluid, collaborative, creative spaces with diversity in identities, skills, perspectives, experiences and political investments. The Internet has not fundamentally altered demographic patterns regarding who is civically engaged. Social networking and crowdsourcing sites often replicate gender, class, race and even caste divisions (Costanza-Chock, 2008: 857). Racial minorities are increasingly online and black and Hispanic mobile users are more likely than whites to participate in mobile activities, including sending and receiving text messages (Horrigan, 2009). But wealthy well-educated élites are generally more active online, including by contacting government officials and signing petitions.

Nonetheless, public journalism's model of collaboration resonated with citizens. It has facilitated open access and organization of creative news and activist projects. For example, 19 per cent of Internet users have posted material online about political or social issues or used a social networking site for some form of civic or political engagement (Smith *et al.*, 2009). Immigrant activists were encouraged to upload video to non-commercial sites, such as IndyMedia.org, on the axiom 'Don't hate the media – become the media' (Costanza-Chock, 2008: 859). Haas (2007) criticized blogs for failing to provide the bottom-up approach, independent original reporting, interactivity and diversity of voices that proponents claim.[12] Nonetheless, blogs, hyper-local sites and journalism sites that programmatically invite citizen interactivity are increasingly enabling people to express themselves, engage in debate, and lead public conversation about issues of they find important. Moreover, the linking and networking among these sites, and the fact that they operate with such different values, definitions and models, may provide the multi-perspectival array that the emerging public sphere requires, especially if this is accompanied, as it should be, by some commitment to ethics and transparency.

Bruns (2008) argues that citizen journalism, with its fluid non-hierarchical networks and ad hoc meritocracy, solves the major tension between those who advocate maximum participation, openness, experimentation and flexibility; and those worried about gatekeeping, and editing. Bruns (2005) offers the notion of gatewatching, referring to relatively continuous, open, communal observation of the 'output gates' (conventional sources and news sites, as well as reports from a range of alternative sources) to see what might be relevant. Gatewatching does not claim to publish, as the *New York Times* does, 'all the news that's fit to print'. Instead it implies that audiences decide for themselves what is important and relevant, a direct descendant of public journalism philosophy.

The criticism that public journalism was financially motivated seems unwarranted; certainly news organizations embarked on far flimsier but more successful efforts to bolster profits. Presumably Pew's impact on coverage was much more diffuse than conventional advertisers'. Citizen journalists, despite a huge range of nonprofit and for-profit experiments and agendas, have not yet invented workable business models for either CJ or LJ. Both are still frantically searching for viability. Dan Gillmor left the *San Jose Mercury News* to see if he could run citizen journalism as a business. His explanation of Bayosphere's failure suggests that he missed important lessons about collaboration and participation (Gillmor, 2006). Yet, neither is money an insurmountable problem. About half of Schaffer's (2007) projects never intended to make money; while advertising provided income for half of the sites generating some revenue, others accepted no advertising or institutional support. Moreover, just as so-called 'public radio' makes use of crowd-funding, CJ and freelance projects can be crowd-funded. Chris Allbritton, a former *Daily News* reporter, used online pleas to fund his Iraq war reporting. Supported by the Knight Foundation, *Spot. Us* asks users to donate money for a news pitch (usually $20). For example, the online site Public Press, with its 50 volunteer and professional journalists in San Francisco, and *Spot.Us* raised $5,000 to support an 18-part series about San Francisco's budget crisis. Eschewing advertising, Public Press promises to enrich civic life: 'Our nonprofit media business model incorporates entrepreneurial use of technology and traditional standards of journalism to provide better local news coverage to underserved audiences, and re-imagines the daily newspaper as a public-media institution accountable to the community' (About SF Public Press, 2009).

A key idea of public journalism was that journalists should include themselves as political actors and fair-minded participants in democratic processes, viewing themselves as part of the public, not objective outsiders. Citizen media offer the engagement that public journalism idealized: citizen journalists adopt journalists' responsibilities in ways that partner with conventional news media and may enrich democratic processes. Acknowledging their work and their responsibilities as political actors, they reconnect journalism and democracy. Again the topics of deliberation do not consistently or completely address the problems of democracy; access and equality remain worrisome. More crucially, the diffuse, decentralized nature of citizen journalism, whose hyper-local versions reach perhaps 1–5 per cent of local citizens, renders the public without a commons. Members of publics cannot see what they have in common. But in the context of new forms of journalism, new ways of collecting, distributing and participating in information sharing, media literacy is increasingly important – for journalists working at mainstream news organizations whose own work would be more effective if they understood how citizens understand news; for citizen journalists, who need to understand the personal, political and ethical stakes of the work that they do (or fail to do), and for citizen audiences, who, even if they are not actively engaged in reporting, need to understand how they can or cannot use various news forms, how they can demand effectively the kinds of news required for various purposes.

CJ does not always work. It is still emerging. On the other hand, the success of citizen journalism should not be equated with the survival of specific organizations; nor does the demise of one site indicate the failure of the larger enterprise. The time has come to develop criteria by which to assess CJ and to assess how it partners with LJ, since citizen reporters are unlikely to undertake sustained rigorous investigation and coverage of important public issues. This leaves LJ with a complementary (i.e., not rival) responsibility for providing comprehensive information, including on topics citizens do not yet regard as relevant. LJ ignores citizen journalism at its peril; such disdain is even more dangerous than its disdain for public journalism. Professional journalists' disdain for partnering with citizens in the general political sense shows disdain for democracy and only serves to undermine the credibility of their profession.

Notes

1   Please address questions to lead author Steiner, at lsteiner@jmail.umd.edu.
2   In 2008 most voters were unimpressed with election coverage; an all-time high number accused reporters of favouring one candidate and most people asked for more information about candidates' policies, but less about who was ahead in polls.
3   The *New York Times* is launching an open-source version of the technology it uses to embed documents in its online stories, to enable readers to comment directly on documents.

4 Moreover, nearly 40 per cent said they are devoting more space to 'hyper-local' news while decreasing the pages devoted to national and international stories, presumably, reasoning that local topics attract less broadcast attention. But, local stories are precisely the ones that citizen journalists can handle.

5 Although 'open source' work is initiated by the public, while crowdsourcing is initiated by a client, the latter term is better known and preferred here; besides, the 'client' is the public. Since crowdsourcing does not pull from a random sample of the population, it is not polling and does not represent community demographics. Nor is it crowdcasting, which refers to commercial and marketing applications for engaging audiences, nor an urtak – the Icelandic word for sample – a collaborative survey for finding out what communities think and care about.

6 (http://blog.washingtonpost.com/story-lab/2009/11/lifting_the_curtain_intro-ducin.html)

7 Len Downie now teaches at Arizona State, and sociologist Michael Schudson teaches at Columbia's journalism school.

8 This excludes opinion blogs and blog aggregators; public relations, marketing and advertising sites; LJ websites posting reader contributions merely for marketing purposes; as well as sites serving a highly specific niche interest.

9 The following month Fowler again drew attention for not identifying herself as a citizen journalist during a three-minute interview with former President Bill Clinton. Rosen regretted the omission, but said, 'We didn't think up guidelines for what to tell her in a situation like this' (Steinberg, 2008).

10 Bruns's produsage as a meritocracy, with standards based on expertise, reclaims the information orientation, but otherwise recognizes the importance of participation *per se*.

11 Although we cannot develop the point here, this makes irrelevant the difference between entertainment and journalism.

12 Blogs entirely devoted to reciting personal activity and opinion – especially if they preclude engagement with alternate positions – are not journalism. Even conventional news media incorporate plural voices in op-ed sections.

References

About SF Public Press (2009) *SF Public Press*. Available : <http://sfpublicpress.org/about> [Accessed 24 November 2009]

Andersen, M. (2009) 'Four crowdsourcing lessons from the Guardian's (spectacular) expenses-scandal experiment', *Nieman Journalism Lab*, 23 June. Available: <http://www.niemanlab.org/2009/06/four-crowdsourcing-lessons-from-the-guardians-spectacular-expenses-scandal-experiment/> [Accessed 24 November 2009]

Arant, D. and Meyer, P. (1998) 'Public Journalism and Traditional Journalism: A Shift in Values?', *Journal of Mass Media Ethics*, 13: 205–218.

Boaden, H. (2008) 'The role of citizen journalism in modern democracy', BBC NEWS, 13 November. Available: <http://www.bbc.co.uk/blogs/theeditors/2008/11/the_role_of_citizen_journalism.html> [Accessed 24 November 2009]

Brabham, D.C. (2008) 'Moving the crowd at iStockphoto: The composition of the crowd and motivations for participation in a crowdsourcing application', *First Monday*, 13(2): 6–12.

Bruns, A. (2005) *Gatewatching: Collaborative Online News Production*, New York: Peter Lang.

Bruns, A. (2008) *Blogs, Wikipedia, Second Life, and Beyond*, New York: Peter Lang.

Calderone, M. and Libit, D. (2009) 'For Election Insight, Twitter Beats Cable', *Politico*, 4 November. Available: <http://www.politico.com/news/stories/1109/29129.html> [Accessed 28 November 2009]

Citizendium (2009) 'Welcome to Citizendium'. Available: <http://en.citizendium.org> [Accessed 12 November 2009]

Costanza-Chock, S. (2008) 'The Immigrant Rights Movement on the Net: Between "Web 2.0" and Comunicación Popular', *American Quarterly*, 60(3): 851–864.

Daugherty, T., Eastin, M.S. and Bright, L. (2008) 'Exploring Consumer Motivations for Creating User-Generated Content', *Journal of Interactive Advertising*, 8(2).

Downie, L. and Schudson, M. (2009) *The Reconstruction of American Journalism*, New York: Columbia University Graduate School of Journalism.

Fowler, M (2008) 'Obama: No Surprise that Hard-pressed Pennsylvanians Turn Bitter', *Huffington Post*, 11 April. Available: <http://www.huffingtonpost.com/mayhill-fowler/obama-no-surprise-that-ha_b_96188.html> [Accessed 14 November 2009]

Friedland, L. and Nichols, S. (2002) *Measuring Civic Journalism's Progress: a Report across a Decade of Activity*, Washington, DC: Pew Center for Civic Journalism.

Gillmor, D. (2006) 'Dan Gillmor's Lessons Learned', *Cyberjournalist.net*, 25 January. Available: <http://www.cyberjournalist.net/dan-gillmors-lessons-learned> [Accessed 4 December 2009]

Glasser, T.L. (2000) 'The Politics of Public Journalism', *Journalism Studies*, 1: 683–686.

Grossman, L. (2006) 'Time's Person of the Year: You', *TIME*, [internet] 13 December. Available: <http://www.time.com/time/magazine/article/0,9171,1569514,00.html> [Accessed 24 November 2009]

Haas, T. (2007) *The Pursuit of Public Journalism: Theory, Practice, and Criticism*, New York: Routledge.

Haas, T. and Steiner, L. (2006) 'Public Journalism: A Reply to Critics', *Journalism: Theory, Practice and Criticism*, 7(2): 238–254.

Hentoff, N. (2002) 'The Future of News', *Editor & Publisher*, 6 May: 26.

Horrigan, J. (2009) *Wireless Internet Access*, (Pew Internet & American Life Project) Washington, DC.

Howe, J. (2006) 'The Rise of Crowdsourcing', *Wired*, 14 June. Available: <http://www.wired.com/wired/archive/14.06/crowds.html> [Accessed 14 October 2009]

Howe, J. (2007) 'Did Assignment Zero Fail? A look back, and lessons learned', *Wired*, 16 July. Available: <http://www.wired.com/techbiz/media/news/2007/07/assignment_zero_final> [Accessed 14 October 2009]

Howe, J. (2008) 'Crowdsourcing: Now With a Real Business Model!', *Wired*, 2 December. Available: http://www.wired.com/epicenter/2008/12/crowdsourcing-n/ [Accessed 14 October 2009]

Huffington, A. and Rosen, J. (2008) 'Thanks to the people who worked on OffTheBus; Here's what comes next', *Huffington Post*, 17 November. Available: <http://www.huffingtonpost.com/arianna-huffington-and-jay-rosen/thanks-to-the-people-who-_b_144476.html> [Accessed 14 October 2009]

Johnson, B.K. (2008) 'Incentives to Contribute in Online Collaboration: Wikipedia as Collective Action', paper presented at the International Communication Association, 58th Annual Conference, Montreal, Quebec, 26 May.

Kanalley, C. (2009) 'Fort Hood Shooting Shows How Twitter, Lists Can Be Used for Breaking News', *PoynterOnline*, 6 November. Available: <http://www.poynter.org/column.asp?id=31&aid=173078> [Accessed 29 November 2009]

Knight Commission (on the Information Needs of Communities in a Democracy) (2009) *Informing Communities: Sustaining Democracy in the Digital Age*, Washington, DC: The Aspen Institute.

Kurpius, D. (2002) 'Sources and Civic Journalism: Changing Patterns of Reporting?' *Journalism & Mass Communication Quarterly*, 79: 853–866.

Leadbeater, C. and Miller, P. (2004) 'The Pro-Am Revolution: How Enthusiasts are Changing our Economy and Society', *Demos*. Available: <http://www.demos.co.uk/files/proamrevolutionfinal.pdf> [Accessed 14 December 2009]

Lenhart, A. and Fox, S. (2008) *Twitter and Status Updating*, Washington, DC: Pew Internet & American Life Project.

Liedtke, M. (2009) 'Editors: Ability to inform diminished'. [Online] 13 May. Available: <http://www.apme.com/soundingboard/newsroom/051309apmesurvey_ap.shtml> [Accessed 16 October 2009]

McNichol, T. (2007) 'The Wales Rules for Web 2.0', *CNNMoney*, 2 July. Available: <http://money.cnn.com/galleries/2007/biz2/0702/gallery.wikia_rules.biz2/5.html> [Accessed 14 October 2009]

Meyer, P. and Potter, D. (2000) 'Hidden Value: Polls and Public Journalism', in Lavrakas, P. and Traugott, M. (eds) *Election Polls, the News Media, and Democracy*, New York: Seven Bridges Press.

Morales, L. (2009) 'Many Americans Remain Distrusting of News Media', *Gallup*, [internet] 1 October. Available: <http://www.gallup.com/poll/123365/Americans-Remain-Distrusting-News-Media.aspx?version=print> [Accessed 1 December 2009]

Morozov, E. (2009) 'Iran: Downside to the Twitter Revolution', *Dissent*, 56(4).

Niles, R. (2007) 'A journalist's guide to crowdsourcing', *Online Journalism Review*, [internet] 31 July 2007. Available: http://www.ojr.org/ojr/stories/070731niles/ [Accessed 13 October 2009]

Palen, L. (2007) 'Online Forums Supporting Grassroots Participation in Emergency Preparedness and Response', *Communication of the ACM*, 50(3).

Pauly, J. (1999) 'Journalism and the Sociology of Public Life', in Glasser, T.L. (ed.) *The Idea of Public Journalism*, New York: Guilford Press.

PEJ (Pew Excellence in Journalism) (2009) *Public Attitudes, the State of the News Media Annual Report 2009*. Available: <http://www.stateofthemedia.org/2009/index.htm> [Accessed 12 December 2009]

Rosen, J. (1999) *What are Journalists For?*, New Haven, CT: Yale University Press.

Rosen, J. (2006) 'Welcome to NewAssignment.Net', 19 August. Available: <http://newassignment.wordpress.com/2006/08/19/welcome-to-newassign-mentnet/> [Accessed 14 October 2009]

Rosen, J. (2007) 'Citizen Journalism Wants You!' *Wired*, 14 March. Available: <http://www.wired.com/techbiz/media/news/2007/03/72970> [Accessed 14 October 2009]

Schaffer, J. (2007) *Citizen Media: Fad or the Future of News?*, College Park: Philip Merrill College of Journalism.

Schudson, M. (1999) 'What Public Journalism Knows about Journalism, But Doesn't Know about the Public', in Glasser, T.L. (ed.) *The Idea of Public Journalism*, New York: Guilford Press.

Smith, A., Schlozman, K., Verba, S. and Brady, H. (2009) *The Internet and Civic Engagement*, Washington, DC: Pew Internet & American Life Project.

St. John, B. III (2007) 'Newspapers' Struggles with Civic Engagement: The U.S. Press and the Rejection of Public Journalism as Propagandistic', *The Communication Review*, 10(3): 249–270.

Steinberg, J. (2008) 'For New Journalists, All Bets, but Not Mikes, Are Off', *New York Times*, 8 June: WK 3.

Surowiecki, J. (2004) *The Wisdom of Crowds*, New York: Random House.

Toffler, A. (1980) *The Third Wave*, New York: Morrow.

Witt, L. (2003) 'This Movement Won't Be Buried: Reports of Public Journalism's Death are Greatly Exaggerated', *Columbia Journalism Review*, November/December: 70.

Witt, L. (2008) 'Representative Journalism Becomes More Appealing', 29 October. Available: http://pjnet.org/representativejournalism/post/33 [Accessed 12 December 2009]

Wolper, A. (2003) 'RIP, Civic Journalism', *Editor & Publisher*, April 16; 26.

Woyke, E. (2009) 'The Struggles of OhmyNews', *Forbes*, 11 March. Available: <http://www.forbes.com/forbes/2009/0330/050-oh-my-revenues.html> [Accessed 12 December 2009]

12 Toward a new(er) sociability: uses, gratifications and social capital on Facebook

Zizi Papacharissi and Andrew Mendelson

Emerging convergent platforms of sociality online generate public interest and invite a reconsideration of traditional theoretical paradigms of media research. Social network sites, specifically, afford a variety of social behaviours that simultaneously expand and challenge our conventional understanding of sociability, audience activity, passivity and involvement. Online platforms such as Facebook, MySpace, LinkedIn, or CyWorld and others provide individuals with the opportunity to present themselves and to connect with existing and new social networks. These networked platforms of socially oriented activity permit an introduction of the self via public displays of connection (boyd and Ellison, 2007; Donath and boyd, 2004; Papacharissi, 2002a, 2002b, 2009). In doing so, they promote multimediated identity-driven performances that are crafted around the electronic mediation of social circles and status. In addition, they provide flexible and personalizable modes of sociability, which allow individuals to sustain strong and weak ties through a variety of online tools and strategies (Ellison *et al.*, 2010). These customized expressions of online sociability allow users to pursue social behaviours through variable levels of involvement, activity, and multi-tasking (Hargittai and Hsieh, 2010; Papacharissi, 2010).

Individuals engage the connective affordances of social network sites (SNSs) so as to combine offline and online communication strategies for interaction. These strategies employ converged media but also converge social, cultural and political practices and spheres (e.g., Walther *et al.*, 2010). Conducting research in a converged media environment requires that researchers develop theories and analytical tools that examine uses, effects, activity, involvement and content across media. These tools must also recognize that in a converged environment, media use allows audiences to serve as both consumers and producers of media, frequently at the same time. The resulting confluence of emerging behaviours escapes the analytical lens of theoretical approaches that associate uses, and user profiles, with particular media and genres of activity. This chapter proposes a theoretical model that combines elements of the uses and gratifications and the social networks approaches so as to explicate patterns of media use, activity and sociability emerging post-convergence.

Uses and gratifications

Uses and gratifications (U&G) is a psychological communication perspective that examines how individuals use mass media, on the assumption that individuals select media and content to fulfil felt needs or wants. Contemporary U&G research is grounded in the following five assumptions:

1 'communication behavior, including media selection and use, is goal-directed, purposive, and motivated';
2 'people take the initiative in selecting and using communication vehicles to satisfy felt needs or desires';
3 'a host of social and psychological factors mediate people's communication behavior';
4 'media compete with other forms of communication (i.e., functional alternatives) for selection, attention, and use to gratify our needs or wants';
5 'people are typically more influential than the media in the relationship, but not always' (A. Rubin, 1994: 420).

U&G has been employed to understand various media uses and consequences, covering for instance soap operas (e.g., Alexander, 1985; Perse, 1986; A. Rubin, 1985), news programmes (e.g., Palmgreen *et al.*, 1980; A. Rubin, 1981), using the VCR (e.g., Levy, 1987; A. Rubin and Bantz, 1989), listening to talk radio (e.g., Turow, 1974), watching cable TV (e.g., Becker *et al.*, 1983), channel surfing (e.g., Ferguson, 1992), magazine reading (Payne *et al.*, 1988; Towers, 1987a), tabloid reading (Salwen and Anderson, 1984), the Internet (e.g., Papacharissi and Rubin, 2000), reality TV (e.g., Papacharissi and Mendelson, 2007) and religious television (Pettersson, 1986).

Specifically related to technological convergence, U&G has been used to understand how individuals employ the Internet to meet different goals, based on their socio-psychological disposition (e.g., Rubin, 1994). Scholars have examined connections between online news and civic engagement, public opinion or political behaviour (e.g., Hardy and Scheufele, 2005; Kaye and Johnson, 2002) or how individuals select or combine online and offline news sources (e.g. Dimmick *et al.*, 2004; De Waal *et al.*, 2006). Research has identified motives for using the Internet, linking them to distinct socio-psychological characteristics and types of Internet use (Perse and Ferguson, 2000; Papacharissi and Rubin, 2000; Papacharissi, 2002a, 2002b, 2007). Consensus suggests that online media serve as functional alternatives to interpersonal and mediated communication, providing options or complements for aspects of an individual's environment that are not as fulfilling. Aligned with time and other medium displacement effects that other studies on the sociability of new media have identified (e.g., Kraut *et al.*, 1998, 2002), these studies help explicate the place of net-based technologies within the individual's media ecology. To this end, U&G has been useful in connecting specific attributes to certain uses of the Internet, and distinguishing between uses that are more goal-oriented or instrumental versus others that are of a habitual or ritualistic nature. The perspective has a long history of being combined with other perspectives, and more recently, it has been integrated with the expectancy value approach to understand online media adoption behaviours (Lo *et al.*, 2005), and with diffusion of innovations to analyse individual differences in gaming adoption (Chang *et al.*, 2006).

However, U&G has not yet identified, in studies of the sociability of new media, a particular social outcome that would be the result of motives, socio-psychological predispositions and uses working together. In fact, lack of conceptual clarity on the concept of gratifications has been repeatedly raised as a theoretical limitation of the perspective (Lometti *et al.*, 1977; Swanson, 1977). The perspective has been critiqued as being too individualistic and underemphasizing the value of interaction (McQuail, 1979). The social networks approach, on the other hand, is structured around the concept of networked interaction. It focuses on the outcome of the interaction, that is, the network and the social capital generated by the network. Still, while the social networks approach is rich in its examination of structural features of networks, it is by definition not concerned with the socio-psychological profile of the individual. This presents a possible area for conceptual integration between the two approaches, so as to present a framework that examines individual orientations toward social network use online.

Online social networks and social network sites

Research on online social networks examines the formation and maintenance of online networks that support existing and new social ties (Wasserman and Faust, 1994; Wellman and Berkowitz, 1997). The unit of analysis is the interaction or relation between people, measured in terms of ties held by individuals maintaining a relation, the types of exchanges, frequency of contact, strength of ties, intimacy, qualitative elements of relations, size of networks, global or local span of networks and numerous other variables (Haythornthwaite, 2000, 2005; Haythornthwaite *et al.*, 1995; Haythornthwaite and Wellman, 1998).

Earlier online social network research examined communication and medium use (email, phone, fax and videoconferencing) in a work network of co-located researchers, to find that pairs of individuals possessing stronger ties tended to communicate more frequently, maintain a greater number of relations and communicate more frequently (Haythornthwaite *et al.*, 1995; Haythornthwaite and Wellman, 1998). This finding has resurfaced in a variety of networks and contexts, including distance learning (e.g., Haythornthwaite, 2000), organizational contexts (e.g., Garton *et al.*, 1997), and social support networks (e.g., Hlebec *et al.*, 2006) allowing researchers to fine-tune the concepts of *social network relation* (type of exchange or interaction, characterized by *content, direction* and *strength*), *tie* (pairs who maintain one or more types of relations, developing *strong, weak* or *latent* ties), *network* as web of person-to-person connectivity (distinguishing between *ego-centred* or *whole* network analysis, which may examine *range, centrality* or *roles*), and *media multiplexity* (the tendency of more strongly tied pairs to make use of more available media). Studies focusing on Netville, a wired suburb of Toronto, revealed that online interaction frequently supplemented or served as an alternative to face-to-face interaction, in ways that had positive effects on social capital (e.g., Hampton and Wellman, 2000; Hampton, 2002).

Social network sites represent a natural extension of this work, as they connect networks of individuals that may or may not share a place-based connection. Social network sites are defined as

> web-based services that allow individuals to (1) construct a public or semi-public profile within a bounded system, (2) articulate a list of other users with whom they share a connection, and (3) view and traverse their list of connections and those made by others within the system (boyd and Ellison, 2007).

They host social networks that are articulated online, and as such, they present one iteration or aspect of social network research. On most SNSs, users are not looking to meet new people or to network, but rather to sustain contact with their existing group of friends and acquaintances (boyd and Ellison, 2007). In doing so, presenting a profile and displaying connections with others publicly forms the basis for interaction on SNSs (boyd and Ellison, 2007; boyd and Heer, 2006; Donath, 2007; Donath and boyd, 2004). SNSs support varying types of interaction on diverse and differing platforms, and SNSs like Friendster, MySpace and Facebook have had a significant influence on the orientation of most other SNSs (for a timeline of SNSs, see boyd and Ellison, 2007).

Social network sites as social architectures

Research on SNSs generates interdisciplinary interest and evidence of evolving social behaviours online. Self presentation online and impression management presents a common starting point for most researchers. boyd and Heer (2006) studied user profiles on SNSs as conversational pieces, and found that Friendster users display friends to suggest or 'signal' aspects of their identity to potential audiences. In this context, 'public displays of connection' present the centre of identity performance, and are typically viewed as 'a signal of the reliability of one's identity claims' (Donath and boyd, 2004: 73).

Several researchers employ the architecture of the SNS as starting point, to discuss and investigate a variety of related topics. Stutzman (2006) tracked the types of personal information most likely to be disclosed on SNSs, pointing out that lexical or architectural differences among these SNSs (Friendster, MySpace and Facebook) contributed to tendencies or variations in personal information disclosure. Gross and Acquisti (2005) further examined how individuals disclose information and protect privacy on Facebook, finding that most users share personal information openly and few modify their default privacy settings for increased protection. For members of a YouTube community, 'publicly private' (private behaviours, exhibited with the member's true identity) and 'privately public' (sharing publicly accessible video without disclosing member's true identity) behaviours were developed within the architectural confines of the system to signal different depths of relationships and to communicate empathy, respect or inclusion among members of the network (Lange, 2007). On MySpace and Friendster, displays of interests were carefully selected and arranged so as to communicate affiliation with a particular taste culture or fabric (Liu *et al.*, 2006; Liu, 2007). These trends are reflective of behaviours that are need-oriented, and are developed around the customization of social attributes of technologies, effected for the communication of social information. They suggest a confluence of user motives, media attributes, and social ties or outcomes that have been previously examined in media research within the approaches of uses and gratifications, social networks, and through a discussion of media attributes or affordances of particular media genres or platforms.

In these networks that are particularly ego-centred, individuals at the centre of their own networks take charge and adapt network norms to fit personal, cultural and social context (boyd, 2006a). Moreover, SNS users frequently interpret cues deposited in member profiles, such as messages on Facebook 'walls' or pictures of member friends to make inferences about the member's character (Walther *et al.*, 2008). In a context that is markedly non-Western, such as Cyworld, architectural SNS features are adapted to match the cultural norms of the users and the high-context relational dialectics of Koreans (Kim and Yun, 2007). These empirical data further document reappropriations of technology that cater to the fulfilment of particular needs associated with the sustenance of social ties with a variety of circles or networks.

Finally, several studies develop around Facebook, the most popular of social networks at present. In particular, studies of Facebook find that users employ the network to learn more about individuals they meet offline, thus further documenting the connection between online and offline behaviours and tendencies (Lampe *et al.*, 2006). Further studies reveal a strong association between bridging social capital, which expands social opportunities and enhances information sharing among primarily weak ties, and individuals reporting low satisfaction and low self-esteem (Ellison *et al.*, 2007). These findings underline connections between user orientations and subsequent generation of social capital, which map out a credible intersection for U&G and the social networks approach.

Rationale

The proposed study is based on a theoretical framework that combines U&G with the social networks approach to study how motives and social-psychological traits affect Facebook use, social network structural factors (size of network, density, types of ties) and social capital generated. The study combines concepts identified and measured by U&G and social network researchers, with a particular focus on social and psychological predispositions, motives, social ties, and social capital. The following paragraphs detail the variables studied within this theoretical framework, and how together they form the conceptual structure for the integration of the two perspectives. The study focuses on the following research questions:

RQ1:   What are salient motives for Facebook use?
RQ2:   How do motives and social and psychological antecedents interact with social capital generated on Facebook?

Method

Sample

A total of 344 students enrolled in introductory communication classes within an urban university were surveyed about their use of Facebook. Participation in the study was voluntary, and participants received extra credit in the courses. The initial sample was then snowballed, through participants asking their Facebook friends to complete the survey. An online survey, administered through Zoomerang.com, was created in order to examine individuals' uses, motivations and effects of Facebook. The sample breakdown was 64.3 per cent female ($n = 221$) and 35.7 per cent male ($n = 123$); 85 per cent of sample were current undergraduates in college. Of those 36.8 per cent were freshmen; 25.1 per cent were sophomores; 26.4 were juniors; and 11.7 per cent were seniors. The majority of participants were between the age of 18 and 25 (88.4 per cent). As regards ethnic origin, 73.7 per cent of the sample was White, 14.5 per cent African American, 7.4 per cent Asian American, 3.6 per cent Hispanic, and 4.1 per cent of multiethnic origin.

Facebook use

Patterns of Facebook use

Participants were surveyed about their general Internet and Facebook use. Overall, participants spent an average of 74 minutes online (SD = 77.53) per week. More specifically, 83.7 per cent of the participants reported checking their Facebook page daily. In fact, participants reported checking their

Facebook pages an average almost 6 times per day ($M = 5.78$; $SD = 5.831$) and spending an average of almost 36 minutes per day on Facebook ($M = 35.83$; $SD = 127.427$). We wanted to get a sense of what participants did when they logged on to Facebook. A series of questions examined a number of activities (on a 1 to 5 scale; 1 = every time I log on; 5 = never). Participants most often sent messages ($M = 2.54$; $SD = 0.901$; median 2.00) and wrote on friends' walls ($M = 2.17$; $SD = 0.907$; median = 2.00). Less frequently participants posted new photographs ($M = 3.04$; $SD = 0.963$; median = 3.00), searched for additional friends ($M = 3.16$; $SD = 0.992$; median = 3.00), and tagged already posted photos ($M = 3.16$; $SD = 1.022$; median = 3.00). They seldom updated their own profile ($M = 3.60$; $SD = 0.885$; median = 4.00), played games ($M = 4.37$; $SD = 0.984$; median = 5.00), took quizzes ($M = 4.26$; $SD = 0.919$; median = 5.00), incorporated new add-ons ($M = 3.97$; $SD = 0.823$; median = 4.00) or used add-ons they already had ($M = 3.97$; $SD = 1.075$; median = 4.00).

Of all participants, 91.3 per cent reported having 51 or more friends; 60 per cent reported having 51 or more photos posted on their page. Also, 55.8 per cent reported having between one and five add-ons on their page, and another 30.7 per cent reported having between 6 and 15 add-ons. Finally, 20 per cent of the participants belonged to between one and five Facebook groups, another 37.9 per cent belonged to between six and 15 groups, and 25.6 per cent more belonged to between 16 and 30. Only 37.8 per cent of the participants reported starting a Facebook group.

Motives

We combined interpersonal (inclusion/companionship), media (entertainment, habit, information, social interaction, escape, pass time, and relaxation), newer media (coolness factor/novelty of technology, self-expression), and professional advancement motives to construct 11 a priori motive categories of possible Facebook motives: pass time, relaxation, entertainment, information sharing, professional advancement, companionship, social interaction, cool and new technology, self expression, habit, escape). Three items were used to represent each of these a priori categories, and we adapted the statements from previous research to Facebook (Papacharissi and Rubin, 2000; Pornsakulvanich *et al.*, 2008). Respondents were asked to indicate how much these reasons were like their own reasons for using Facebook on a 5-point Likert scale (5 = *exactly*, 1 = *not at all*). We used principal components analysis with Varimax rotation to extract and interpret possible Facebook motive factors. We required an eigenvalue of 1.0 or greater to retain a factor, which also had to contain at least three items meeting a 60/40 loading criteria. Responses to the retained items were summed and averaged to form the scales representing each factor. The analysis accounted for 69 per cent of the variance, and the results are summarized in response to RQ1 below.

Social and psychological antecedents

Contextual age

Contextual age is a construct that was developed to account for the inaccuracies resulting from only using chronological age in communication research and was developed as 'a transactional, life-position index of aging' (A. Rubin and Rubin, 1986). Depending on contextual age, people may also use mediated channels as functional alternatives (over interpersonal ones) for the fulfilment of interpersonal needs (A. Rubin and Rubin, 1982, 1986; R. Rubin and Rubin, 1982). A. Rubin and Rubin's (1982) Contextual Age Scale was used to assess life position, consisting of the following dimensions: physical health, interpersonal interaction, mobility, life satisfaction, social activity, and economic security. The physical health and economic security dimensions were not included due to low expectation of significant variation within the population under study. Each remaining dimension – life satisfaction, mobility, social activity, and interpersonal interaction – contained five items (A. Rubin and Rubin, 1982; R. Rubin and Rubin, 1982). Respondents stated their levels of agreement with these statements on a 5-point Likert-type scale (5 = *strongly agree*, 1 = *strongly disagree*). Responses to the items of each subscale were summed and averaged. The mean scores for the separate dimensions were: life satisfaction ($M = 3.32$, $SD = 0.75$, a = 0.68); mobility ($M = 3.68$, $SD = 0.87$, a = .62); social activity ($M = 3.67$, $SD = 0.70$, a = 0.67); and interpersonal interaction ($M = 3.75$, $SD = 0.66$, a = 0.45).

Unwillingness to communicate

Burgoon (1976) conceptualized unwillingness to communicate as 'a chronic tendency to avoid and/or devalue oral communication' (p. 60). The construct has been linked to anomie and alienation, introversion, lower self-esteem, communication apprehension, and reticence (Burgoon 1976). It has been applied to mass media research to help explain differences in media and new technology use and has been linked to a preference for online or mediated channels of communication for individuals who did not find face-to-face channels as convenient, readily available, or comfortable. It has two dimensions: (a) approach avoidance (UCAA), which indicates anxiety, introversion, and diminished participation in general communication, and (b) reward (UCR), which includes distrust, perceived isolation, and an evaluation of the overall utility of communication. We adapted Burgoon's (1976) 20-item scale to 10 items for use in this study. The scale was coded so that high scores for UCAA imply a tendency to welcome and seek out interpersonal encounters, and high scores for UCR reflect an individual who feels valued by their environment and perceives interpersonal communication to be rewarding. We used a 5-point Likert-type scale (5 = *strongly agree*, 1 = *strongly disagree*) to be consistent with the rest of the measures in the study, and summed and averages responses to the items. The mean for the UCAA dimension was (M = 3.69; SD = 0.65, a = 0.79) and for the UCR (M = 4.07; SD = 0.52, a = 0.70).

Communication outcomes

Social capital

Social network ties are frequently assessed by making use of the concept of social capital. Previous literature on social capital conceptualizes three different forms of social capital. Bonding social capital focuses on resources people have for strengthening the connection between people in their closely-connected groups. Bridging social capital focuses on reaching outside traditional in-groups to link with those unlike you. And maintained social capital focuses on staying connected to groups from previous moments in one's life (Ellison *et al.*, 2007). Fifteen items (five for each type of social capital), modified from Williams (2006) and Ellison *et al.*, (2007) were included (maintained (M = 3.94; SD = 0.62; a = 0.75), bridging (M = 3.43; SD = 0.63; a = 0.72), and bonding (M = 3.38; SD = 0.67; a = 0.72)).

Affinity with media has been linked to many motives, such as arousal, habit, pass time, escape, entertainment, companionship, and information seeking, in the television and online context (e.g., A. Rubin, 1981; Papacharissi and Rubin, 2000). The Television Affinity Scale (A. Rubin, 1981) was adapted to assess liking for or *affinity* with Facebook. This was a 5-item Likert scale (5 = *strongly agree*, 1 = *strongly disagree*), reflecting how attached people are to the platform, how much they might miss it if gone, or how much they depend on it for their daily routines. Responses to the items were summed and averaged. The mean for the scale was 2.50 (SD = 0.33, a = 0.88).

Open ended questions

Participants were given the opportunity to expand upon their views of Facebook through three open ended questions. These responses were analysed qualitatively, pulling out the major themes that arose. We asked: 'In your own words, what is it about Facebook that makes it appealing? What do you like the most about Facebook? What do you like the least about Facebook?' Responses are employed in the discussion section, to illuminate and substantiate quantitative findings.

Results

RQ1: Motives for Facebook use

The factor analysis of the motive statements yielded nine interpretable factors: expressive information sharing, habitual pass time, relaxing entertainment, cool and new trend, companionship, professional advancement, escape, social interaction, and new friendships. The first factor, *expressive information sharing* (a = 0.85), accounted for 11.39 per cent of the variance after rotation. It combined five items from the *information sharing* and *self expression* a priori categories, pointing to a need to share both general and personal information with others, and alluding to a lack of distinction between the two that is characteristic on Facebook. The second factor, *habitual pass time* (a = .85), consisted of five items from the a priori categories *habit* and *pass time*, and explained 10.54 per cent of the variance. The items all pointed to pass time uses of Facebook of a ritualistic nature, possibly attesting to the addictive nature of the genre. The third factor, *relaxing entertainment* (a = 0.82), combined five items from the *relax* and *entertainment* motive categories, and accounted for 9.4 per cent of the variance. The factor indicated a passive and entertainment-oriented mode of engaging with Facebook. The fourth factor, *cool and new trend* (a = 0.80), accounted for 7.03 per cent of the variance contained all three items of the same a priori motive category, representing a clean loading of this factor. This motive category suggested that individuals were on Facebook because it is 'the thing to do', 'it is cool', and because 'everybody else is doing it', thus pointing to the social desirability cost of staying off Facebook. The fifth factor, *companionship* (a = 0.83), retained all three items from its respective a priori category, and explained 6.76 per cent of the variance, pointing to the ability of the medium to simulate companionship in the absence of other channels. The sixth factor, *professional advancement* (a = 0.80), also did not deviate from its a priori conceptualization, and accounted for 6.74 per cent of the variance. The seventh factor, *escape* (a = 0.75), also emerged in its a priori formation post rotation, and accounted for 6.56 per cent of the variance. This factor suggested procrastinatory uses of Facebook, to avoid tasks or individuals. The eighth factor, *social interaction* (a = 0.83), explained 6.16 per cent of the variance, but only contained two items from its a priori category, and thus was not employed in subsequent analysis. The ninth and final factor was a single item factor ('Meet new people'), explaining 4.3 per cent of the variance. While the item attested to the importance of Facebook in making new connections, unfortunately the make-up of the factor did not meet the criteria for inclusion in statistical analysis. Future studies may try to expand and perfect these last two factors, as they appear to allude to important social needs fulfilled by Facebook.

Habitual pass time (M = 3.82, SD = 0.75) and *relaxing entertainment* (M = 3.02, SD = 0.68) had the highest mean scores, rendering them the motives more likely to be salient to most. *Expressive information sharing* (M = 2.75, SD = 0.80), *escapism* (M = 2.54, SD = 0.87), and *cool and new trend* (M = 2.50, SD = 0.92) were also fairly salient factors, along with *companionship* (M = 2.35, SD = 0.95), to a lesser extent. *Professional advancement* (M =1.92, SD = 0.84) was the least salient, indicating that it was more likely to be significant for a specific and smaller part of the study population. Most motives correlated moderately, with the highest correlations noted between companionship and escapism (r = 0.45), companionship and relaxing entertainment (r = 0.40), escapism and habitual pass time (r = 0.43), and escapism and relaxing entertainment (r = 0.44), p < 0.001. These tendencies sketched out rather ritualistic and socially-oriented uses of the Facebook genre.

RQ2: Motives, antecedents and social capital

The most significant and highest correlations were noted among inter-personal interaction and the approach-avoidance (UCAA) (r = .43, p < 0.001) and the reward (UCR) (r = 0.53, p < 0.001) dimensions of the unwillingness to communicate scale. UCAA also correlated highly with life satisfaction (r = 0.49, p < 0.001) and social activity (r = 0.40, p < 0.001), as did UCR with life satisfaction (r = 0.46, p < 0.001) and social activity (r = 0.45, p < 0.001). Maintained, bonding and bridging social capital correlated positively and significantly with all motives, with the highest and most significant relations noted between bridging social capital and expressive information sharing (r = 0.43, p < 0.001), as well as relaxing entertainment (r = 0.38, p < 0.001).

Four separate hierarchical multiple regression analyses were conducted to further investigate the nature and direction of these relationships. Facebook affinity, bonding, bridging and maintained social capital each served as the dependent variable for the four regressions. Variables associated with the amount of time spent online, number of times individuals check Facebook daily, estimated time spent on Facebook per week, and number of years of experience with the Internet were entered on the first step of the regression analysis. Contextual age dimensions (mobility, interpersonal interaction, life satisfaction and social activity), UC-Approach Avoidance and UC-Reward were entered on the second step, as antecedent variables. The Motives for Facebook Use scales were entered on the third step of the analysis. For *affinity*, two predictors emerged at the final step of the analysis: total time spent on Facebook per week (F = 4.90, p = 0.03) and the motive of escapism (F = 4.13, p = 0 0.5), in an overall significant equation (R = 0.73, R2 = 0.54, F [7, 29] = 2.02, p = 0.01). This indicated that the more people used Facebook, the greater the affinity they developed for it, especially for uses associated with escapist needs.

The same hierarchical regression procedure was repeated for the three types of social capital. The equation for bonding social capital yielded two significant predictors, both of which increased in significance in the final step of the analysis: total time spent online per day off work (F = 5.76, p = 0.02), and the contextual age dimension of social activity (F = 11.13, p = 0.002), in an overall significant equation (R = 0.81, R2 = 0.66, F [7, 28] = 3.22, p = 0.003). These results indicated stronger social ties were best served by more time spent online, for those individuals who enjoyed a greater amount of social activity. These findings support the idea that time spent online allows those individuals to maintain or increase their level of social connectivity.

The regression equation calculated for bridging social capital produced an overall significant equation (R = 0.86, R2 = 0.74, F [7, 28] = 4.72, p = 0.000), with four significant predictors, all of which emerged on the final step: Mobility (F = 5.68, p = 0.02), and the motives of relaxing entertainment (F = 5.63, p = 0.02), cool and new trend (F = 5.64, p = 0.02), and professional advancement (F = 6.12, p = 0.02). The results of the equation indicated that those with increased mobility, using Facebook for entertainment, relaxation, because it is a new trend, and for professional advancement tended to increase and sustain weaker ties with distanced friends or individuals in extended or non-traditional in-groups of contact. The findings support the idea that mobile individuals tend to use Facebook to support and extend their mobility to spheres of contact that may not be readily available or accessible.

Finally, the regression equation for maintained social capital was overall not significant and failed to produce significant predictors. It is possible this is related to the variables examined or the demographic characteristics of the population surveyed.

Discussion

This study focused on the social utility of Facebook, by employing a theoretical model that combined the uses and gratifications perspective with social networks theory, especially centred on the concept of social capital. The conceptual framework proposed that antecedent variables, together with user motives, morph the Facebook experience and influence the type of social capital generated by Facebook use. In order to provide supporting evidence for this model, relationships among the included concepts were examined.

Prevalent motives that emerged from the analysis included the motives of habitual pass time and relaxing entertainment, both of which combined motive categories for traditional media. Not only did this reflect the converged nature of the services provided by Facebook, but it also suggested salient uses for most users tended to be of a ritualistic and relatively passive nature. The more instrumental uses of expressive information sharing and professional advancement were not as salient with this sample. At the same time, escapism and companionship, two traditional media use motives usually associated with television use, were moderately salient for this population, thus confirming the ability of Facebook to converge traditional and new media needs. In the open ended responses, participants referred to the ability of Facebook to help relieve boredom or distract them from or relieve them of daily stresses. As one respondent said: '[Facebook] is entertaining enough to spend time on to get away from homework.' Another said, 'It is fun, and not stressful like schoolwork can be.' This can verge on addiction, according to one user: 'Its easy to get sucked into', while another respondent added, 'I think the reason Facebook is so appealing is because it offers a wide variety of ways to distract people from the stress.'

The regression analyses documented some substantial links between social capital, Facebook motives, and social and psychological predisposition. Overall, these tended to support an image of a user who employs this particular technology genre to amplify opportunities at his or her disposal. Unlike earlier studies of the Net in general, which pointed to the paradox of a social technology that isolates individuals in private sphere of communication, and in contrast to the popular stereotype of the anti-social computer geek, these results indicate those mobile and leading a socially active life are able to reap the social benefits of Facebook, and employ it to increase bonding and bridging social capital. Thus, this online social network sustains the social connectivity of members that are already fairly active and mobile. Interestingly enough, these users rarely have the generation of social capital in mind, as they tend to approach Facebook from the not-so-goal-directed, relatively passive, and ritualistic motives for relaxing entertainment and habitual pastime. For these users, this becomes a daily routine that conveniently maintains and extends individuals' spheres of contact. Through the open ended responses, participants revealed some apprehension of the addictive nature of Facebook, typically presented as a third-person effect, affecting others but not them directly. For example, one person said, 'The obsessive way some people are about checking Facebook, updating their page, etc. It's annoying.'

Additional responses to open ended questions further solidified our interpretations.

Participants repeatedly stressed the communicative aspects of Facebook, specifying that they relied on Facebook for staying connected to those they already know and for meeting new people. Participants valued Facebook for helping them keep up with people at a distance, inform others about themselves and find people with similar interests. For example, one respondent stated: [Facebook is appealing because of] 'the ability to be a part of someone's everyday life no matter how far away they are'. Another respondent stated: 'I can connect to my friends across the country and world easily and see what they're up to which used to be somewhat of a hassle. I can stay more easily connected to friends from high school as well.' One person summarized Facebook's ability to meet people in terms of building on those they already know. 'The ability to meet someone randomly and make that person a part of the people you know in your life time.' Participants enjoyed being able to keep up with their friends' achievements, news, relationship status and life developments. Several indicated that not being part of Facebook would equal being left out of these developments and sphere of contact, thus alluding to the social cost of not joining.

Qualitative and quantitative responses on dominant uses of Facebook pointed to a user state that palindromes between the socially active and idle, or more colloquially put, describes a social couch potato. Users happily connect with others socially, as long as they may do so from the comfort an electronically mediated couch, in a state that permits the stationary pursuit of social activity. This antithesis reflects the realities of our contemporary everyday routines, which blur spheres of work and play, friends and co-workers, public and private life. Future research could place social networks in the greater context of public life, and specifically examine how they support and reinforce dominant work–life patterns and routines. Beyond the point of fulfilling short-term needs for relaxation, entertainment and social contact simultaneously, these networks are telling of contemporary trends that include globalization, trasnational mobility and work, social spheres that are local, global and glocal, and in general, with what Zygmunt Bauman (2005) refers to as a more liquid pace of life. Challenging our conventional understanding of sociability as an activity-driven imperative, these results suggest a contemporary interpretation of sociability that includes static social behaviours enabled through online technology. In a relaxed state that converges passivity and sociality, social network site users traverse spheres of social interaction to learn about and interact with others they connect to.

Moreover, equipped with a toy that enables social connections, individuals are able to fulfil traditional mediated and interpersonal needs simultaneously, while at the same time expanding their social connections and so-called social net worth in satellite social spheres. Relaxing entertainment also provided a way in which Facebook became useful for the generation of bonding social capital, thus reaffirming users' ties and connections to their close sphere of family and friends.

In conclusion, for communication researchers, these findings both affirm and challenge our understanding of audience activity and passivity. The relevance of traditional mediated and interpersonal motives for Facebook users confirms the permanence of these needs and their fulfilment via mediated communication. At the same time, these needs emerge in a converged state, capturing intermittently active and idle states of engagement that challenge the binary manner in which we, as communication scholars, understand active and passive uses. Future research on online media could move away from linear understandings of user motivations and social outcomes, to networked theoretical conceptualizations that permit us to follow the organic generation of developing forms of sociability. The social networks approach incorporates the organic appropriation of social ties, social capital generation, and the frequently non-linear rationale of social behaviour. The uses and gratifications approach, on the other hand, adopts a more conventional linearity in its approach, but, at the same time, is particularly useful for a systematic understanding of the connections between user profiles, motivations, orientations, practices and resulting outcomes.

A combined perspective examining the uses, networks and affordances of convergent media would connect antecedent variables and motives to particular uses of networks, which are sensitive to the affordances of online media. Such an approach would be guided by the following assumptions, *remediated* from Rubin (1994) that:

1   'socially motivated behaviours, including media selection and use, are both purposive and ritualistic';
2   'a host of social and psychological factors mediate people's communication behavior';
3   'people adopt or adapt the affordances of convergent media to satisfy felt needs and to form and maintain social networks';
4   'media compete and converge with other forms of communication for selection, attention, and use to gratify our individual and collective needs';
5   'mediated behaviors possess social outcomes, which result in varying qualities and quantities of social capital generated.'

This is a socio-psychological communication perspective that examines how individuals use converged media, to fulfil felt needs or wants that are personal and collective, and generate social outcomes that permit a networked sociality.

References

Alexander, A. (1985) 'Adolescents' soap opera viewing and relational perceptions', *Journal of Broadcasting and Electronic Media*, 29: 295–308.

Bauman, Z. (2005) *Liquid Life*, Cambridge: Polity Press.

Becker, L., Dunwoody, S. and Rafaell, S. (1983) 'Cable's impact on use of other news media', *Journal of Broadcasting*, 27: 127–142.

boyd, d. and Ellison, N.B. (2007) 'Social network sites: Definition, history, and scholarship', *Journal of Computer-Mediated Communication*, 13(1): article 11. Available: <http://jcmc.indiana.edu/vol13/issue1/boyd.ellison.html>.

boyd, d. and Heer, J. (2006) 'Profiles as conversation: Networked identity performance on Friendster', Proceedings of 39th Hawaii International Conference on System Sciences. Los Alamitos, CA: IEEE Press.

Burgoon, J.K. (1976) 'The Unwillingness to Communicate Scale: Development and Validation', *Communication Monographs*, 43: 60–69.

Chang, B., Lee, S. and Kim, B. (2006) 'Exploring factors affecting the adoption and continuance of online games among college students in South Korea: Integrating uses and gratification and diffusion of innovation approaches', *New Media and Society*, 8 (2): 295–319.

De Waal, E., Schoenbach, K. and Lauf, E. (2006) 'Online newspapers: A substitute or complement for print newspapers and other information channels?', *Communications: The European Journal of Communication Research*, 30(1): 55.

Dimmick, J., Chen, Y. and Li, Z. (2004) 'Competition between the Internet and traditional news media: The gratification-opportunities niche dimension', *Journal of Media Economics*, 17(1): 19–33.

Donath, J. and boyd, d. (2004) 'Public displays of connection', *BT Technology Journal*, 22 (4): 71.

Ellison, N.B., Lampe, C., Steinfield, C. and Vitak, J. (in press) 'With a Little Help from My Friends: How Social Network Sites Affect Social Capital Processes', in Papacharissi, Z. (ed.) *The Networked Self: Identity, Community and Culture on Social Network Sites*, New York: Routledge.

Ellison, N.B., Steinfield, C. and Lampe, C. (2007) 'The benefits of Facebook "friends": Social capital and college students' use of online social network sites', *Journal of Computer-Mediated Communication*, 12(4), article 1. Available: <http://jcmc.indiana.edu/vol12/issue4/ ellison.html>.

Ferguson, D.A. (1992) 'Channel repertoire in the presence of remote control devices, VCRs and cable television', *Journal of Broadcasting and Electronic Media*, 36: 83–91.

Garton, L., Haythornthwaite, C. and Wellman, B. (1997) 'Studying online social networks', *Journal of Computer-Mediated Communication*, 3 (1). Available: <jcmc. indiana.edu/vol3/issue1/garton.html>.

Gross, R. and Acquisti. A. (2005) 'Information Revelation and Privacy in Online Social Networks'. Paper presented at the ACM Workshop on Privacy in the Electronic Society, Alexandria, VA.

Hampton, K. (2002) 'Place-based and IT mediated "community"', *Planning Theory and Practice*, 3 (2): 228–231.

Hampton, K. and Wellman, B. (2003) 'Neighboring in Netville: How the Internet supports community and social capital in a wired suburb', *City and Community*, 2 (4): 277–311.

Hardy, B. and Scheufele, D. (2005) 'Examining differential gains from Internet use: Comparing the moderating role of talk and online interactions', *Journal of Communication*, 55(1): 71–84.

Hargittai, E. and Hsieh, Y.L. (in press) 'From Dabblers to Omnivores: A Typology of Social Network Site Usage', in Papacharissi, Z. (ed.) *The Networked Self: Identity, Community and Culture on Social Network Sites*, New York: Routledge.

Hargittai, E. (2007) 'Whose space? Differences among users and non-users of social network sites', *Journal of Computer-Mediated Communication*, 13(1): article 14. Available: <http://jcmc.indiana.edu/vol13/issue1/hargittai.html>.

Haythornthwaite, C. (2000) 'Online personal networks: Size, composition and media use among distance learners', *New Media and Society*, 2(2): 195–226.

Haythornthwaite, C. (2005) 'Social networks and internet connectivity effects', *Information Communication and Society*, 8(2): 125–147.

Haythornthwaite, C. and Wellman, B. (1998) 'Work, friendship and media use for information exchange in a networked organization', *Journal of the American Society for Information Science*, 49 (12): 1101–1114.

Haythornthwaite, C., Wellman, B. and Mantei, M. (1995) 'Work relationships and media use: A social network analysis', *Group Decision and Negotiation*, 4 (3): 193–211.

Hlebec, V., Manfreda, K.L. and Vehovar, V. (2006) 'The social support networks of internet users', *New Media and Society*, 8(1): 9–32.

Kaye, B. and Johnson, T. (2002) 'Online and in the know: Uses and gratifications of the Web for political information', *Journal of Broadcasting and Electronic Media*, 46(1): 54–71.

Kim, K.-H. and Yun, H. (2007) 'Crying for me, Crying for us: Relational dialectics in a Korean social network site', *Journal of Computer-Mediated Communication*, 13 (1), article 15. Available: <http://jcmc.indiana.edu/vol13/issue1/kim.yun.html>.

Kraut, R., Patterson, M., Lundmark, V., Kiesler, S., Mukophadhyay, T. and Scherlis, W. (1998) 'Internet paradox: A social technology that reduces social involvement and psychological well-being?', *American Psychologist*, 53: 1017–1031.

Kraut, R., Kiesler, S., Boneva, K., Cummings, J., Helgeson, J. and Crawford, A. (2002) 'Internet paradox revisited', *Journal of Social Issues*, 58(1): 49–74.

Lampe, C., Ellison, N.B, Steinfield, C., (2006) 'A Face(book) in the crowd: Social searching vs. social browsing', in *Proceedings of the 2006 20th Anniversary Conference in Computer Supported Cooperative Work*, New York: ACM Press.

Lange, P.G. (2007) 'Publicly private and privately public: Social networking on YouTube', *Journal of Computer-Mediated Communication*, 13(1), article 18. Available: <http://jcmc.indiana.edu/vol13/issue1/lange.html>.

Levy, M.R. (1987) 'VCR use and the concept of audience activity', *Communication Quarterly*, 35: 267–275.

Liu, H. (2007) 'Social network profiles as taste performances', *Journal of Computer-Mediated Communication*, 13(1): article 13. Available: <http://jcmc.indiana.edu/vol13/issue1/liu.html>.

Liu, H., Maes, P. and Davenport, G. (2006) 'Unraveling the taste fabric of social networks', *International Journal on Semantic Web and Information Systems*, 2 (1): 42–71.

Lo, V., Li, Y., Shih, Y. and Yang, S. (2005) 'Internet adoption, uses, and gratifications obtained', *Mass Communication Research*, 83(1): 127–165.

Lometti, G.E., Reeves, B. and Bybee, C.R. (1977) 'Investigating the assumptions of uses and gratifications research', *Communication Research*, 7: 319–334.

McQuail, D. (1979) 'The uses and gratification approach: Past, troubles, and future', *Massacommunicatie*, 2: 73–89.

Mendelson, A. and Papacharissi, Z. (in press) 'Look at us: Collective Narcissism in College Student Facebook Photo Galleries', in Papacharissi, Z. (ed.) *The Networked Self: Identity, Community and Culture on Social Network Sites*, New York: Routledge.

Palmgreen, P.C., Wenner, L.A. and Rayburn, J.D. (1980) 'Relations between gratifications sought and obtained: A study of television news', *Communication Research*, 7: 161–192.

Papacharissi, Z. (2009) 'The Virtual Geographies of Social Networks: A Comparative Analysis of Facebook, LinkedIn and ASmallWorld', *New Media and Society*, 11 (1–2): 199–220.

Papacharissi, Z. (2007) 'The Blogger Revolution? Audiences as Media Producers' in Tremayne, M. (ed.) *Blogging, Citizenship, and the Future of Media*, New York: Routledge.

Papacharissi, Z. and Mendelson, A. (2007) 'The Reality Appeal: Uses and gratifications of reality shows', *Journal of Broadcasting and Electronic Media*, 51(2): 355–371.

Papacharissi, Z. (2002a) 'The self online: The utility of personal home pages', *Journal of Broadcasting and Electronic Media*, 46(3): 346–368.

Papacharissi, Z. (2002b) 'The presentation of self in virtual life: Characteristics of personal home pages', *Journalism and Mass Communication Quarterly*, 79(3): 643–660.

Papacharissi, Z. and Rubin, A. (2000) 'Predictors of Internet use', *Journal of Broadcasting and Electronic Media*, 44(2): 175–196.

Payne, G., Severn, J. and Dozier, D. (1988) 'Uses and gratifications motives as indicators of magazine readership', *Journalism Quarterly*, 65: 909–915.

Pettersson, T. (1986) 'The audiences' uses and gratifications of TV worship services', *Journal for the Scientific Study of Religion*, 25: 391–409.

Perse, E. (1986) 'Soap opera viewing patterns of college students and cultivation', *Journal of Broadcasting and Electronic Media*, 30: 175–193.

Perse, E. and Ferguson, D. (2000) 'The benefits and costs of Web surfing', *Communication Quarterly*, 48(4): 343–359.

Pornsakulvanich, V., Haridakis, P. and Rubin, A.M. (2008) 'The influence of dispositions and Internet motivation on online communication satisfaction and relationship closeness', *Computers in Human Behavior*, 24: 2292–2310.

Rubin, A.M. (1981) 'A multivariate analysis of "60 Minutes" viewing motivations', *Journalism Quarterly*, 58, 529–534.

Rubin, A.M. (1985) 'Uses of daytime television soap opera by college students', *Journal of Broadcasting and Electronic Media*, 29: 241–258.

Rubin, A.M. (1994) 'Media uses and effects: A uses-and-gratifications perspective', in Zillmann, J. and Bryant, D. (eds) *Media Effects: Advances in Theory and Research*, London: Lawrence Erlbaum Associates.

Rubin, A. and Bantz, C. (1989) 'Uses and gratifications of videocassette recorders', in Salvaggio, J. and Bryant, J. (eds) *Media Use in the Information Age: Emerging Patterns of Adoption and Consumer Use*, Hillsdale, NJ: Lawrence Erlbaum Associates.

Rubin, A.M. and Rubin, R.B. (1982) 'Contextual age and television use', *Human Communication Research*, 8: 228–244.

Rubin, A.M. and Rubin, R.B. (1986) 'Contextual age as a life-position index', *International Journal of Aging and Human Development*, 23: 27–45.

Rubin, R.B. and Rubin, A.M. (1982) 'Contextual age and television use: Re-examining a life-position indicator', *Communication Yearbook*, 6: 583–604.

Salwen, M.B. and Anderson, R.A. (1984) *The Uses and Gratifications of Supermarket Tabloid Reading by Different Demographic Groups*, East Lansing, MI: National Center for Research on Teacher Learning.

Stutzman, F. (2006) 'An evaluation of identity-sharing behavior in social network communities', paper presented at the iDMAa and IMS Code Conference, Oxford, Ohio.

Swanson, D.L. (1977) 'The uses and misuses of uses and gratification', *Human Communication Research*, 3: 214–221.

Turow, J. (1974) 'Talk-show radio as interpersonal communication', *Journal of Broadcasting*, 18: 171–179.

Walther, J.B., Carr, C., Choi, S.S.W., DeAndrea, D., Kim, J., Tong, S.T. and Van Der Heide, B. (in press) 'Interaction of Interpersonal, Peer, and Media Influence Sources Online: A Research Agenda for Technology Convergence', in Papacharissi, Z. (ed.), *The Networked Self: Identity, Community and Culture on Social Network Sites*, New York: Routledge.

Walther, J.B., Van Der Heide, B., Kim, S.Y., Westerman, D. and Tong, S.T. (2008) 'The role of friends' appearance and behavior on evaluations of individuals on Facebook: Are we known by the company we keep?', *Human Communication Research*, 34(1): 28–49.

Wasserman, S. and Faust, K. (1994) *Social Network Analysis*, Cambridge, MA: Cambridge University Press.

Wellman, B. and Berkowitz, S.D. (eds) (1997) *Social Structures: A Network Approach*, 2nd edn, Greenwich, CT: JAI Press.

Wellman, B., Haase, A.Q., Witte, J. and Hampton, K. (2001) 'Does the Internet increase, decrease, or supplement social capital? Social networks, participation, and community commitment', *American Behavioral Scientist*, 45 (3): 436.

Williams, D. (2006) 'On and Off the Net: Scales for Social Capital in an Online Era', *Journal of Computer-Mediated Communication*, 11: 593–628.

13 Minding the digital gap: why understanding digital inequality matters

Eszter Hargittai

A large body of literature exists looking at differential rates of Internet diffusion both across and within countries (e.g., see Billon *et al.*, 2009 for a review of the international comparative literature; and DiMaggio *et al.*, 2004 for a review of mainly US-based studies). An important shift in this work over the past decade has been the recognition that inequalities related to digital media[1] use will exist beyond mere issues of connectivity (e.g., Barzilai-Nahon, 2006; DiMaggio *et al.*, 2004; Hargittai, 2002; Mossberger *et al.*, 2003; van Dijk, 2005). That is, even after people gain access to the Internet and cross the so-called digital divide, differences will remain in how they use the medium, namely, how skilled they are at it, how free they are to use it in different situations and toward what purposes they put it. Ultimately, the question for scholars of social stratification is whether the increasing diffusion of this new resource will exacerbate or lessen inequities across the population (Hargittai, 2008). But a concern about this matter should not be restricted to those specifically interested in matters of social inequality, given that differentiated adoption of various information and communication technologies has consequences for numerous areas of media studies.

Many of the questions being asked about whether or how digital media are changing our world and our lives assume universal outcomes across population segments. That is, regardless of the attributes of the actors under consideration (whether individuals, organizations, industries, etc.), many inquiries tend to assume that there is one overarching answer that applies to all cases. Questions such as 'What are the Internet's political effects?', 'Are digital media democratizing the public sphere?', 'How are new media changing cultural consumption?', 'What is the relationship between playing video games and one's health?', 'How do virtual worlds influence identity expression and development?', 'Are notions and expectations of privacy changing?' often disregard that the answers may not apply uniformly across different strata of the population. Such an overarching approach has little basis in empirical evidence yet continues to inform much scholarship and public debate. It is reflected both in questions being asked and methodologies employed to study them. By framing our approach to the study of digital media in such a way

– whether intentionally or not – work becomes deterministic, because it suggests that new media result in certain generalizable outcomes regardless of the particular contexts in which their uses are examined.

Take for example one of the questions from above: 'Are digital media democratizing the public sphere?' It would be wrong to assume that there is a response to this question that is universally applicable to everybody yet the way it is phrased suggests such expectations. It may be that for some segments of the population (i.e., those in more privileged positions), new opportunities offered by information and communication technologies (or ICTs) are having a democratizing effect by allowing easier access to participation in public debates. However, it may be that for some segments of the population, new media have made little difference. If the overall conclusion we then draw is that 'yes, digital media are democratizing the public sphere', based on the fact that we find positive associations for *particular* population segments (i.e., the already privileged) then we are ignoring the situation of those who are seeing no such outcomes and walking away with a mistaken conclusion. Indeed, by offering different opportunities to different groups, ICTs may be *increasing* inequalities on the whole.

In order to produce findings that represent a diverse set of users, investigations must take a more careful approach to the study of ICTs than is currently often the case. Of course, plenty of scholarship over the decades has suggested the importance of taking nuanced approaches to the study of media's social, political, economic and cultural implications both in the realm of traditional media (e.g., Cook *et al.*, 1975; Liebes and Katz, 1993; Morley, 1980; Vidmar and Rokeach, 1974) and ICTs (see many of the citations later in this chapter). It is important to recognize that some work does take more refined approaches and learn from such projects. Nonetheless, many ongoing questions and debates about digital media ignore such refined approaches and thus an explicit consideration of this matter seems warranted. Although the particular focus here is on questions of social inequality as related to digital media uses, the overall argument advocates recognizing and staying conscious of differentiated ICT uses in all areas of inquiry about digital media usage if we are to avoid overly simplistic approaches to the study of their social, political, economic and cultural implications.

Since the mid-1990s, there has been widespread recognition of the fact that ICTs are not spreading equally across the population, whether in an international or national context. Some work has considered this inequality at the global level (e.g., Hargittai, 1999; Norris, 2001; Ono and Zavodny, 2007; Wilson, 2004), while much other research has focused on inequities within national borders (e.g., Bimber, 2000; Bucy, 2000; Compaine, 2001; National Telecommunications and Information Administration, 1995). Initial investigations – most widely known under the term 'digital divide' – simply asked who had access to the Internet and who did not, or who was using it at all versus who was not. Subsequent work introduced more refined approaches by considering differentiated uses (e.g., Barzilai-Nahon, 2006; Bonfadelli, 2002; DiMaggio *et al.*, 2004; Howard *et al.*, 2001; Jackson *et al.*, 2008; Livingstone and Helsper, 2007; Norris, 2001; van Dijk 2005; Wilson, 2000) also expanding investigations to other technologies such as mobile and gaming devices (e.g., Lenhart *et al.*, 2008; Rice and Katz, 2003). While variation in basic usage rates continues to exist and consequently remains an important area of inquiry (Jones and Fox, 2009; Zhang *et al.*, 2008), the goal here is to focus on refined studies of digital inequality, that is, differences that remain among users even after we control for basic access and usage.

The term 'digital inequality' is an alternative to the more widely-used 'digital divide' and serves to highlight that inequality cannot simply be seen as a dichotomous notion when it comes to ICT usage (DiMaggio *et al.*, 2004). Rather, it is essential to acknowledge and incorporate into our studies the diverse aspects of inequality – especially differentiated contexts of usage and variation in skills – related to digital media uses if we are to have a realistic understanding of the many diverse ways in which people are incorporating new media into their lives across population groups. Beyond arguing that these are important considerations for scholars primarily focused on the study of social stratification, the goal here is to emphasize that the reality of digital inequality – at this point documented by sufficient empirical evidence to be accepted as reality (e.g., DiMaggio and Bonikowski, 2008; Hargittai and Hinnant, 2008; Livingstone and Helsper, 2007; Zillien and Hargittai, 2009) – should be of concern to and be considered by investigators focusing on other areas of inquiry as well. Research in numerous domains needs to be conscious of – and when possible should avoid – assumptions about the universality of processes being examined. And while it is not possible to include these considerations front-and-centre in every project, they need to be at least part of the discussions enumerating the more general implications of findings.

What are the nuanced approaches to understanding ICT usage beyond access? They concern both the technical and the social contexts in which people engage with digital media. Related to these is an additional important factor: people's level of skill with ICTs. These then all in turn influence how people incorporate digital media into their lives (i.e., their types of uses), which can range from the mundane to the serious with different potential implications for beneficial (or in some cases problematic) outcomes in people's lives.

The mix of one's technical resources and social circumstances regarding ICT usage results in a context that will be more or less optimal for various types of digital media usage and will influence the extent to which a user is likely to engage with digital media in the most advantageous ways. Not surprisingly, better technical resources are likely to be more supportive of diverse uses than outdated equipment and slow connections. Access to more advanced hardware is likely to benefit the user when trying to access websites using state-of-the-art technology. Additionally, easy access to equipment (e.g., computers one does not have to share with many other household members) as well as lack of monitoring (whether technical or social) is likely to lead to more freedom in using the Internet, resulting in more exploration, more advanced skills and more diverse uses (e.g., Hargittai and Hinnant, 2008; Hassani, 2006; Lim, 2009; Zillien and Hargittai, 2009).

Although less research has focused on the social context of people's Internet uses, there is some evidence that people rely on their networks to navigate the Web (Frohlich and Kraut, 2003; Kiesler *et al.*, 2000). Not surprisingly, it helps to have people nearby who know how to troubleshoot issues that come up during one's online activities. Moreover, beyond situations involving specific problems, a user can also benefit from know-how passed along informally in everyday life from those in one's networks. In sum, both technical and social aspects of a user's environment influence whether the particular usage context will enable or constrain one's ICT uses.

An important aspect of people's digital media uses that has been shown to be unequally distributed across the population concerns people's skills in using information and communication technologies (Hargittai, 2010; Hargittai, 2002; Hargittai and Hinnant, 2008; van Deursen and van Dijk, 2009). While many online actions may seem trivial to the experienced user, most online activities require some level of know-how, which is why skill is an essential factor to understanding how people incorporate ICTs into their lives. Consider the need to access support networks when one runs into a situation requiring assistance. Even if one lacks knowledgeable people in one's surroundings, one may be able to draw on helpful advice from online sources. However, recognizing that such support is available on the Web and being able to find it and tap into it effectively requires a certain level of skill that is not uniformly distributed among people.

In a different vein, a certain level of know-how is important in order to sidestep potential negative consequences of Internet use. While in some circles it may be baffling that anyone would fall for scams such as those coming in through emails promising instant access to millions of dollars from far-away lands, indeed there are people out there who respond to such messages and suffer the consequences (Hinde, 2002). While fraud of this type is certainly not restricted to the Internet age, the low cost of email and ease of access to mailing lists has made their proliferation quicker. Such phenomena can have problematic consequences for those not savvy enough to hunt down information that would make them rethink their responses to such solicitations. Consequently, while online skills can improve the ways in which people take advantage of their Internet uses, they can also help prevent people from engaging in potentially risky online behaviour.

Many users also lack skills that limit the extent to which they can benefit from their usage optimally. From knowing how best to handle large volumes of email or send a message to someone maximizing chances for a response (Bunz, 2004; van Dijk, 2005), to appreciating what material is available online and being able to find it efficiently (e.g., Eastin and LaRose, 2000; Hargittai, 2002; van Deursen and van Dijk, 2009); from knowing how to contribute to online content production (Hargittai and Walejko, 2008; Jenkins *et al.*, 2006), to knowing where and how to find relevant contacts; from having the ability to evaluate content credibility (e.g., Metzger, 2007) to being vigilant about privacy and security concerns and also recognizing one's legal rights in the online environment (Palfrey *et al.*, 2009), informed uses of digital media rely on many important skills (Hargittai, 2007). The factors enumerated earlier – the technical and social contexts of usage – all influence users' online abilities and what they are able to accomplish using digital media.

Antecedent to all of these factors, however, is the social position that a user inhabits. Figure 13.1 presents a graphical representation of the relationships between the factors enumerated in this piece. One's demographic characteristics and socio-economic background are likely to influence the technical and social contexts of usage in addition to one's skills. These all, in turn, have implications for how one uses information and communication technologies. Finally, usage feeds back into additional skills leading to a potentially reinforcing effect.

Prevalent in popular accounts of digital media use is the assumption that young people are universally savvy with information and

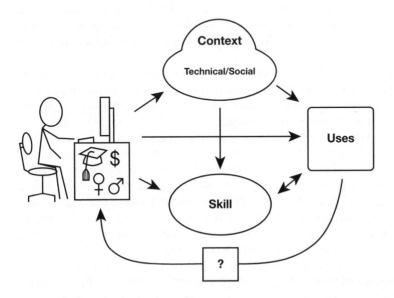

Figure 13.1 The relationship of factors that influence people's ICT uses and their implications for people's social status and well-being

communication technologies (Prensky, 2001; Tapscott, 1998). However, as critiques of that perspective have pointed out, such approaches tend to lack empirical evidence (Bennett *et al.*, 2008). Although the majority of youth are now online in many countries and thus access differences (i.e., the so-called 'digital divide') are no longer the main barrier to bene-fiting from digital media for this particular segment of the population, know-how and actual uses exhibit considerable differences even among universally wired youth (e.g., many cohorts at American universities). Far from being randomly distributed, online skills and uses vary by socio-economic status suggesting that rather than meeting its potential to level the playing field, the Internet may be contributing to increasing social inequality (Hargittai, 2010).

Take, for example, a group of over one thousand students in the first-year cohort of an urban public university in the midwestern United States surveyed about their Web uses in 2007. When asked to rate their level of understanding, on a five-point scale, of such Internet-related items as 'reload', 'advanced search' and 'bookmark', most suggested that they had anywhere from a good to full understanding of what these terms mean. However, asked to rate their level of understanding of terms like 'RSS' and 'social bookmarking', most indicated that they have anywhere from no to little understanding of the items. These same questions were posed to the 2009 first-year cohort at this same university and while average knowledge of the more recent Web terms had gone up slightly (at the level of the hundredth decimal point for the group as a whole), for the most part the results were consistent with those from two years earlier. While most students understand terms that have been around for over a decade, many remain unaware of more recent Web functionalities despite those having been around for several years themselves.

In addition to affording more and more opportunities for finding diverse types of content, an important aspect of recent Web developments concerns increasing opportunities for people to contribute to online materials and conversations themselves (e.g., Benkler, 2006). Research on youth has suggested that many are indeed taking part in such activi-ties online (Ito *et al.*, 2009; Jenkins *et al.*, 2006; Palfrey and Gasser, 2008; Resnick, 2007). The question remains, however, to what extent these types of engagement are widespread. Based on the same cohort of first-year college students surveyed in 2009 mentioned above, findings suggest that active participation is quite limited even among a group of highly wired young adults. For example, less than half of the group indicated contributions to sites through writing reviews or voting on content posted by others. Moreover, such engagement is not randomly distributed across the group. Rather, those from more privileged backgrounds (i.e., students whose parents have higher levels of education) report taking part in such activities considerably more than those from less educated families. Work on the data from the 2007 study found that students also differ in the extent to which they are sharing content they create online (Hargittai and Walejko 2008). Results such as these suggest caution when interpreting the outcome of any study that does not represent the online behaviour of a wide range of users. Returning to the example mentioned in the beginning of this chapter, while data on students who contribute to online content and conversation may suggest that ICTs are democratizing the public sphere, considering data about the participation of a wide range of students makes the answer less obvious.

Disparities in people's ICT abilities and uses have the potential to augment social inequalities rather than lessen them. Those who know how to navigate the Web's vast landscape and how to use digital media to address their needs can reap significant benefits from their uses while those who lack skills in these domains will miss out on opportunities. The Matthew Effect – 'unto every one that hath shall be given' – introduced by Robert Merton (Merton, 1979: 445) to sociological investigations applies well to this domain like many others. Findings from this emerging field suggest that initial advantages translate into increasing returns over time for the digitally connected and digitally skilled (DiMaggio and Bonikowski, 2008). The implications of these findings are far from limited to work focused on questions of social stratification. Rather, investigations across all domains of digital media research must remain conscious of this fact if they are to avoid incorrect generalizations of findings across all population segments concerning the social, political, economic and cultural implications of ICTs.

Note

1 I use 'digital media' and 'information and communication technologies' interchangeably to refer mainly to the Internet, but also the use of mobile and other devices (e.g., games).

References

Barzilai-Nahon, K. (2006) 'Gaps and Bits: Conceptualizing Measurements for Digital Divide/s', *The Information Society*, 22: 269–278.

Benkler, Y. (2006) *The Wealth of Networks*, New Haven, CT: Yale University Press.

Bennett, S., Maton, K. and Kervin, L. (2008) 'The "digital natives" debate: a critical review of evidence', *British Journal of Educational Technology*, 39: 775–786.

Billon, M., Marco, R. and Lera-Lopez, F. (2009) 'Disparities in ICT adoption: A multidimensional approach to study the cross-country digital divide', *Telecommunications Policy*, 33: 596–610.

Bimber, B. (2000) 'The Gender Gap on the Internet', *Social Science Quarterly*, 81: 868–876.

Bonfadelli, H. (2002) 'The Internet and Knowledge Gaps. A Theoretical and Empirical Investigation', *European Journal of Communication*, 17: 65–84.

Bucy, E. (2000) 'Social Access to the Internet', *Harvard International Journal of Press/Politics*, 5: 50–61.

Bunz, U. (2004) 'The Computer-Email-Web Fluency Scale: Development and Validation', *International Journal of Human-Computer Interaction*, 17: 477–504.

Compaine, B.M. (ed.) (2001) *The Digital Divide: Facing a Crisis or Creating a Myth?*, Cambridge, MA: The MIT Press.

Cook, T.D., Appleton, H. Conner, R.F. Shaffer, A., Tamkin, G. and Weber, S.J. (1975) *'Sesame Street' Revisited*, New York: Russell Sage Foundation.

van Deursen, A.J.A.M. and van Dijk, J.A.G.M. (2009) 'Using the Internet: Skill related problems in users' online behavior', *Interacting with Computers*, 21: 393–402.

van Dijk, J.A.G.M. (2005) *The Deepening Divide*, London: Sage Publications.

DiMaggio, P. and Bonikowski, B. (2008) 'Make Money Surfing the Web? The Impact of Internet Use on the Earnings of U.S. Workers', *American Sociological Review*, 73: 227–250.

DiMaggio, P., Hargittai, E., Celeste, C. and Shafer, S. (2004) 'Digital Inequality: From Unequal Access to Differentiated Use', in Neckerman, K. (ed.) *Social Inequality*, New York: Russell Sage Foundation.

Eastin, M.S. and LaRose, R. (2000) 'Internet Self-Efficacy and the Psychology of the Digital Divide', *Journal of Computer-Mediated Communication*, 6.

Frohlich, D.M. and Kraut, R. (2003) 'The Social Context of Home Computing', in Harper, R. (ed.) *Inside the Smart Home*, London: Springer-Verlag.

Hargittai, E. (1999) 'Weaving the Western Web: Explaining difference in Internet connectivity among OECD countries', *Telecommunications Policy*, 23: 701–718.

Hargittai, E. (2002) 'Second-Level Digital Divide: Differences in People's Online Skills', *First Monday*, 7.

Hargittai, E. (2007) 'A Framework for Studying Differences in People's Digital Media Uses', in Kutscher, N. and Otto, H.U. (eds) *Cyberworld Unlimited?*, Wiesbaden: VS Verlag für Sozialwissenschaften/GWV Fachverlage GmbH

Hargittai, E. (2008) 'The Digital Reproduction of Inequality', in Grusky, D. (ed.) *Social Stratification*, Boulder, CO: Westview Press.

Hargittai, E. (2010) 'Digital Na(t)ives? Variation in Internet Skills and Uses among Members of the "Net Generation"', *Sociological Inquiry*, 80.

Hargittai, E. and Hinnant, A. (2008) 'Digital Inequality: Differences in Young Adults' Use of the Internet', *Communication Research*, 35: 602–621.

Hargittai, E. and Walejko, G. (2008) 'The Participation Divide: Content creation and sharing in the digital age', *Information, Communication and Society*, 11: 239–256.

Hassani, S.N. (2006) 'Locating Digital Divides at Home, Work, and Everywhere Else', *Poetics*, 34: 250–272.

Hinde, S. (2002) 'Spam, scams, chains, hoaxes and other junk mail', *Computers and Security*, 21: 592–606.

Howard, P.N., Rainie, L. and Jones, S. (2001) 'Days and Nights on the Internet: The Impact of a Diffusing Technology', *American Behavioral Scientist*, 45: 383–404.

Ito, M., Baumer, S., Bittanti, M., boyd, d., Cody, R., Herr, B., Horst, H.A., Lange, P.G., Mahendran, D., Martinez, K., Pascoe, C.J., Perkel, D., Robinson, L., Sims, C. and Tripp, L. (2009) *Hanging Out, Messing Around, and Geeking Out: Kids Living and Learning with New Media*, Cambridge, MA: MIT Press.

Jackson, L.A., Zhao, Y., Kolneic, A., Fitzgerald, H.E., Harold, R. and Von Eye, A. (2008) 'Race, Gender, and Information Technology Use: The New Digital Divide', *CyberPsychology and Behavior*, 11: 437–442.

Jenkins, H., Purushotma, R., Clinton, K., Weigel, M. and Robison, A.J. (2006) *Confronting the Challenges of Participatory Culture: Media Education for the 21st Century*, Chicago, IL: John D. and Catherine T. MacArthur Foundation.

Jones, S, and Fox. S. (2009) *Generations Online in 2009*, Washington, DC: Pew Internet & American Life Project.

Kiesler, S., Zdaniuk, B., Lundmark, V. and R. Kraut, R. (2000) 'Troubles With the Internet: The Dynamics of Help at Home', *Human–Computer Interaction*, 15: 323–351.

Lenhart, A., Kahne, J., Middaugh, E., Macgill, A., Evans, C. and Vitak, J. (2008) *Teens, Video Games and Civics*, Washington, DC: Pew Internet & American Life Project.

Liebes, T, and Katz, E. (1993) *The Export of Meaning: Cross-Cultural Readings of Dallas*, Cambridge, MA: Polity Press.

Lim, S.S. (2009) 'Home, School, Borrowed, Public or Mobile: Variations in Young Singaporeans' Internet Access and their Implications', *Journal of Computer-Mediated Communication*, 14: 1228–1256.

Livingstone, S. and Helsper, E. (2007) 'Gradations in Digital Inclusion: Children, Young People, and the Digital Divide', *New Media and Society*, 9: 671–696.

Merton, R.K. (1979) *The Sociology of Science: Theoretical and Empirical Investigations*, Chicago: University of Chicago Press.

Metzger, M.J. (2007) 'Making sense of credibility on the Web: Models for evaluating online information and recommendations for future research', *Journal of the American Society for Information Science and Technology*, 58: 2078–2091.

Morley, D. (1980) *The Nationwide Audience: Structure and Decoding*, London: British Film Institute.

Mossberger, K., Tolbert, C.J. and Stansbury, M. (2003) *Virtual Inequality: Beyond the Digital Divide*, Washington, DC: Georgetown University Press.

National Telecommunications and Information Administration (1995) *Falling Through the Net: A Survey of the 'Have Nots' in Rural and Urban America*, Washington, DC: NTIA.

Norris, P. (2001) *Digital Divide: Civic Engagement, Information Poverty and the Internet in Democratic Societies*, New York: Cambridge University Press.

Ono, H. and Zavodny, M. (2007) 'Digital Inequality: A five country comparison using microdata', *Social Science Research*, 3.

Palfrey, J., Gasser, U., Simun, M. and Barnes, R.F. (2009) 'Youth, Creativity and Copyright in the Digital Age', *International Journal of Media and Learning*, 1: 79–97.

Palfrey, J. and Gasser, U. (2008) *Born Digital: Understanding the First Generation of Digital Natives*, New York: Basic Books.

Prensky, M. (2001) 'Digital Natives, Digital Immigrants', *On the Horizon*, 9: 1–6.

Resnick, M. (2007) 'Sowing the Seeds for a More Creative Society', in *Learning and Leading with Technology*. Available: <http://web.media.mit.edu/~mres/papers.html>.

Rice, R.E., and Katz, J.E. (2003) 'Comparing internet and mobile phone usage: digital divides of usage, adoption, and dropouts', *Telecommunications Policy*, 27: 597–623.

Tapscott, D. (1998) *Growing Up Digital: The Rise of the Net Generation*, New York: McGraw Hill.

Vidmar, N. and Rokeach, M. (1974) 'Archie Bunker's Bigotry: A Study in Selective Perception and Exposure', *The Journal of Communication*, 24: 36–47.

Wilson, E.J. (2000) *Closing the Digital Divide: An Initial Review: Briefing the President*, Washington, DC: Internet Policy Institute.

Wilson, E.J. (2004) *The Information Revolution and Developing Countries*, Cambridge, MA: MIT Press.

Zhang, C., Callegaro, M. and Thomas, M. (2008) 'More than the Digital Divide? Investigating the Differences between Internet and Non-Internet Users', in *Midwest Association of Public Opinion Research*, Chicago, Illinois.

Zillien, N. and Hargittai, E. (2009) 'Digital Distinction: Status-Specific Types of Internet Usage', *Social Science Quarterly*, 90: 274–291.

Index